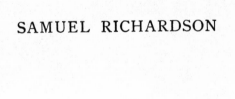

SAMUEL RICHARDSON

SAMUEL RICHARDSON
FROM A PAINTING BY HIGHMORE

SAMUEL RICHARDSON

A BIOGRAPHICAL AND
CRITICAL STUDY

BY

CLARA LINKLATER THOMSON

KENNIKAT PRESS
Port Washington, N. Y./London

SAMUEL RICHARDSON

First published in 1900
Reissued in 1970 by Kennikat Press
Library of Congress Catalog Card No: 74-103214
SBN 8046-0851-2

Manufactured by Taylor Publishing Company   Dallas, Texas

PREFACE

NEARLY a hundred years have elapsed since Mrs
Barbauld's edition of Samuel Richardson's Correspondence appeared. This was preceded by
a biographical sketch which still forms the chief
source of information concerning a writer whose
importance in the development of English fiction
would seem to render necessary a cheaper and
more accessible biography. The present book
is an attempt to gather into a moderate compass
the essential facts of his life. It is based on Mrs
Barbauld's Memoir, which, however, has been
largely supplemented by information obtained
from Richardson's unpublished correspondence in
the Forster Library at the South Kensington
Museum, from the registers of Charterhouse
Chapel and St Bride's, Fleet Street, and from
other contemporary sources. The critical chapters
are intended chiefly as a guide to those readers
who are quite unacquainted with Richardson's
novels, and it is hoped that the references to
the works of the principal English, French, and
German writers on the subject may be found
useful by those wishing to pursue the study
further. In the chapters on the Development
of the Novel, and on Richardson's Influence, I

am greatly indebted to the works of MM. Brunetière, Le Breton and Texte, and Dr Erich Schmidt.

I wish also to express my sincere thanks to Mr C. H. Firth, M.A., of Oxford, to whom the inception of this book is due; and to Lord Balcarres; the Rev. Canon Thompson, M.A., Rector and Chancellor of St Saviour's, Southwark; and Mr W. G. Whitear, of Chiswick, for help kindly given during its preparation.

A bibliography will be found at the end of the volume.

CLARA LINKLATER THOMSON.

SOLIHULL,
April 1900.

CONTENTS

PAGE

PREFACE v

CHAPTER I

BIOGRAPHY, 1689-1748 1

CHAPTER II

BIOGRAPHY, 1748-1761 44

CHAPTER III

RICHARDSON'S FRIENDS 77

CHAPTER IV

RICHARDSON'S FRIENDS (*continued*) . . . 104

CHAPTER V

THE DEVELOPMENT OF THE NOVEL . . 124

CHAPTER VI

" PAMELA " 147

CHAPTER VII

" CLARISSA HARLOWE " 171

CONTENTS

PAGE

CHAPTER VIII

"Sir Charles Grandison" . . . 209

CHAPTER IX

The Art of Richardson 242

CHAPTER X

Richardson's Influence 266

Bibliography 292

Index 303

SAMUEL RICHARDSON

CHAPTER I

1689-1748

UNLIKE his great contemporary and rival, Henry
Fielding, Samuel Richardson could boast of no
connection, however remote, with an aristocratic
house. He himself has informed us that he came
of a family "of middling note," in the county of
Surrey, from which we may conjecture that his
ancestors were small landed gentry or respectable
yeomen. But by degrees, its property not increasing in the same proportion as its members, the
family came down in the world; the sons were
put to trades, and the daughters were married to
tradesmen.

Richardson's father was a joiner, but seems to
have combined with that calling some knowledge
and practice of architecture; he settled in London,
and married a lady of a family "not ungenteel,"
whose parents had died within half-an-hour of
each other, in the great plague. He was a
partisan of the Duke of Monmouth and the Earl
of Shaftesbury, and must have been concerned in
the rebellion of the former; for his son tells us
that their "known favour for him, having, on the

duke's attempt on the crown subjected him to be
looked upon with a jealous eye, notwithstanding
he was noted for a quiet and inoffensive man, he
thought proper, on the decollation of the first
named unhappy nobleman, to quit his London
business, and to retire to Derbyshire, though to
his great detriment." [1]

It is quite likely that the complicity of his father
in treasonable practices accounts for Richardson's
great reticence concerning his parentage, especially
as in later life he was not at all reluctant to talk
of himself and his domestic concerns. He never
even revealed the name of the town in Derbyshire,
where, in 1689, he was born, and all research has
hitherto failed to discover it. His father probably
returned to London not long after the accession
of William and Mary, for a rumour, reported in
Nichols' *Literary Anecdotes*, states that Samuel
was a pupil at Christ Church Hospital.[2] This is
not confirmed by the register of scholars, and it
seems improbable that he received so good an
education, unless in the years of drudgery that
followed he forgot the knowledge of the classics
that he had acquired at school. He seems to
have had some smattering of Latin, but only
sufficient to translate short sentences, or, as Mrs
Barbauld says, for hackneyed quotation. For the
letter of the pedant Brand in *Clarissa Harlowe*,
which is full of classical allusions, he is supposed
to have had recourse to the help of friends ; and

[1] Barbauld, i. 31.
[2] Nichols' *Literary Anecdotes*, iv. 579.

it is most likely that, wherever he received his education, he left school too early to have advanced further than the Latin accidence or the reading of easy texts. His written style, fluent, homely, and diffuse, is just what might be expected from such circumstances, and is altogether deficient in the concentration and polish that are hardly ever absent in the writing of one who has had much practice in Latin prose. And as education at that time was almost exclusively classical, this "little Latin and less Greek" points to a general inadequacy of intellectual training. Nor was this supplemented to any considerable extent by subsequent reading; for, though from references in the letters, it may be assumed that Richardson had a fair acquaintance with the great English poets, and for trade purposes kept in touch with current literature, he himself laments his incapacity for study, and regrets that the habit of writing has so grown upon him as to leave him little leisure for any other pursuit.

Notwithstanding the paucity of information respecting his boyhood, we can gather from his own relation that the favourite occupations of the child already foreshadowed those of the elderly novelist. The ponderous didacticism excusable in an old gentleman who had lived a blameless and industrious life, and was respected equally for his genius and his benevolence, was less amiably characteristic of the schoolboy, and once, at least, involved him in some difficulty. "I was not eleven years old," he tells us, "when I wrote spontaneously a letter to a widow of near fifty, who, pretending to a zeal for religion, and being a constant frequenter of church ordinances, was continually fomenting quarrels and disturbances by backbiting and scandal among all her acquaintance. I collected from the Scripture texts that made against her. Assuming the style and address of a person in years, I exhorted her, I expostulated with her. But my handwriting was known. I was challenged with it, and owned the boldness, for she complained of it to my mother with tears. My mother chid me for the freedom taken with a woman of her years; but knowing that her son was not of a forward nature, but on the contrary shy and bashful, she commended my principles though she censured the liberty taken." [1]

It is small wonder that Richardson's father at first designed him for the church, or that he was unpopular with his school-fellows, who nick-named him "Serious and Gravity." But though he did not care for games and could not win the liking of his companions by his skill in the play ground, they soon found that he could be the source of infinite amusement in another way. "Five of them particularly delighted to single me out, either for a walk, or at their fathers' houses, or at mine to tell them stories, as they phrased it. Some I told them from my reading, as true; others from my head, as mere invention, of which they would be most fond and often were affected by them. One of them particularly I remember was for putting me

[1] Barbauld, i. 38.

to write a history, as he called it, on the model of Tommy Pots ;[1] I now forget what it was, only that it was of a servant man who was preferred by a fine young lady (for his goodness) to a lord who was a libertine. All my stories carried with them, I am bold to say, a useful moral."[2]

Such subjects as those hinted at above seem rather curious themes for schoolboy romances, and one is glad to think that contemporary childhood has a healthier taste in fiction. But Richardson was evidently a morbid, precocious child in days when precocity was regarded as a sign of grace. The doctrine of original sin had much to answer for, and, as every child was supposed to be bad by nature, the sooner he put away childish things the nearer was he considered to salvation. Far from being looked upon as fresh from the hand of God, and bearing on him, still pure and uncorrupted, the marks of his divine origin, the child was treated as a creature whose natural perversity necessitated the most severe discipline. The application of such principles as these resulted too often in the development of priggishness and a premature adoption of adult manners. A hundred years later than Richardson's boyhood, Hannah More, writing in 1809, makes her pattern child say :—

"I am eight years old to-day. I gave up all my gilt books with pictures this day twelvemonth, and to-day I give up all my little story-books,

---

[1] "A character in Ritson's *Ancient Ballads*" (Scott).
[2] Barbauld, i. 37.

and I am now going to read such books as grown
men and women use."

In his own small circle, then, the future novelist
was evidently treated as a prodigy, and encouraged
in that native priggishness which the years that
developed other and finer qualities never quite
eradicated.   Even in his boyhood he was the
centre of a little company of feminine admirers
who gathered together to hear him read aloud.

"As a bashful and not forward boy," he says, " I
was an early favourite with all the young women
of taste and reading in the neighbourhood.   Half-
a-dozen of them, when met to work with their
needles used, when they got a book they liked
and thought I should, to borrow me to read to
them ; their mothers sometimes with them, and
both mothers and daughters used to be pleased
with the observations they put me upon making.

" I was not more than thirteen when three of
these young women, unknown to each other, having a high opinion of my taciturnity, revealed to
me their love secrets in order to induce me to
give them copies to write after, or correct, for
answers to their lovers' letters, nor did any one of
them ever know that I was the secretary to the
others.   I have been directed to chide and even
repulse when an offence was either taken or given,
at the very time that the heart of the chider or
repulser was open before me, overflowing with
esteem and affection ; and the fair repulser, dread-
ing to be taken at her word, directing *this* word or
that expression to be softened or changed.   One,

highly satisfied with her lover's fervour and vows
of everlasting love, has said when I have asked her
direction, 'I cannot tell you what to write, but
(her heart on her lips) you cannot write too
kindly.' All her fear was only that she should
incur slight for her kindness." [1]

Thus Richardson was already reading in the
book from which he drew most of his information.
It was this early experience that enabled him to
describe with such astonishing accuracy the intricacies of feminine passion, and to realise the
fallacy of the prejudice that requires a woman's
affections to be passive till roused to activity by
the declaration of a lover. He understood what
the present generation is beginning to realise, that
the similarities between the sexes are greater than
their divergences, and that the ordinary heroine of
the masculine dramatist or novelist is rather an
exposition of what he thinks a woman should be,
than an illustration of what she is. "Indeed, my
good Lady Bradshaigh," he wrote years afterwards, "one generally finds in the writings of
even ingenious men that they take up the characters of women too easily, and either on general
opinions or particular acquaintances. Shakespeare
knew them best of all writers in my humble
opinion. He knew them better than they know
themselves, for pardon me for saying that we
must not always go to women for general knowledge of the sex. Ask me now with disdain, my
dear Lady Bradshaigh, if I pretend to know

[1] Barbauld, i. 40.

them. No, I say, I only guess at them. And yet I think them not such mysteries as some suppose. A tolerable knowledge of men will lead us to a tolerable knowledge of women. Mrs Shirley [1] has said well where she says the two sexes are too much considered as different species. He or she who soars not above simplicity is most likely to understand the human heart best in either sex, especially if he can make allowance for different modes of education, constitution, and situation." [2]

Want of means frustrated the intentions of Richardson's parents, and instead of being educated for the church he was, at the age of seventeen, apprenticed to Mr John Wilde, of Stationers' Hall, a printer. He chose this trade, he tells us, chiefly because he thought it would give him opportunity for reading, but he seems to have had very little time for such amusement, and perhaps the want of facilities for gratifying his taste had the effect of partially removing it. Wilde was a hard taskmaster, and grudged him every moment not spent in his service ; besides this, the lad found another recreation in a correspondence with a gentleman, "greatly his superior in degree and of ample fortune," which encroached on the time he could give to reading. "Multitudes of letters passed between this gentleman and me," he says; "he wrote well, was a master of the epistolary style. Our subjects were various, but his letters were

---

[1] A character in *Sir Charles Grandison*.

[2] Forster MS., Bradshaigh Correspondence.

mostly narrative, giving me an account of his proceedings, and what befell him in the different nations through which he travelled. I could, from them, had I been at liberty, and had I at that time had the thought of writing as I have since done, have drawn great helps: but many years ago, all the letters that passed between us, by a particular desire of his (lest they should ever be published), were committed to the flames."[1]

Thus passed the days of his apprenticeship, and from his own account he might very well have stood as a model for Hogarth's hero. For he tells us that none of the efforts he made at self-improvement—the above-mentioned correspondence being the chief—were allowed in any way to interfere with his obligations to his employer. Even the candle by the light of which he wrote these letters was his own purchase, and he was careful not to impair his efficiency in his work by over-taxing his strength in his own pursuits. All this virtue brought him the deserved approbation of his master, who used to call him "the pillar of his house."

After his apprenticeship was over Richardson worked for some time as a journeyman printer and corrector of the press, rising at last to the position of overseer. His naturally methodical habits, not always a striking characteristic of literary men, were greatly strengthened by this long training, and he seems to have obtained a high reputation as an honourable and punctual

[1] Barbauld, i. 43.

man of business. In 1719 he was at length able
to set up for himself as a master printer, at first
at a court in Fleet Street, whence he afterwards
removed in 1724 to Salisbury Court. Two years
after the commencement of his independent career
he married Martha Wilde, concerning whose
parentage there has been some confusion. Mrs
Barbauld states that she was the daughter of his
first master, John Wilde, while Mr Leslie Stephen,[1]
probably following Nichols' *Literary Anecdotes*, says
that her father was another "high-flying" printer,
by name Allington Wilde. But in the registers of
Charterhouse Chapel I find under date 1692 that
John Wilde, widower, of the Parish of St Bartholomew the Great, married Martha A. Allington,
spinster, of the Parish of St Bartholomew the
Less; and under date Nov. 23, 1721, Samuel
Richardson (cœlebs), of the Parish of St Bride's,
married Martha Wilde (soluta) of the Parish of
St Botolph's, Aldersgate. It seems likely that this
Martha was the daughter of the John and Martha
mentioned in the first entry, and as, from Richardson's will, we know that he had a brother-in-law,
Allington Wilde, Nichols probably confused the
son, who was named after his mother's family, with
the father, who died in 1728, and is mentioned by
Dunton in 1705 as having "a very noble printing-
house in Aldersgate Street." So that we may
conclude that Richardson carried out his resemblance to the industrious apprentice by marrying his master's daughter.

[1] Dict. Nat. Biog. Art., *Richardson*.

For the domestic details of Richardson's early
married life there is little information except what
can be obtained from the parish registers of St
Bride's. From these we learn that by his first
wife he had six children, five sons and one
daughter, all of whom save the third, William,
died in infancy; and even he lived only to the
age of four years. Richardson was always happy
in his domestic relations, but there are grounds
for supposing that both his marriages were
prompted mainly by prudential considerations.
His intense earnestness in arguing that a first
love is not invincible, together with his sympathetic
delineation of disappointed affection, support this
theory, though it must not be pushed too far. It
is easy to imagine that a man of his susceptible,
though not ardent, temperament must have stood
in sentimental relations to many women in the
years that elapsed before his increasing prosperity
enabled him, at the age of thirty-two, to marry
and settle down. In a letter to Lady Bradshaigh
he alludes to some of these early love affairs.

" The fortune of the man you hint at was very
low ; his mind, however, was never mean. A bash-
fulness, next to sheepishness, kept him down ; but
he always courted independence, and, being contented with a little, preserved a title to it. He
found friends who thought they saw merit in him
through the cloud that his sheepishness threw over
him, and knowing how low his fortune was, laid
themselves out to raise him ; and most of them
by proposals of marriage, which, however, had

always something impracticable in them. A
pretty idiot was once proposed, with very high
terms, her circumstances considered; her worthy
uncle thought this man would behave compassion-
ately to her. A violent Roman Catholic lady was
another, of a fine fortune, a zealous professor,
whose terms were (all her fortune in her own power
—a very apron-string tenure!) two years' probation and her confessor's report in favour of his
being a true proselyte at the end of them.
Another, a gay, high-spirited, volatile lady whose
next friend offered to be his friend in fear of
her becoming the prey (at the public places she
constantly frequented) of some vile fortune-
hunter. Another there was whom his soul loved;
but with a reverence. Hush! Pen lie thee
down!"

"A timely check; where else might I have
ended? This lady—how hard to forbear the
affecting subject! but I will forbear. This man
presumed not—again going on! Not a word
more this night." [1]

Mrs Barbauld has expressed her belief that the
heroine of this early love affair gave the hint for
the character of Mrs Beaumont, the friend and
confidante of Clementina in *Sir Charles Grandison*.
Mrs Barbauld had her information from Mrs Duncombe, then a very old lady, who, as Susannah
Highmore, had been one of the brightest ornaments
of Richardson's circle, and it is therefore very
probably correct; and if we may make the further

[1] Barbauld, i. 160.

conjecture that *The History of Mrs Beaumont*[1] was founded on that of this unknown lady, we may conclude that she was somewhat above Richardson in position, an orphan heiress, who had been deprived of her fortune by a fraudulent uncle. Whether, like Mrs Beaumont, she actually became attached as " gouvernante " to an Italian family is still more conjectural, but in that case the incident may well have provided the first hint for the Italian scenes in *Sir Charles Grandison.*

During these years of his first marriage Richardson supplemented his income as a printer by writing prefaces, indexes, and dedications for the booksellers. Fortunately for him he was not dependent for his livelihood on these desultory literary adventures, by which so many denizens of Grub Street were supported or starved. The heart-breaking battle with poverty, which was largely responsible for the pessimism of Johnson, and in which Fielding received so many wounds, he seems to have known only as a spectator ; and though he was always ready to help the sufferers in the fray, he had little sympathy with the habits and morals of Bohemia. Close to his door rolled by the restless tide of striving human life ; importunate poets carried their manuscripts to unappreciative publishers, or solicited subscriptions to works that might never appear ; impecunious parsons touted for custom ; beggars and statesmen, hawkers and peers, jostled each other in the narrow paths ; and up that hill, which to how few of their

[1] Barbauld, v. p. 301.

number has at length proved a Parnassus, the
aspirants to literary fame toiled and panted and
despaired, even as do their descendants to this
very day.

But in all this Richardson seems to have had
no part. " He preferred," says Mr Leslie Stephen,
" to keep his shop that his shop might keep him."
The country was settling down after a long period
of financial and military excitement. Walpole's
strong government gave it an opportunity for recu-
peration. Trade revived; the middle class throve
and became, at the same time, more materialistic
and more powerful, and the antagonism to the
government, which afterwards became so loud, was
at present hushed and subdued. And among those
who profited by this period of quiet, not the least
prosperous was Richardson. Once, indeed, we
find him concerned in an enterprise of some
danger, though he appears to have withdrawn
from it before he became very deeply implicated.
This was the publication of *The True Briton*, a
journal conducted by Philip, Duke of Wharton,
and one of the first of the many papers devoted
to attacks on the existing government. Wharton
is perhaps best remembered by the scathing lines
of Pope :—

> " Wharton, the pride and wonder of our days,
>   Whose ruling passion was the lust of praise ;
>   Born with whate'er could win it from the wise,
>   Women and fools must like him or he dies ;
>   Though wondering senates hung on all he spoke,
>   The club must hail him master of the joke.

.   .   .   .

Grown all to all, from no one vice exempt,
And most contemptible to shun contempt :
His passion still to covet general praise,
His life to forfeit it a thousand ways ;
A constant bounty which no friend had made ;
An angel tongue which no man could persuade ;
A fool with more of wit than half mankind,
Too rash for thought, for action too refined ;
A tyrant to the wife his heart approves,
A rebel to the very king he loves ;
He dies, sad outcast of each church and state,
And harder still, flagitious and not great."

It was a strange combination, that of the little
methodical printer, absorbed in business and domesticity, with this young aristocrat, whose career was at
once so brilliant and so tragic. When he died in
1731, an exile in Catalonia, having run through an
enormous fortune and won and lost the reputation
of the greatest politician of his age, he was only
thirty-three. His life was, indeed, "a miracle of
thirty years, which to relate were not a history,
but a piece of poetry, and would sound to common
ears like a fable." It has been suggested, with
some appearance of probability, that Richardson
owed to him the first suggestion for the character
of Lovelace, and it is quite possible that the
brilliant young nobleman, so remote from himself in
rank, circumstances and character, may have had
some curious fascination for the future author of
Clarissa Harlowe. Richardson, however, printed
only six numbers (there were seventy-four altogether) of *The True Briton,* though Nichols declares

that it seems highly probable that the sixth (June 21, 1723) was written by him, "as it is much in his style and manner." However this may be, informations were lodged against Payne, the publisher, for numbers 3, 4, 5 and 6 as being more than common libels, "as they not only insulted every branch of the legislature, but manifestly tended to make the constitution itself odious to the people. Payne was found guilty, and Mr Richardson escaped as his name did not appear in the paper." This prosecution probably alarmed Richardson, and caused him to break his connection with his patron; it seems likely that he had all the time disapproved of Wharton's political views, but was flattered by the attention and patronage of so notorious a character. Their connection, however, accounts for the fact that Richardson is classed among the "high flyers" in the curious classification of printers according to their political views which may be found in the first volume of Nichols' *Literary Anecdotes*. Some years afterwards he was the printer of two other papers, *The Daily Journal* (1736-1737) and *The Daily Gazetteer* (1738).

These years were for Richardson a period of much domestic trouble. His first wife, overwhelmed by grief at the loss of all her children, died in 1731. He did not long remain a widower, and the next year married Elizabeth Leake, the daughter of a bookseller at Bath. She was not a very young woman, having been born in 1696. Their eldest child, Elizabeth, born in 1733, lived only a few months; but Mary, born in 1734, Martha, born in 1736, Anne, born in 1737, and Sarah, born in 1740, all survived their father. There was also a son, Samuel (the third to whom Richardson had given his name), born in 1739 and buried in 1740. Richardson was a very affectionate man, and felt his bereavements deeply. " No less than eleven affecting deaths in two years! " he wrote afterwards to Lady Bradshaigh, and these repeated shocks so affected his health that he ascribed to them the chronic infirmities from which he afterwards suffered.

All this time the opposition to the government was gradually increasing in strength. It is a curious fact that nearly all the literary men of the day belonged to its ranks—a somewhat serious state of things for the ministry at a time when, as parliamentary reporting was in its infancy, pamphlets were the chief weapons of political agitation. Oratory had but a narrow range, and the accounts of speeches that penetrated to the outside world were at best garbled and distorted, but the pamphleteer could appeal to a much wider public. Pope, Swift, Gay, Bolingbroke, Carteret, Glover, Lyttelton, Thomson, Fielding—all these writers of varying greatness were opposed to Walpole, and the storm of ridicule which greeted the appointment of Colley Cibber as poet laureate in 1730 was due quite as much to political causes as to his own shortcomings. One particularly bitter epigram ascribed to Pope alludes to the appointment in the following terms :—

B

" In merry old England it once was the rule,
  The King had his Poet and also his Fool.
  But now we're so frugal, I'd have you to know it,
  That Cibber can serve both for Fool and for Poet." [1]

The persecution of the government by the most
distinguished literary men of the day had the effect
of driving the less accomplished, who, by the
example of Pope in the *Treatise on Bathos* and
the *Dunciad* became their natural enemies, into
the opposite camp. The votaries of the Goddess
of Dulness would naturally be forced into antagonism to the satirist who thus characterised
them, and to the party to which he belonged, and
thus another literary coterie consisting mainly of
his victims sprang up. To this coterie, which included Cibber and Aaron Hill, Richardson belonged, and it is from his correspondence with the
latter poet that we gather most of our information
concerning this period of his life. Hill was then
living at Westminster, and in a letter dated July
19, 1736, writes thus :—

" Corney House is much oftener in my thoughts
than perhaps you imagine, and it is not without
some impatience that I long for the delight of
becoming a witness of that friendly and agreeable
freedom wherein you divide and enjoy a retreat
that carries temptation even in description. If it
had the effect on your health that it has on your
pleasure, it would be a perfect enjoyment. But
I am afraid you want leisure to reap that rural

[1] *Apology for the Life of Colley Cibber*, Ed. Lowe, p. 46,
note.

RICHARDSON'S HOUSE AT NORTH END
FROM AN ENGRAVING IN MRS BARBAULD'S EDITION OF THE CORRESPONDENCE (1804)

advantage to the full degree requisite for the change that is wished on your spirits."[1]

This letter is interesting because one may glean from it, first, that Richardson had by this time sufficiently prospered to indulge in a "rural retreat" as a refuge from the city; and secondly, that the ill health from which he suffered so long had already begun to vex him. The reference to Corney House is somewhat perplexing. The house of that name in Chiswick, which was demolished in 1832, was the ancient seat of the Russell family, and it does not seem very likely that Richardson could ever have lived there. But from Lyson's Account of Chiswick we learn that the Hon. Percy Widdrington, to whom it belonged in 1745, purchased in that year certain tenements and a piece of land called Corney Houses and Corney Close, adjoining his own premises.[2] It is possible that Richardson occupied one of these houses, though from another of Hill's letters, dated the same year as the one already quoted, he seems to have been already living at North End. Yet there is other evidence that he did not move to the house which he afterwards occupied in that village till 1738; for writing to Thomas Edwards in 1754 he says that he has paid rent for it for sixteen years.

This second country house of Richardson, which still exists, and was for many years in the possession of the late Sir Edward Burne Jones, has formed the subject of much discussion. It lies on

---

[1] Forster MS., Hill Correspondence.
[2] Phillimore and Whitear, *Chiswick*, pp. 28-29, and p. 271.

the left hand side of the way as one approaches
from the Hammersmith Road, and is now one of
the few remaining traces of the old world beauty
of the place, once "the pleasantest village within
ten miles of London." The large houses that once
kept it company are rapidly making way for blocks
of flats; the fine old cedar trees which gave its
name to a neighbouring estate have nearly all
disappeared, and are only commemorated by the
name of a huge public-house; and within a few
yards of this once secluded spot, omnibuses rumble,
and the trains of the District Railway pursue their
noisy and untiring way.

It is a moot question whether the two houses,
of which "The Grange" is one, did not originally
form one large one. Faulkner, in his *Historical
Account of Fulham*, published in 1813, says that
it "has been lately altered, and is now occupied
as two houses." This testimony is borne out by
the fact that there is only one set of stables, and
these belong to the left hand house, which is
not the one traditionally said to be Richardson's,
though we know from his correspondence that his
house had a stable which he did not use. The
picture in Mrs Barbauld's *Life* may have been
sketched after the division was made, though it
should be stated that she says in her note on the
plate, "that the half of this mansion which is
nearest the eye was occupied by Mr Richardson,
and the other half by Mr Vanderplank." But
Mrs Barbauld is not invariably correct. If in this
instance she is mistaken, and Richardson occupied

the whole building, so large a house points to much prosperity on the part of its tenant, and Richardson's home must certainly have been capacious, for he entertained crowds of guests, and always had accommodation for chance visitors to whom the sweet country air might prove beneficial. On the other hand, the rent, twenty-five pounds, which he paid, does not seem adequate to so large a house, though it must be remembered that it represented a greater value at that time than at present. A former tenant had been Lady Ranelagh, "who would have thought herself disgraced had she lived in a house under sixty pounds a year; and they made her (besides paying fifty pounds a year) build the house and stables, and having done so, she thought she had a bargain at sixty pounds." Lady Ranelagh's successor in the house was a Mr Sherwood, who paid thirty pounds, but when Richardson took it, as he had no use for the stables, the rent was reduced to twenty-five pounds.[1]

At first, however, he seems to have spent most of his time at Salisbury Court, which his wife, who was a lady of strong prejudices, preferred. It was perhaps only in later years, when increasing prosperity gave him more leisure, that he built the famous grotto or summerhouse, of which a drawing by Susannah Highmore is preserved, and where he was accustomed to spend the morning hours reading his latest manuscript to a group of admiring friends. It is probably safe to assume that *Pamela* was composed in the city house.

[1] Forster MS., Edwards Correspondence.

It was in the year 1739, at the age of fifty, that Richardson was asked by the publishers, Rivington and Osborne, to compose a little book of familiar letters on the most useful concerns in common life. "At last," says he, "I yielded to their importunity, and began to recollect such subjects as I thought would be useful in such a design, and formed several letters accordingly. And, among the rest, I thought of giving one or two cautions to young folks circumstanced as Pamela was. Little did I think at first of making one, much less two, volumes of it. But when I began to recollect what had[1] so many years before been told me by my friend, I thought the story, if written in an easy and natural manner, suitably to the simplicity of it, might possibly introduce a new species of writing, that might possibly turn young people into a course of reading different from the pomp and parade of romance writing, and dismissing the improbable and marvellous with which novels generally abound, might tend to promote the cause of religion and virtue. I therefore gave way to enlargement, and so *Pamela* became what you see her. But so little did I hope for the approbation of judges, that I had not the courage to send the two volumes to your ladies, until I found the books well received by the public.

"While I was writing the two volumes my worthy hearted wife and the young lady who is with us, when I had read them some part of the story, which I

[1] See below p. 153.

had begun without their knowing it, used to come into my little closet every night with : 'Have you any more of *Pamela*, Mr Richardson ? We are come to hear a little more of *Pamela*, etc. This encouraged me to prosecute it, which I did so diligently, through all my other business, that by a memorandum on my copy I began it November 10, 1739, and finished it January 10, 1740. And I have often, censurable as I might be thought for my vanity for it, and lessening to the taste of my female friends, had the story of Molière's old woman in my thoughts upon the occasion.

" If justly low were my thoughts of this little history, you will wonder how it came by such an assuming and impudent preface. It was thus : The approbation of these two female friends, and of two more who were so kind as to give me prefaces for it, but which were much too long and circumstantial as I thought, made me resolve myself on writing a preface. I therefore, spirited by the good opinion of these four, and knowing that the judgments of nine parts in ten of my readers were but in hanging sleeves, struck a bold stroke in the preface you see—having the umbrage of the editor's character to screen myself behind ; and now, sir, all is out."[1]

Pamela was thus published anonymously, and interrupted for a time the composition of the volume of *Familiar Letters* which had caused its inception. But as, in point of date, these came

[1] Barbauld, i. 76.

first, it will be as well to give them a brief consideration here.

The book, as stated above, was primarily intended as a "complete letter-writer," containing
models for every type of intimate correspondence.
But it was impossible for the author to let slip so
good an opportunity for pointing a moral, and the
title-page sets forth its advantage in "directing
not only the requisite style and forms to be
observed in writing familiar letters, but how to
think and act justly and prudently in the common
concerns of human life." This purpose is further
emphasised in the preface, which tells us that the
author has endeavoured to point out the duties of
masters, servants, fathers, children, and young men
entering the world. But especially—and this is
characteristic of the future novelist—he has given
much attention to the subject of courtship, aiming
"to point out such methods of address to a young
man as may stand the test of the parent's
judgment as well as the daughter's opinion; and
at the same time that they should not want the
proper warmth of expression which complaisance
and passion for the beloved object inspire (and is
so much expected in addresses of this nature); they
should have their foundation in common sense and
manly sincerity, and, in a word, be such as a
prudent woman need not blush to receive, nor a
discreet man be ashamed to look back upon, when
the doubtful courtship is changed into the matrimonial certainty." This passage strikes the key-
note to all that Richardson afterwards wrote on

the subject.   Love is his predominant theme, but he treats it always as a passion to be sternly controlled and kept within due bounds.

The moral intention so plainly stated might lead one to suppose that the letters are somewhat dull, but this is far from being the case.   They are extremely entertaining, not only for the light they throw on contemporary custom, but also for the humour and shrewd insight into human nature that they display.   They are supposed to be written on all sorts of occasions, and include warnings to young women of the dangers of London ; exhortations to apprentices to obey their masters ; dissuasions from imprudent marriages ; applications to parents for their daughters' hands ; reproaches of deserted damsels to their lovers ; demands of creditors for payment, and the piteous entreaties of distressed debtors ; together with letters of condolence, which, as the author remarks, " with small variations may be used to a husband on the death of his wife, and on other melancholy occasions of the like nature."   One of the most amusing is supposed to be addressed by a villager to an old crony who has gone abroad, and is full of the most lively gossip ; for instance : " John Jones the organist is married to Sykes' daughter Peggy, who proves an arrant shrew, and has broke about his head his best Cremona fiddle, in the sight of half-a-dozen neighbours."

But the best of all, as may be imagined, are those on Richardson's favourite subject of courtship and marriage, such as the following, in which a diffident wooer relates his difficulties in coming to the point.

"I first declared my regard for her in a manner I thought most suitable for that purpose. She very encouragingly made me no answer, and when I spoke again on the subject she asked me how you did, and was glad to hear you were well. Being put out of my play, I talked of indifferent things a good while, and at last fell again upon the reason of my attending her. She ordered the cloth to be laid, and complaisantly hoped I would stay to supper. I had no more opportunity for that time. . . . Yet next visit I began again. I told her how happy I should think myself if I could be encouraged to hope for the smallest share of her favour. But she made me such an odd answer, as plainly demonstrated to me that I had more of her contempt than her approbation. This made me as earnest as she to waive the subject, and so we went on upon the weather for a whole week as before; and when we had done that we talked politics; so that, in short, after two months' study how to accomplish the happiness you pointed out for me, I find myself not one single step advanced, for when I see her now we both talk with seeming satisfaction on any subject where love has no part."[1]

Unfortunately, there is nothing to show whether this persevering lover won his mistress, for the model correspondent now turns his attention to the other sex, and gives a delightful epistle from a

[1] *Familiar Letters*, pp. 109, 110.

lively young lady "ridiculing her serious lover";
it is so amusing in itself, and so interesting as
a forerunner of the letters of Anna Howe and
Charlotte Grandison, that it is worth quoting at
some length.

"The first time the *honest man* came to see me,"
writes this disdainful damsel, "in the way you were
pleased to put into his head was one Sunday after
sermon time. He began by telling me, what I
found at *my* fingers' ends, that it was very cold,
and politely blowed upon *his*. I immediately
perceived that his passion for me could not keep
him warm; and, in complaisance to your recom-
mendation, conducted him to the fireside. After
he had pretty well rubbed heat into his hands, he
stood up with his back to the fire; and with his
hand behind him, held up his coat, that he might be
warm all over; and, looking about him, asked with
the tranquility of a man a twelvemonth married,
and just come off a journey, 'How all friends did
in the country?' I said, 'I hoped very well, but
would be glad to warm my fingers.' . . . 'Cry
mercy, madam!' and then he shuffled a little
further from the fire, and after two or three hems,
and a long pause :—

"'I have heard,' said he, 'a most excellent
sermon just now. Dr Thomas is a fine man, truly.
Did you ever hear him, madam?' 'No, sir, I
generally go to my own parish church.' 'That's
right, madam, to be sure. What was your subject
to-day?' 'The Pharisee and the Publican, sir.'
'A very good one, truly. Dr Thomas would have

made a fine work upon that subject. His text to-day was, "Evil communications corrupt good manners."' 'A good subject, sir. I doubt not that the doctor made a fine discourse upon it.' '*O, ay,* madam, he can't make a bad one on any subject.' I ran for the tea-kettle, for, thought I, we shall have all the heads of the sermon immediately. . . . At last came the happy moment of his taking leave, for I would not ask him to stay supper. And, moreover, he talked of going to a lecture at St Helen's. And then (though I had an opportunity of saying little more than yes and no all the time, for he took the vapours he had put me into for devotion or gravity, at least, I believe), he pressed my hand, looked *frightfully* kind, and gave me to understand that if upon further conversation and inquiry into my character he should happen to like me as well as he did from my behaviour and person, why, truly, I need not fear in time being blessed with him for my husband." [1]

One more quotation, this time from the letter of a country cousin visiting London, which is in its way as graphic as a drawing by Hogarth, must close these extracts.

"From thence we went into the (Greenwich) Park, where I beheld divers odd scenes of holiday folks. Here appeared a rakish young fellow, with two or three women who looked like servant-maids ; the hero delighted, the nymphs smiling round him. There, a careful looking father with

[1] *Familiar Letters,* pp. 115, 116.

his children on each side; trains of admiring lovers, ready paired, followed one another in thronging crowds at the gate; a sea officer with a lady not over-burdened with modesty in her behaviour; a crowd of city apprentices, some with, some without, their lasses; half-a-dozen beaux ogling all they met, and several seemingly disconsolate virgins walking alone. The concourse of middling objects pressed chiefly towards a high hill in the middle of the park, where, as they arrived, their business was to take hold of hands, and run down as fast as possible, amidst the huzzas of a multitude of people. . . . This, madam, is a diversion you would not expect near the polite city of London; but I assure you such a levity possessed almost everybody assembled on this occasion as made the park, though most beautiful in itself, no way entertaining to your most dutiful niece."[1]

The first edition of the *Familiar Letters* was published anonymously, and it was not till after his death that the novelist's name appeared on the title-page. It seems to have served its end as a complete letter-writer (and moral guide) for the lower classes; for Mrs Barbauld mentions it as a favourite book in the servants' kitchen-drawer. "But when so found," she says, "it has not infrequently detained the eye of the mistress, wondering all the while, by what secret charm she was induced to turn over a book apparently too low for her perusal, and that charm was— Richardson."

[1] *Familiar Letters*, pp. 219, 220.

It is possible that while writing these letters
the author often became so much interested in
his imaginary correspondents that he would have
liked to develop the circumstances at which they
hint. But the necessity for variety and for dealing
with a large range of topics prevented him from
turning this book, whose primary motive was edu-
cational, into a story. He deliberately kept to
the lines marked out for him, and seems to have
taken some pains to adapt his language to the
class for which he was writing ; for, many years
afterwards, apologising for the book as being too
low for the perusal of a friend who had asked to
see it, he states that he laid aside several letters,
after he had written them, as "too high for the
view of my two friends" (Rivington and Osborne).
It is worthy of note that this "lowness" of style
gave Lord Jeffrey an opportunity for a characteristic criticism. In his review of Mrs Barbauld's
Life of Richardson, he commends the volume of
Familiar Letters as being excellently adapted to
its purpose, but adds that "it may be of singular
use to Mr Wordsworth and his friends in their
great scheme of turning all our poetry into the
language of the common people. In this view
we commend it very earnestly to their consideration."

Pamela as has been already seen, was composed at a white heat, and was written in three
months. It had an immediate success, especially
among the middle classes, but Mrs Barbauld tells
how the fine ladies at Ranelagh held up the

volumes containing it to each other to show
"they had got the book everyone was talking
of." This must be a mistake, as Ranelagh was
not opened till 1742,[1] but we may perhaps sub-
stitute Vauxhall for the name of the rival place
of entertainment. Aaron Hill[2] relates how Dr
Slocock, Chaplain of St Saviour's, Southwark,
recommended it from the pulpit, and it was at
once seized upon by the instructors of the young
as a book to be pressed into their service.

Even Mr Pope for once condescended to be
generous, and said that *Pamela* "would do more
good than many volumes of sermons." At
Slough, near Windsor, the inhabitants used to
gather round the village forge while the black-
smith read the story aloud. As soon as he came
to the place where the fate of the heroine is
decided by a happy marriage, his hearers were

[1] See *Correspondence of Horace Walpole*, May 26, 1742, "Two
nights ago Ranelagh Gardens were opened at Chelsea."

[2] "January 6, 1740-1741. All the blessings of inward content
and of outward fidelity on that hearty good friend of yours, Dr
Slocock of St Saviour's. When you call him a worthy divine, you
but speak with your usual propriety. So uncommon a truth as he
dared to recommend from his pulpit did an honour not only to
Pamela but to the speaker and the place where it was spoken."
This extract from an unpublished letter in the South Kensington
MSS. confirms Mrs Barbauld's statement that "Dr Slocock recommended *Pamela* from the pulpit," and proves that Slocock in this
passage is not a misprint for Sherlock, as has been supposed.
Moreover, Canon Thompson, Rector and Chancellor of St
Saviour's, kindly informs me that Dr Benjamin Slocock commenced
his ministry at St Saviour's in 1725, and also says, on the authority
of the Rev. O. E. Slocock, that the doctor was chaplain from 1728
to 1753.

so excited that they cheered for joy, ran for the church keys, and rang the bells to give expression to their gladness.

Richardson was at once overwhelmed with letters from eager readers who longed to know whether the story was true. Six ladies pressed him to declare on his honour, which they were sure he was too much of a gentleman to violate, whether the story was true or false, and they hoped Mrs B. (*i.e.* Pamela), if there was such a lady, would not be against satisfying a request which redounded so much to her honour. They added that they had taken an oath to keep the secret, should he intrust it to them, and that they would never cease writing till he obliged them. To this Richardson answered, in his usual manner of " polite raillery," that no secret entrusted to six ladies could long remain inviolate, and that as they maintained their own anonymity they could hardly expect Mrs B. to resign hers. Another laudatory letter concludes with a postscript which runs thus :—

" *P.S.*—I think that nothing can more evidently prove how much your performance resembles nature than the effect it produced on a young miss not twelve years old, who was so struck with the reading of it that she broke out in these pretty verses :—

> " O Pamela, thy virtuous mind
> Riches and honour has resigned ;
> Riches were but dross to thee,
> Comparéd with thy modesty.

" But since the case is altered thus,
With thankfulness thou may'st rehearse
The many combats thou hast made,
And think with joy thou'rt fully paid.

" Praise God for all his mercies past,
Beg that His favours still may last,
And in obedience due express
Thy highest love and thankfulness." [1]

This is only one out of many poetical compliments to Richardson. Aaron Hill, who probably shrewdly suspected his friend's responsibility in the matter, was the writer of another, addressed " to the unknown author of the beautiful new piece called *Pamela.*" The substance of this effusion is a lament over the degraded state of contemporary morality, which causes the example of " Sweet Pamela, for ever blooming maid," to be wasted on an age too gross to profit by it.

" Tho' thine each virtue that a God could lend,
Thine every help that every heart can mend ;
'Tis thine in vain !   Thou wak'st a dying land ;
And lift'st departed hope with fruitless hand.
Death has no cure, thou hast mistimed thy aim,
Rome had her Goths, and all beyond was shame." [2]

Hill's correspondence is full of similar tributes to the novelist, expressed in a vein of extreme exaggeration ; for, as Mr Leslie Stephen has remarked, he was a " florid flatterer," even in those days of polite hyperbole, and, moreover, was under substantial pecuniary obligations to

[1] Forster MS., " Philaretes " to Richardson, June 22, 1741.
[2] " Hill, *Works,*" iii. 348.

Richardson. "Who could have dreamed he should find," he wrote once, "under the modest guise of a novel, all the soul of religion, good breeding, discretion, good nature, wit, fancy, fine thought, and morality? . . . It has witchcraft in every page of it, but it is the witchcraft of passion and meaning. . . . Yet I confess there is one in the world of whom I think with still greater respect than of *Pamela*, and that is the wonderful author of *Pamela*. Pray, who is he, dear sir? and where has he been able to hide hitherto such an encircling and all-mastering spirit?" Such, indeed, was Hill's enthusiasm, that he read the book aloud for the entertainment of his guests; and another amusing letter tells how a little boy of six who, during the reading, had hidden himself behind the ladies' hoops, was overcome with emotion at the tale of the heroine's woes. "I turned his innocent face to look towards me, but his eyes were quite lost in his tears, which running down from his cheeks in free currents had formed two sincere little fountains on the part of the carpet he hung over. All the ladies in the company were ready to devour him with kisses, and he has since become doubly a favourite, and is, perhaps, the youngest of Pamela's converts." [1]

Amidst this almost universal chorus of praise, there were, however, some discordant notes. In a letter to the publisher, Osborne, an anonymous writer took exception to the preface. "You were bewitched," he said, "to print that bad stuff in the

[1] Barbauld, i. 58.

introduction, for it has made enemies, as the writer, indeed, calls us all fools, and of coarse discernment ; 'tis as a requital to your readers. He is too full of himself and too gross in his praise of the author, though I confess he deserves much. But I believe he has done himself no good in accepting of such greasy compliments. He would do well to alter it and make it shorter." [1] What would this ingenious critic have said had he known that the writer of the story and of the introductory panegyric were identical ?

The great success of the book led to two immediate results. A spurious continuation, called *Pamela in High Life*, induced Richardson to publish a genuine sequel in two volumes, relating the history of Pamela's married life. Pope and Warburton had advised Richardson "to make it a vehicle for satire upon the follies and fashions of the great world by representing the light in which they would appear to the rustic Pamela when she was introduced to them." But the author had too little knowledge of society, and too much respect for "high life" to ridicule it ; and the second part of *Pamela*, far from being an entertaining exposure of polite vice, is a heavy treatise on the domestic virtues.

The other result of Richardson's success was more noteworthy. The faults of *Pamela*, being those that arise especially from a narrow judgment and a too literal turn of mind, were just such as would strike a man like Henry Fielding, who,

[1] Forster MS. Miscell. Corr.

though Richardson's junior by nearly twenty years, possessed twice his knowledge of the world. He had been writing plays—good, bad, and indifferent—for many years, till the hand of the licenser, provoked by his daring attacks on the government, had interfered with their production. Probably, too, he tired of the harassing career of playwright, for about this time he returned to the legal profession, for which he had originally been intended. He did not, however, entirely relinquish literary work, and the appearance of *Pamela* presented him with an opportunity that he could not refrain from using. Fielding's good women, if of somewhat robust character, are always perfectly refined and generous in their dealings with men; the idea of a woman making capital out of her virtue, which is the pivot on which Richardson's story turns, was to him equally absurd and distasteful.

As early as 1741 there appeared, under the pseudonym of Mr Conny Keyber,[1] a very gross, but at the same time witty parody of *Pamela*, entitled: *An Apology for the Life of Mrs Shamela Andrews, in which the many notorious falsehoods and misrepresentations of a book called "Pamela" are exposed and refuted, and all the matchless arts of that young politician set in a true and just light.* The occasion of the book is supposed to be the presentation of a copy of *Pamela* by a certain

---

[1] Apparently a parody on the name of Colley Cibber, whom Fielding was never weary of satirizing. See *Joseph Andrews*, bk. i. chap. i.

Parson Tickletext to his friend Parson Oliver. "Herewith I transmit you a copy of sweet, dear, pretty *Pamela*, a little book which this winter hath produced ; of which I make no doubt you have already heard mention from some of your neighbouring clergy, for we have made it our common business here, not only to cry it up, but to preach it likewise. The pulpit as well as the coffee-house hath resounded with its praise, and it is expected shortly that his L——p will recommend it in a letter to our whole body." To this Parson Oliver replies that he is sorry the story has so great a reputation, for, as he lives in the neighbourhood where its events took place, he has a better opportunity of judging of the facts of the case, and sends letters to prove that the lady, far from being the virtuous character she is represented, is, in fact, a most disreputable person, while the hero is a fool to be deceived by her. These letters are parodies of those in Richardson's book, and unmercifully expose its many weak points, especially the mingled piety and cunning of the heroine. For instance, Shamela tells us that when she heard her master coming, " I ran up into my room, and washed and dressed myself as well as I could, and put on my prettiest round-eared cap, and then I practised all my airs before the glass, and then I sat down and read a chapter in *The Whole Duty of Man*." The book concludes with a short summary by Parson Oliver of the shortcomings of the original, which, he says, is not the kind of story he would give his daughter

or his servant-maid.   Thus the parody was quite
seriously intended as a protest against the immoral
tendency of *Pamela*, and from internal evidence
I am inclined to think that it was not improbably
written by Fielding, to whom Richardson, at any
rate, attributed it.   There is, for example, a very
strong suggestion of Fielding in the introductory
letter " from the Editor to himself," which is, of
course, a skit on Richardson's prefatory puff to the
anonymous first edition of *Pamela*.

However this may be, it is certain that Fielding was already meditating his immortal parody,
Joseph Andrews, which appeared in 1742.   It represents Pamela's brother in circumstances of
similar difficulty from the advances of Lady Booby
(a wicked expansion of Richardson's Mr B.,
which first occurs in the *Life of Mrs Shamela
Andrews*, and thus affords a further proof of its
authorship).   But it was not long before Fielding
became so much interested in his story that he
forgot his original plan, and found himself producing a *picaresque* novel on the lines of *Gil
Blas*, but better constructed, and less weighted
with episodes.   For the sake of consistency, and
prompted by the sense of artistic unity gained by
his long training as a playwright, he makes Lady
Booby reappear in the last chapters, in company
with Pamela and Mr B.

Richardson naturally resented the liberty that
had been taken, and though he knew Fielding,
whose sister was a frequent visitor at North End,
he never forgave him ; the correspondence is full

of jealous references to his rival's success, which will be noticed in another place.

The same year that saw the publication of *Pamela* found its author engaged in very different labours. He was employed by a Society for the Encouragement of Learning to edit the letters of Sir Thomas Roe, who, in the reign of James I., had been employed in diplomatic missions in India and Turkey. The portion of the correspondence that Richardson edited relates to his negotiations at the Ottoman Porte, and occupies, in double columns, a large folio. It is introduced by a preliminary epistle, addressed to the king, who is reminded of the special interest, which he, as a descendant of James I., should take in the subject; and there is also a preface which gives some account of the life and writings of Roe. Finally, the editor supplied a very exhaustive and laborious index, which, as one of his correspondents remarked, rendered almost unnecessary the perusal of the letters. By such labours Richardson acquired the documentary habit that is less pleasantly noticeable in his romances. Method had been the guiding star of his life; it had led him through the intricacies of a vast amount of business and had enabled him to acquire a competency. No wonder, then, that he exalted this virtue beyond its deserts, making his sentimental misses take copies of their very love-letters, and regulate their duties and pleasures by an elaborate division of hours and minutes.

It was in this year also that an edition of

Æsop's Fables, with morals and reflections adapted
from L'Estrange, was published by Richardson's
friend, Osborne. The name of the editor is not
given, but as we know that Richardson did edit
these fables "with reflections," it is reasonable to
suppose that the work is his. The introduction,
moreover, bears clear traces of his hand, especially
in the careful classification of the fables according
to the alterations made in L'Estrange's morals.
There is also an elaborate alphabetical index to
the titles.

Two years after this, another book, which seems
to have had a wide popularity, appeared under
Richardson's supervision. This was Defoe's *Tour
through Great Britain*, a descriptive survey of
England and Scotland, which had first been
published in 1723. It was now somewhat out of
date, and an unsigned preface, probably by
Richardson, states that the editor "has spared no
expense to make the present (edition) as complete
as the nature of the work would admit"; many
particulars have been added, especially concerning
Scotland; and, says the writer, "he was glad of
doing some further justice to that country which
has generally been slightly considered by those
who know little of it." This kindly reference to
the sister kingdom is worth noticing, when one
considers the contemporary antipathy to Scotland.
Richardson had probably reprinted the work in
its original form before this, as Hill, in a letter
written in 1739, refers to a *Survey of Great*

Britain, and the title-page of the copy in the British Museum, dated 1742, states that it is the third edition.

Another labour of these years was the printing of the Journals of the House of Commons, a commission which Richardson had obtained through the friendship of Mr Onslow, the Speaker. He did not, however, receive the payment for this work as promptly as he could have wished; for when, in 1748, Hill, whose money difficulties appear to have been chronic, appealed to him for aid, he replied that his great weekly disbursements and a still remaining debt due to him for upwards of £1500, for printing the ten folio volumes of the Journals, prevented him from helping him as much as he would have liked.[1]

Thus the time that elapsed between the appearance of *Pamela,* and that of *Clarissa* was full of business, and it is not surprising that the completion of the latter work was so long delayed. It was probably begun not long after the publication of the *Tour through Great Britain,* since Hill, in an unpublished letter of February 1745, alludes to "the charming Miss Harlowe," and expresses his impatience to hear of her elopement and its consequences. This proves that Richardson had already invited his friend's criticism on the book, which forms the chief subject of their correspondence between the years 1745 and 1748. As a study in the relations of two literary men,

[1] The debt was still unpaid in 1756.   See below, p. 57.

each thoroughly believing in his own powers, yet
politely crediting the other with the greater genius,
these letters are extremely interesting ; for while
the novelist's vanity impels him to discuss his
work under the pretence of asking advice about
it, he cannot endure the slightest approach to
adverse criticism.   Hill, with a singular want of
tact, but from motives with which most readers of
Clarissa will sympathise, suggested an abridgement of the first two volumes, and actually made
some attempts in this direction.   Richardson replied
in a letter full of grateful acknowledgments, but
excused himself from using the summaries on the
score that his friend's "time and genius would
be derogatorily employed in an undertaking so
grovelling and puerile," and further, he says, "all
that I designed by it, I doubt, cannot be answered
in so short a compass, without taking from it
those simple and diffuse parts which some like, and
have (however unduly), complimented me upon,
as making a new species of writing.   I am sure
you will not be displeased with me, if I rather
alter verbally, than verbally copy from you —
and this the rather, as there are some passages
and descriptions omitted, which have been approved by persons of judgment, who would be
disappointed if ever it be published, not to find
them."[1]

Hill, however, was not daunted by the polite
rejection of his abridgement, and of his proposed

[1] Forster MS., Correspondence with Hill.

alternative titles for the novel,[1] which are also to be found in the correspondence at South Kensington. He continued to send his suggestions and criticisms, till, having ventured to call Clarissa's flight with Lovelace "a rash elopement," he offended Richardson so much that a quarrel nearly ensued. They were, however, soon reconciled and continued to be on friendly terms till Hill's death in 1750.

[1] One of these suggested titles runs as follows :—

THE LADY'S LEGACY,

or,

The Whole Gay and Serious Compass of the Human Heart
Laid Open
For the Service of Both Sexes
In the History of the Life and Ruin of
A Lately Celebrated Beauty,

Miss CLARISSA HARLOWE ;

including

Great Variety of other Lives and Characters
Occasionally Interested in the Moving Story,
Detecting and Exposing
The Most Secret Arts and Subtlest Practices
Of
That Endangering Species of Triumphant Rakes
Called

WOMEN'S MEN,

Assisted by Corrupt and Vicious Engines of the Sex they plot
against.

Published in compliance with the Lady's order, on her deathbed,
as a warning to the unguarded, vain or credulous.

CHAPTER II

1748-1761

AT last *Clarissa* was finished. The book was published in 1748, the first four volumes appearing in the spring, the last four in the autumn of that year. Its success was even greater than that of *Pamela*, and at once raised Richardson to the first rank among living writers. For although fine ladies and gentlemen like Lady Mary Wortley Montagu, Horace Walpole, or Lord Chesterfield, might give but grudging approval, and while bearing testimony to the moving power of the story criticise its tediousness and prolixity, the middle classes, for whom it was written, and whose tone and sentiment it may be justly taken to represent, were seized with wild enthusiasm for it. In the interval between the publication of the volumes the author was besieged with earnest entreaties that he would give the story a happy ending. Dr Young begged that the title-page of the *Night Thoughts*, which were issued from Richardson's press, should bear the inscription "published by the author of *Clarissa*." "This," he says, "is a trick to put it into more hands. I know it would have that

effect." [1] Cibber, the veteran laureate, "read a
course of full five hours and a half, without
drawing bit" ; [2] and Aaron Hill, as he described
the effect of the concluding volumes on his family
circle, became for once actually poetical. "At
this moment," he wrote, "I have three girls round
me—each a separate volume in her hand, and all
their eyes like a wet flower in April." [3]

But, as in the case of *Pamela*, some adverse
opinions found voice. An anonymous correspondent, writing in May 1748, when only four volumes
had appeared, dared to say that all the readers he had
met with " were offended at the tedious repetitions,
and when they hoped to come to something of
moment, they were hardly anything advanced in
the story. Others wished the author had remembered Mr Prior's advice, ' not to tire his
friend to grace his story.' Another (and that a
man of learning) decided ' 'twas much ado about
nothing,' and many things of the like nature." [4]
Moreover, Richardson's friend Channing tells him
how one day he "happened into the company of
a Mowbray and Beau Fribble, each of whom had
a volume of your work in his hands, skipping like
monkeys from letter to letter. ' Yours, gentlemen ;
what so busily employed about ? ' ' This d—d
Clarissa. Zounds, what a rout is here about a
woman ! ' ' Don't you like her character ? ' ' I can
only tell you she's such a woman as I never met with
yet, and hope never to have to do with.' ' What

---

[1] Barbauld, ii. 28.   [2] *Ibid.*, ii. 169.
[3] Forster MS., Corr. with Hill.   [4] *Ibid.*, Miscellaneous letters.

say you, sir ?' 'Lawd, such a multitude of reading
without coming at the story, 'tis quite tiresome; a
man can never get through with any patience, by
my sawl!'"[1]   From this it may be conjectured that
the very people whom Richardson hoped to benefit
by his performance were exactly those for whom
it had no attraction; though Urania Hill, the
only one of Hill's daughters who inherited his
faculty for indifferent verse, declared that the
domestic life of unborn generations would profit
by it :—

> " Thence maids shall learn to shun the wiles of art,
>   And early prudence guard the female heart,
>   Thence thousands yet unborn shall owe thee praise,
>   That duteous wives and daughters bless their days ;
>   Friends, parents, children, lovers, duty know,
>   And all with worthy emulation glow !" [2]

It was in the autumn of this year, 1748, when
all England was still in suspense as to the ultimate
fate of Clarissa, that Richardson paid the memorable visit to Tunbridge Wells, which forms the
basis of the well-known picturesque pages in
The Virginians.   Thackeray puts the date of the
visit eight years later, but it is the earlier stay for
which we have most information, and if Richardson
repeated his visit in 1756, failing health must have
prevented him from playing so active a part as
his brother novelist describes.   The sketch by
Logan of the "remarkable characters who were at
Tunbridge Wells with Richardson in 1748," with

---

[1] Forster MS., Channing to Richardson.   [2] Forster MS.

its explanatory key in his own hand, testifies to the intense pleasure that the author of *Clarissa* felt in his growing fame, and in the attention that he received from the notable people who visited this fashionable Spa. For here are Garrick and Onslow and Lyttelton; and greatest of all, though the period of his triumph was still to come, Mr Pitt. And here is one of Richardson's intimate friends, Colley Cibber, who at seventy-seven had by no means lost his liking for a pretty face. The Dr Johnson mentioned can hardly be the great lexicographer, who in 1748 was still struggling with poverty and the dictionary, which did not appear till 1755. Moreover, he was at that time plain Mr Johnson, and though Thackeray, probably following Malone, includes him, with Lord Chesterfield and Miss Mulso, and others who are not represented in the picture, in the company at the Wells, it is not very likely that he was there at this time.

But this sketch is not the only record of Richardson's visit. In a letter to Miss Highmore he gives a graphic account of the society at the Spa. "Do come," he says, "and see how your other old lover (Cibber) spins away, hunting after new faces at seventy-seven. You will see him in his kingdom, and he will read to you a new performance, calculated indeed for the perts of the place: *A Dialogue between a Father and a Daughter*, very sprightly. . . . What figures do Mr Nash and Mr Cibber make, hunting after new beauties, and with faces of high importance tra-

versing the walks! God bless you, come and
see them! And if you do, I will show you a still
more grotesque figure than either—a sly sinner,
creeping along the very edges of the walks, getting
behind benches, one hand in his bosom, the other
held up to his chin as if to keep it in place, afraid
of being seen as a thief of detection. The people
of fashion, if he happen to cross a walk (which he
always does with precipitation), unsmiling their
faces, as if they thought him in the way ; and he as
sensible of so being, stealing in and out of the bookseller's shop, as if he had one of their glass cases
under his coat. Come and see this odd figure!"[1]

But, notwithstanding the evident gusto with
which he describes these gay scenes, Richardson,
in another letter,[2] earnestly disclaims the idea of
altogether approving of so much frivolity. The
manners of the ladies, especially, are not quite
what they should be, although "there are very
few pretty girls here. Modesty, humility, graciousness, are now all banished from the behaviour
of these public-place frequenters of the sex.
Women are not what they were." And if Miss
Chudleigh, the famous maid of honour, who afterwards became Duchess of Kingston, was typical
of the ladies present, these strictures were probably
not too severe. "Mr Cibber," continues his friend,
"was over head and ears in love with Miss Chudleigh ; her admirers (such was his happiness!) were
not jealous of him ; but, pleased with that wit in
him which they had not, were always for calling

[1] Barbauld, ii. 204-206.   [2] Barbauld, iii. 315-317.

THE REMARKABLE CHARACTERS WHO WERE AT TUNBRIDGE WELLS IN 1748, FROM A DRAWING IN HIS POSSESSION
WITH REFERENCES IN HIS OWN WRITING

1748 Aug:
1. Dr. Johnson
2. Bp. of Salisbury (Dr. Gilbert)
3. Ld. Harcourt

4. Mr. Cibber (Colley)
5. Mr. Garrick
6. Mrs. Frasi (The Singer)
7. Mr. N. A

8. Miss Chudleigh (Dutch of Kingston)
9. Mr. Pitt (Earl of Chatham)
10. Mr. Onslow (The Speaker)
11. Ld. Powis

12. Dutch of Norfolk
13. Miss Banks
14. Lady Lincoln
15. Mr. Littleton (Afterwards Lord Lyttelton)

16. The Baron (A German Gamester)
17. Monsym (Mr. Richardson)
18. Mrs. Onslow

19. Miss Onslow
20. Mrs. Johnson (The Dr's Wife)
21. Mr. Whiston
22. Crispian the Gout
23. The Woman of the Wells

him to her. She said pretty things—for she was Miss Chudleigh. He said pretty things—for he was Mr Cibber; and all the company, men and women, seemed to think they had an interest in what was said, and were half as well pleased as if they had said the sprightly things themselves; and mighty well contented were they to be second hand repeaters of the pretty things. But once I faced the laureate squatted upon one of the benches, with a face more wrinkled than ordinary with disappointment. 'I thought,' said I, 'you were of the party at the tea-treat—Miss Chudleigh is gone into the tea-room.' 'Pshaww!' said he, 'there is no coming at her, she is so surrounded by the toupets.' And I left him upon the fret. But he was called to soon after, and in he flew, and his face shone again and looked smooth."

It was not long after Richardson returned from Tunbridge Wells that he received his first letter from Lady Bradshaigh, who, writing under the name of Belfour, implored him to convert Lovelace and give *Clarissa* a happy ending. This led to a correspondence, and during the eighteen months that elapsed before they met in 1750, he and his "incognita," as he called her, kept up a brisk interchange of letters, from which, though they are principally concerned with literary discussions, a few details as to Richardson's private life may be gleaned. From one of them (Dec. 16, 1749),[1] we learn that the novelist's health was so bad that he had long neglected going to church.

[1] Barbauld, iv. 298.

D

As his family attended Fulham Parish Church, quite three miles away, this is scarcely surprising; perhaps, too, he was glad of the rest that Sunday morning brought, for while prospering more and more, he was harassed by many business cares. A strike among his compositors in 1748 gave him a good deal of trouble, and he was apparently still annoyed by the delay he experienced in obtaining payment for printing the Journals of the House of Commons. In spite of these anxieties, however, he was already planning a fresh book, and in the midst of his engagements was ready to give a helping hand to his friend Johnson, who had just begun to issue *The Rambler*.

This paper, which was a bi-weekly sheet on the model of *The Spectator*, but, as may be imagined from the character of the author, much more ponderous and far less graceful, first appeared on March 20, 1750. It was too serious and didactic to find much favour with the general public, and its circulation was only about five hundred. But its sombre tone at once appealed to Richardson, who wrote to Cave, the publisher, to express his pleasure at the new publication. "I should rejoice," he said, "to hear that they succeed; for I would not for any consideration that they should be laid down through discouragement." To this Cave replied that, owing perhaps to the price of twopence, or the unfavourable season of their first publication, no great boast could be made of the sale.[1] But the paper continued to appear, and on

[1] Barbauld, i. 170.

Tuesday, February 19, 1751, there was published number 97, with the following introduction by the editor :—

" The reader is indebted for this day's entertainment to an author from whom the age has received greater favours, who has enlarged the knowledge of human nature, and taught the passions to move at the command of virtue."

" This day's entertainment " consisted of a lamentation in Richardson's ordinary vein over the corruption of feminine manners, which he declares have greatly deteriorated since the days of *The Spectator*, and a comparison between the method of courtship practised in the days of Queen Anne, and that in vogue in the last years of George II. It is satisfactory to know that Richardson's efforts in his friend's behalf were so far successful that more copies of this number were sold than of any other.

Meanwhile, he had been composing the first chapters of *Sir Charles Grandison*. As early as 1749 Lady Bradshaigh had written to him, urging him to complete his efforts towards raising the moral standard of the age by giving a masculine counterpart of *Clarissa*. " It is a character we want," she says, " I am sorry to say it ; but few there are who deserve it," and then follow some slighting reflections on *Tom Jones*, whose popularity the writer is quite at a loss to account for. It was perhaps not the least inducement to Richardson to draw a model hero, that his rival had created one who was so much open to criticism.

However this may be, the new book proceeded apace, and by 1751 much must have been written, for in a letter of that date Susannah Highmore comments on its progress to her friend Hester Mulso. "We have this day had the satisfaction of hearing Miss Grandison extricate herself from those difficulties you left her involved in. Oh! my dear, Sir Charles will be all we wish him—I am sure he will—and is destined to show the world what the purest love should be, when inspired by an object irresistibly amiable, like Miss Byron!"[1] But the composition of the book was not unattended by difficulty, for Richardson, in choosing for his hero a man belonging to a higher social plane than he had hitherto attempted to describe, was hampered by insufficient knowledge of such society. "How shall a man," he asked plaintively of Lady Bradshaigh, "how shall a man obscurely situated, never delighting in public entertainments, nor in his youth able to frequent them from narrowness of fortune had he a taste for them; one of the most attentive of men to the calls of his business; his situation for many years producing nothing but the prospects of a numerous family . . . naturally shy and sheepish . . . how shall such a man pretend to describe and enter into characters in upper life? How shall such a man draw scenes of busy yet elegant trifling?"[2] Nevertheless, he went boldly on, drawing bravely on his imagination for these scenes in high life, and for the yet more remote subject of the deportment of

[1] Barbauld, ii. 259.   [2] *Ibid.*, vi. 86.

the Italian nobility; fortified by the applause of all his feminine audience, he could afford to despise the possible sneers of Lord Chesterfield and Lady Mary Wortley Montagu. And so the story of Sir Charles continued to grow in bulk, till, as he complained, he was forced to commit violence in order to bring it into seven twelves volumes, which he was determined it should not exceed. Meanwhile, he had the benefit of a running criticism from the many correspondents to whom he lent copies of his manuscript, and from the guests, who, gathered together at North End, awaited further news of Harriet and Clementina with as much eagerness as the modern public exhibits for military despatches in time of war. Richardson was just one of those people for whose productive power the gentle titillation of undiscriminating flattery is almost a necessity ; an unconscionable egoist, who was never weary of discussing his own work, yet withal so diffident that he needed the continual stimulus of reiterated approval. He was largely sustained in his toil by the encouragement of his feminine disciples, nor should we be far out in saying that the prolixity of his third novel is due as much to their perseverance in flattery as to his own indefatigable industry.[1]

[1] *Cf.* " Correspondence of Mrs Carter and Miss Talbot," i. 361. " Do you know the Grandison family? If you do not, you will to your cost. Oh, Miss Carter, did you ever call Pygmalion a fool for making an image and falling in love with it ? And do you know that you and I are two Pygmalionesses? Did not Mr Richardson ask us for some traits of his good man's character : and did we not give him some ? And has not he gone and put these and his own

The book was published in the autumn of
1753, thus following *Clarissa Harlowe* at a
much shorter interval than separated the appearance of the latter novel from that of *Pamela*.
Its publication was hastened by a fraud practised
on the author by some Dublin booksellers, who, by
corrupting Richardson's compositors, managed to
get the sheets in advance of the time fixed for its
appearance in London, and brought it out without
the author's sanction and in an incomplete form.
Richardson was justly indignant at this piracy,
and issued a long statement of the affair, entitled,
" *The Case of Samuel Richardson of London, Printer,
at the Invasion of his Property in the History of
Sir Charles Grandison.*" " The work thus invaded,"
he complains,—and this he seems to consider an
immense aggravation of the offence—" is a moral
work." Moreover, the English edition is printed
and published at his own expense, without having
recourse to subscription. " Never was work more
the property of any man than this is his." But it
was impossible to obtain any redress, and though
he afterwards sent his own edition to Dublin to
be sold there at a low price, the pirates under-
sold him, and for what he did dispose of he did
not get the money. His letters of this period
plainly betray the perturbation caused by the
matter, and are full of naïve surprise at the

charming ideas into a book and formed a Sir Charles Grandison?
And though all the rising generation should copy after him, what
good will that do poor us, who must sigh and pine till they are
educated?

iniquity of the rogues who can thus defraud an honest man. "These Irishmen!" he exclaims to Edwards, "they do vex me; for I am informed that they are driving on with five volumes at five different presses, and are agreeing with some Scottish booksellers to print them in Scotland, and intend to make the most of their wickedness by sending copies to France before publication. What have I done, my dear friend, to be thus treated?"

To balance this vexation, the enthusiasm evoked by Richardson's third book was not less than that which had greeted its predecessors. "Oh, sir, you ought to have been a bishop!" wrote Lady Brad-shaigh, after reading the last volume; and Colley Cibber declared that he would rather have the fame deserved by Richardson's zeal for virtue than be preferred as a poet to Pope or his Homer. John Chapone, who afterwards married Hester Mulso, considered that Sir Charles was the noblest representation that ever did honour to man; Mrs Delany filled her letters with eulogies of both author and hero; and Urania Hill, now Mrs Johnson, and Thomas Edwards, contributed fresh poetical compliments. But unique among all these tributes to the genius of the novelist is the following effusion from an imprisoned debtor, who attributed his recent conversion to Richardson's teaching :—

" May 2, 1754.

" SIR,—Gratitude compels me to return you my most unfeigned thanks for effecting in a few hours

by your *Sir Charles Grandison* what five years'
imprisonment with all the want and indigence
imaginable annexed to it could not. I've had my
horrors and terrors in a great degree, and thoughts
of future economy, when discharged by an insolvent
act; but still with shame confess I retained in
great measure my old principles of libertinism,
and often flattered myself with enjoying my old
acquaintances' company once more in affluence;
but happily met with your Sir Charles, where I
saw virtue so charmingly delineated, so delightfully
described, that it immediately affected me in the
highest degree, more especially when I read the
contrast in the unhappy Sir Hargrave Pollexfen's
character and his dreadful catastrophe.

"Yes, sir, I'm now determined during my stay in
confinement and when in the world to make virtue
and honour to be the standard and governor of all
my actions; and, as real happiness must infallibly
be the consequence, I shall always esteem you as
the source of every good that may hereafter accrue
to one who is with the greatest respect and sincerity,—Sir, Your much obliged humble servant,

"B. F." [1]

Here was success indeed, and Richardson had
some reason to plume himself on the realisation of
his aims as a moral reformer. Nor was "B. F."
the only impecunious gentleman to whom the story
afforded moral support. Eusebius Sylvester, an
"attorney of Warwick," also testified to the utility

[1] Forster MS., Miscellaneous Correspondence.

of the example given, and on the strength of his admiration wrote to the author for further instruction. Richardson, evidently flattered by this mark of respect, entered into a correspondence with him, and everything went well until Sylvester began to ask for pecuniary, as well as for ethical, aid. Richardson, who was always ready to help his friends, but expected to be repaid, if not in kind, at least by an immoderate amount of gratitude and flattery, sent £25, and apologised for the smallness of the loan on the score of the many calls on his purse. He had hoped to spare more, he says, "from the promises of a gentleman who is indebted to me in a very large sum, upwards of £1500, for printing a very large work, 'The Journals of the House of Commons.' He has put me off (though I pressed him very earnestly for but a part of it) for some time, and now tells me that he will soon discharge the debt, and intimates that he expects to pay me interest for the time he shall trespass upon me. I have in a manner contracted for a little land lying contiguous to a small estate of my late deceased brother, which will be a great convenience to that good family. And I fear, as the above gentleman has disappointed me, that I must sell out of the little matter I have in the stocks £500 at ten or eleven per cent. disadvantage to complete the purchase. £450 I lent to a dear friend and relation about a year ago to make his last hours easy. My removal the summer preceding this from North End, Hammersmith, to Parson's Green, sunk me upwards of £300 from my current cash, and the

building I erected last summer for my printing-office
and what it will cost me to remove from the house
I so long lived in to the new one adjoining to my
new building has and will cost me upwards of
£400.   My expenditures weekly are between £30
and £40 to journeymen, etc."[1]

But Mr Sylvester was too far sunk in debt for
£25 to be more than a temporary relief, and
though the correspondents continued for some
time on friendly terms, and Richardson sent
further monetary help, accompanied by many
pages of closely written counsel, the non-payment
of the debt at last led to an open rupture. Nothing
could throw more light on the character of the
novelist — credulous, excessively susceptible to
flattery, generous yet tenacious, and goaded to a
fury of irritability by ingratitude on the part of
one he had benefited—than these letters. Whether
the money was ever forthcoming is doubtful ;
Richardson's dunning epistles seem to have had
no effect, and the correspondence closes in 1759
with an angry remonstrance written on his behalf
to Sylvester, accusing him of base ingratitude
and deceit.

The letter quoted above gives some idea of
Richardson's pecuniary position in 1756. Two
years before he had left the house at North End,
where he had lived for sixteen years, owing to a
disagreement with his landlord. The property
had changed hands, and the new owner, Mr
Pratt, on the strength of Richardson's own

[1] Forster MS., Correspondence with Eusebius Sylvester.

improvements, had raised the rent from £25 to £40 a year. In a long letter to Edwards[1] he sets forth his grievances at this increase. His predecessor, he complains, had paid only £30 a year, and when he took the house the rent was reduced because he had no use for the stables and because his first landlord, Mr Vanderplank, lived near, and having " two girls that were growing up and would have handsome fortunes, he was cautious of whom he admitted into so near a neighbourhood." Mr Pratt, however, held to his demand, and Richardson then moved to another house on the south side of Parson's Green, which has since disappeared. He had hesitated between this and one at Finchley, but the latter place was undesirable on account of its popularity with highwaymen. " If there you dwell," wrote one anxious correspondent, " I foresee death and destruction in your next work ; and bitter will be the complaints of all your fair readers. As our thoughts are, in some degree, influenced by what we hear and see, rapes, robberies and murders must ensue if you are planted so near their scene of action as to be continually hearing of highwaymen, and viewing of gibbets." To this Richardson replied that his friend's kind concern was now unnecessary, since he had settled on his new home —" an old monastery-like house, with a porch at the door, wherein he proposed often to reconnoitre the green and watch for the visits of his friends." [2]

---

[1] Forster MS., Correspondence with T. Edwards.
[2] Barbauld, ii. 299.

It was not long after this change of abode that Richardson became Master of the Stationers' Company, an office of which he was admirably fitted to perform all the duties except that of hearty participation in the banquets. " I cannot but figure to myself," said Thomas Edwards, " the miserable example you will set at the head of their loaded tables, unless you have two stout jaw-workers for your wardens and a good hungry court of assistants. Yours, indeed, is an example, which were the company to follow, your cook's place would be in effect a sinecure." [1] For the new Master's weak health had for some time necessitated a vegetarian and water diet, which in those days of heavy feeding and deep drinking must have made him somewhat remarkable.

Meanwhile, he had some difficulty in reconciling his wife to their change of residence. She was evidently a quiet, domesticated person, who found her chief pleasure in household cares, and in extending a kindly welcome to her husband's numerous guests, even to those young ladies whose frank adoration of his genius might have had a disquieting effect on a less sensible woman. By degrees, however, she came to prefer the new house, though another shock was in store for her the next year, when Richardson decided that the warehouse in Salisbury Court was unsafe and set about building another. This necessitated a change in the town dwelling-house also, for in order to have convenient access to the new offices the family moved

[1] Barbauld, iii. 97.

to a smaller and less handsome house adjoining
them, and opening on to the paved court between
the two blocks into which they were divided. In
undertaking this extensive enterprise at his advanced age Richardson was consulting the interests
of his daughters, for he tells Lady Bradshaigh that,
as he has a sixty years' lease at an easy rent, the
money he has laid out will turn to good account
to his children. "Everybody," he continues, "is
more pleased with what I have done than my wife.
But that, I flatter myself, is because she has not
seen either the offices or the house she is to
live in, since the former were little better than a
heap of rubbish (eight houses being demolished to
make room for them) and the latter was a dirty
warehouse. The necessity of removing being absolute let me tell your ladyship that I shall be
both grieved and disappointed if my wife is not
pleased with them both on her coming to town,
which will be next Tuesday. But having three-
quarters of a year to come of the lease of my present house she insists on passing one more winter
in it. And I must comply, though to my inconvenience, and though the surveyors have hinted
that the house has stood its time."[1] Mrs Richardson, indeed, seems to have tried her husband's
patience considerably in this matter of building,
as may be gathered from another letter. "Last
time my good wife was in town," he writes, "I sent
for the master carpenter to find fault with his
slowness, the bricklayers standing still for him.

[1] Forster MS., Correspondence with Lady Bradshaigh.

He came while we were sitting lovingly at supper.
My wife had a little before peeped at the work
from my spy window; she told him she had. I
was just forming my features into a complaining
air. 'Don't you think, madam,' said the sly thief,
'that we make a great show for the time?' (He
had just got up a range of window-frames, of
eighty foot long, that ought to have been up ten
days before.) 'Indeed you do, Mr Burnell,'
answered promptly the good woman. 'I did not
expect to see the building so much advanced.' I
was forced to pull in my horns, as the saying is.
The charge of unreasonableness seemed to be im-
plied on the husband, who knew something of the
matter; and the wife, who knew nothing at all of
it, went off at her honest man's expense with the
character of a very reasonable, courteous, good
sort of woman."[1]

In spite of the trouble caused by the builders,
Richardson found time in this year to gather from
his three books *A Collection of the Moral and Instructive Sentiments, Maxims, Cautions and Reflections, contained in the Histories of Pamela, Clarissa
Harlowe, and Sir Charles Grandison, Digested
under Proper Heads*. This was intended to con-
centrate the cream of the moral teaching of the
three novels, and to those who care for sententious
observations, sometimes commonplace, but often
betraying great shrewdness and penetration, the
little book may still afford entertainment. But, as
might be expected, it could boast of nothing like

[1] Barbauld, iii. 227.

the vogue of its predecessor, and some correspondents expressed a wish, probably shared by many others, that the time devoted to its compilation had been given to the composition of a new novel.

But Richardson's working days were nearly over. One by one his old friends were passing away. Aaron Hill died in 1750, and Colley Cibber and Thomas Edwards in 1757, while he also lost two brothers about this time. And by the various references in his correspondence to the provision he was making for his family, it is clear that the novelist thought his own death not far off. In 1757, on the marriage of his eldest daughter Polly, he made his will, and in 1760 he purchased a half of the patent of law printer, the other half being in the hands of Miss Catherine Lintot. He was probably somewhat anxious about the future of his daughters, of whom only Polly was married in her father's lifetime. "I have a very good wife," he said to Edwards. "I am sure you think I have. But the man who has passed all his days single is not always a loser. Children are careful comforts, though good. Daughters, when marriageable, especially." [1] But when a suitor did present himself for Polly, in the person of Mr Ditcher, a surgeon of Bath, whom she had probably met while staying with her uncle at that place, her father, after the manner of fathers, was not altogether pleased. Polly had had a previous love affair, and he complains "that Mr Ditcher's task

[1] Forster MS., Correspondence with T. Edwards.

was as easy as he could wish, too easy, considering another affair had so recently gone off." [1]   Still, as the bridegroom was "commended for his sobriety, skill, and good sense, and had an increasing business, and a well-conditioned little estate," which he settled on his wife, no serious objection to the match could be made.

Of Richardson's other daughters, Patty is often mentioned as being her father's principal amanuensis, an office which, as he kept duplicates of all his extremely prolix letters, must have taken a good deal of time.   Patty was married in 1762 to a Mr Bridgen, and Sarah, the youngest, to a Mr Crowther, who, like Polly's husband, was a doctor. Nancy, the third daughter, to whose ill-health there are frequent references in the correspondence, died unmarried in 1803, the last survivor of the family.   Richardson was undoubtedly a good father, and very much attached to his daughters, especially to Nancy, whose constitutional delicacy caused him perpetual anxiety; but he never seems to have been treated by them with as much confidence as was shown him in their girlhood by Hester Mulso, Susannah Highmore, or Sarah Westcomb.   From passages in *Clarissa Harlowe* and *Sir Charles Grandison* it is obvious that he had an exaggerated idea of filial duty, and he probably kept his daughters at too great a distance for intimate affection.   "My girls," he says, "are shy little fools"; but he apparently never realised that their reserve was the effect of over

[1] Forster MS., Correspondence with Lady Bradshaigh.

repression. Only one person, the audacious Lady
Bradshaigh, dared to hint at this. Richardson's
reply to her suggestion may be quoted as representing his own views on the subject. "As for
your general instruction on stiffness, as you call
it ; as too much reverence is not the vice of the
age, I had rather lay down rules that should stiffen
into apparent duty than make the pert rogues
too familiar with characters so reverend that it
can never be thought want of breeding to demon-
strate a reverence for them in all companies, in
all conversations; while I would have the parent
so behave to the child as to show that he or
she was above the pride and stiffness of exacting the reverence. Condescension becomes the
character of the parent. It behoves the child to
show it is not hurt by it. . . . 'I have heard you
complain of the want of freedom in your amiable
children.' You have, madam, and so have they,
and all those with whom I have the honour to
be acquainted. I have been always ready to
blame myself, as if there appeared to them in
my behaviour a stiffness that I was willing to
correct in myself if found guilty of it. I have
rallied them all in turn ; I have jested with them ;
I have freely spoken my mind before them on
every occasion, and I hope they are come off
a good deal of the distance I have sought to make
them break through." [1] And Richardson, with
characteristic vanity, goes on to account for their
formality by the respect which it is inevitable

[1] Forster MS., Correspondence with Lady Bradshaigh.

E

they should feel for one so greatly, however un-
deservedly, honoured by his friends.

It is somewhat remarkable that the great
champion of woman in the eighteenth century,
who everywhere in his novels endeavours to
vindicate her claim to be considered a rational
as well as a fascinating being, and who was
certainly not lacking in deference towards the
numerous ladies with whom he corresponded,
should always assume a half bantering, patronising
tone in speaking of his own women-kind. This
is very plainly apparent in the passage already
quoted, concerning the new offices, which, it may
be observed, was addressed to Hester Mulso,
who was young enough to be Mrs Richardson's
daughter. And though he invariably speaks of
his wife with affection, his playful allusions to
her obstinacy and love of management are not
always in the best taste.

"Many who think they know us well (God help
them, or rather, God help me!) imagine I carry
every point. So meek my wife! Be quiet, standers
by, you don't *always* see more than those who
play. Let me warn you to doubt your own judgments when you take upon you to decide in favour
of the yielding qualities of a meek wife. Not obstinacy itself is more persevering." [1] It is possible
that Mrs Richardson, like Mrs Primrose, was chosen
for qualities that would wear well, and that in his
second marriage her husband was chiefly concerned
to procure a sensible and amiable housekeeper.

[1] Forster MS., Correspondence with Lady Bradshaigh.

She hardly belonged to the same social class as
the ladies whom she afterwards entertained on his
behalf, and an allusion in Mrs Delany's correspondence leads one to imagine that she was a shy
woman, with little knowledge of the world.[1] "I
don't know," writes Mrs Delany, "whether Mrs
Richardson is a proper person to find a servant
for you ; she is a quiet, retired sort of woman,
who, I believe, cannot have had any opportunity of
knowing of a suitable servant of that sort." But at
least she must have been a good-hearted, patient
wife, since she filled her house with her husband's
friends, and actually nursed two of them, Thomas
Edwards and Miss Dutton, in their last illnesses.
And it must not be forgotten that it was her sympathy that stimulated Richardson in the production
of *Pamela*, while their mutual good understanding is sufficiently indicated by the following letter
which he presented to her "with a set of *Clarissa
Harlowe*."

" *Dec.* 1, 1748.

"DEAR BET,—Do you know that the beatified
Clarissa was often very uneasy at the time her
story cost the man whom you favour with your
love ; and that chiefly on your account ?
"She was.
"And although she made not a posthumous

---

[1] *Cf.* also *Correspondence of Mrs Carter and Miss Talbot*, ii. 173.
" I am doomed this afternoon to stick myself out and pay my compliments to a new inhabitant of this place, who makes curtsies ' qui
ne finissent point,' and at least as many in number as good Mrs
Richardson."

apology to you on that account, as she did on
other occasions to several of those who far less
deserved to be apologised to, I know so well her
mind that she would have greatly approved of this
acknowledgment; and of the compliments I now
make you, in her name, of the volumes which contain her history.

"May you, my dear Bet, may I, and all ours,
benefit by the warnings of the example given in
them! And may our last scenes be closed as
happily as her last scene is represented to have
done,

"Are the prayers of,

"Yours most affectionately, whilst

"SAMUEL RICHARDSON." [1]

Richardson's esteem for his wife is further
proved by the fact that he appointed her one of
the executors of the will which he made in 1757,
though by a curious oversight it is dated 1727,
at which date many of the persons mentioned in
it, including the two witnesses, Catherine Lintot
and Harry Campbell, were not yet born. By it
he left one-third of his estate to his widow, while
the remaining two-thirds were to be divided between his three single daughters, Polly having
been sufficiently provided for at the time of
her marriage. Various bequests to his relations, especially to the children of his brothers
Benjamin and William, indicate that he, as the
rich member of his family, had already done much

---

[1] Forster MS., Miscellaneous Correspondence.

to help them.   One niece, Susannah, the daughter
of his brother Benjamin, whom he seems to have
adopted, is especially commended to his wife's
kindness; but irritable references to others show
that his generosity had not always met with the
grateful acknowledgment it deserved.   His nephew
William, who had for some time acted as his
overseer, but had left him in 1758 to set up on
his own account, is referred to in codicils of increasing bitterness as a selfish young man who
is well able to take care of himself.[1]   Perhaps if
William's case could be heard there might appear
some justification for his conduct.   Richardson's
increasing infirmities can scarcely have improved
a temper naturally irritable and exacting, and in
the last years of his life he was probably not a
very amiable companion.   This view is confirmed
by a letter written by Miss Talbot to Mrs Carter
announcing his last illness.   "Poor Mr Richardson," she says, "was seized on Sunday evening
with a most severe paralytic stroke.   How many
good hearts will be afflicted by this in many more
countries than England!   To how many will he
be an inexpressible loss!   But to consider him
at present as lost to himself and perhaps with
some sense of that loss is most grievous.   It sits

[1] Nichols' *Literary Anecdotes*, iv., p. 594, states that William
succeeded his uncle in the printing-office, and this assertion is borne
out by the proposal which he quotes for an edition of Richardson's
works by "William Richardson, his nephew and successor in the
printing-office."   Possibly between 1760, the date of the second of
the two codicils referred to, and July 1761, a reconciliation took
place, and William was reinstated in his former position.

pleasantly upon my mind that the last morning
we spent together was particularly friendly and
quiet and comforting.   It was the twenty-eighth
of May—he looked then so well !   One has long
apprehended some stroke of this kind ; the disease
made its gradual approaches by that heaviness
which clouded the cheerfulness of his conversation,
that used to be so lively and so instructive ; by
the increased tremblings which unfitted that hand
so peculiarly formed to guide the pen ; and by
perhaps the querulousness of temper most certainly not natural to so sweet and so enlarged a
mind, which you and I have lately lamented as
making his family at times not so comfortable as
his principles, his study and his delight to diffuse
happiness wherever he could, would otherwise
have done.   Well, his noble spirit will soon now
I suppose be freed from its corporeal encumbrance ;
it were a sin to wish against it, and yet how few
such will be left behind." [1]

Richardson lingered unconscious for two days,
and died on the 4th of July 1761.   He was buried
beside his first wife in the middle aisle of St Bride's
church, which had witnessed the baptism of all his
large family.

Plenty of anecdotes about Richardson's character and habits exist, and they all tend to confirm
the impression produced by his novels and correspondence.   He was a kind master, and there is a
tradition that he used to leave half-crowns among
the type in the workshop as a reward for the most

[1] *Correspondence of Mrs Carter and Miss Talbot*, ii. 209.

punctual among his men.   He was fond of children,
and delighted in making them little presents, though
these seem generally to have consisted of books of
an improving nature.   Full of benevolent intentions, he never tired of assisting his friends with
money and advice, but he preferred always to be
in the position of the donor ; of that higher generosity, which consists in the graceful reception of
favours not always desired, he seems to have had
little, and really hurt Lady Bradshaigh's feelings
once by refusing some needle-work that she had
prepared as an adornment for the house at Parson's
Green.   His letters contain many allusions to
presents made to needy friends, such as Miss
Collier, the friend of Sarah Fielding, who was so
poor that she slept in a garret without a door till
Richardson sent her five pounds to buy one.   Dr
Webster, Aaron Hill and Mr Chapone, senior,
were under much greater pecuniary obligations to
him, to say nothing of the less respectable de-
pendents on his bounty, such as Mrs Pilkington
and Eusebius Sylvester.   "His generosity," says
Mrs Barbauld, "knew no bounds but the necessary
attention to the welfare of a growing family."   His
house, moreover, as has been seen, was always open
to his friends, on whom he repeatedly pressed
cordial invitations.   But though Richardson liked
society, especially that of young people, he was
not a man of many words.   Johnson said that he
could be voluble only on the subject of his own
works, and on one occasion determined to draw
him out on this topic.   "But he failed ; for in that

interview Richardson said little else than that there lay in the room a translation of *Clarissa* into German." Boswell, who relates this story, adds in a footnote the well-known anecdote of the gentleman who, having just returned from France and wishing to compliment Richardson, told him that he had seen a copy of *Clarissa* lying on the king's brother's table. As some of the company present were engaged in conversation and missed this remark, Richardson affected to lose it also, and, waiting till there was a pause so that everyone might hear the compliment, said to his visitor, "I think, sir, you were saying something about —" But the gentleman, provoked at his inordinate vanity, resolved not to indulge it, and with an exquisite air of indifference answered, "A mere trifle, sir, not worth repeating." The mortification of Richardson was visible, and he did not speak more than ten words the whole day.

This vanity was closely allied to the irritability and intense egoism which have already been noticed. Another somewhat unamiable trait was his intense consciousness of class distinctions and his almost servile address to those in a superior social position. Not that he was ashamed of his trade, for he justly prided himself on the position he had won by his unaided energy and ability, and made no secret of his early struggles ; but he took it as a matter of course that the possession of wealth and family entitled the owner to a superlative degree of respect. "There is a bar between us," he says, writing to Mrs Delany of another fine

lady, Mrs Desborough, " Temple Bar.   Ladies
who live near Hill Street and Berkeley and
Grosvenor Squares love not to pass this bar.
They speak of it as if it were a day's journey
from them."   This objectionable note runs through
all Richardson's work, for, as will be seen later,
although he made a serving-maid the heroine of
his first novel, and thereby inaugurated a social
as well as a literary revolution, he never for a
moment supposed, as some critics would have us
think, that Pamela's virtue levelled her up to
the rank of her lover.   The whole point of the
book is that superior morality can be adequately
rewarded by worldly elevation, and the exaltation
of rank and money could scarcely go further.

Other unamiable characteristics that are very
prominent in Richardson's correspondence are his
extreme sensitiveness to criticism, and his jealousy
of all writers outside his own clique.   It has been
seen how the well-meant but blundering advice
of Aaron Hill nearly led to a quarrel, and while
Richardson frequently invited his lady correspondents to give him their counsel on questions
of feminine deportment, to follow it was a compliment beyond his magnanimity.   The most striking
exhibition of this temper, however, is shown in his
relations with Fielding, whom he was never weary
of depreciating, though, somewhat inconsistently,
he declared that his rival had learnt his art from
him.   " The *Pamela* which he abused in his
Shamela, taught him how to write to please,
though his manners are so different.   Before his

Joseph Andrews (hints and names taken from that story, with a lewd and ungenerous engraftment), the poor man wrote without being read."[1] . . . And again, "Mr Fielding has over-written himself, or rather *under*-written; and in his own journal seems ashamed of his last piece; and has promised that the same Muse shall write no more for him. The piece (*Amelia*) in short is as dead as if it had been published forty years, as to sale." After this it is rather surprising to turn the page and read, "You guess I have not read *Amelia*."[2] This bitterness betrays a lack of self-reliance as well as of dignity, and looks as if Richardson was more conscious of Fielding's merits than he cared to allow. So long as a novel was obviously inferior to his own work he could afford to be generous—witness his eulogy of Sarah Fielding's *David Simple*; but as soon as his own literary position was challenged there was a sudden diminution in his appreciative power. And this jealousy of success in his own peculiar field accounts for his hostile criticism of Sterne as well as of Fielding.

As to Richardson's personal appearance there is plenty of information, supplied alike by portraits and verbal description. The word portrait which he gave of himself to Lady Bradshaigh is well known, but will bear repetition. "Short, rather plump, about five feet, five inches, fair wig, one hand generally in his bosom, the other a cane in it, which he leans upon under the skirts of his coat that it may imperceptibly serve him as a support

---

[1] Barbauld, iv. 286.   [2] *Ibid.*, 59.

when attacked by sudden tremors or dizziness which too frequently attack him, but, thank God! not so often as formerly ; looking directly foreright, as passers-by would imagine, but observing all that stirs on either hand of him without moving his short neck ; hardly ever turning back ; of a light brown complexion, teeth not yet failing him ; smooth-faced and ruddy-cheeked ; at some times looking to be about sixty-five, at other times much younger ; a regular even pace, stealing away the ground rather than seeming to rid it; a grey eye, too often overclouded by mistiness from the head, by chance lively—very lively it will be, if he have hope of seeing a lady whom he loves and honours." [1] Of the regular portraits of Richardson the best known is that by Highmore, of which an engraving is prefixed to Mrs Barbauld's edition of the Correspondence. It represents him as a comfortable little gentleman having a double chin, a fair wig, and a dark coat; one hand is thrust into the front of his waistcoat, the other holds a book, perhaps meant for one of his own volumes. Behind him, in the arm of his chair, is inserted his inkhorn, out of which a quill is sticking. This was the portrait which he had reproduced to present to his friends, and which, according to Mrs Barbauld, was always esteemed his best likeness.

Highmore was also responsible for a companion painting of Mrs Richardson, a dark-eyed amiable-looking lady in a yellow gown. There is little information as to her history after her husband's

---

[1] Barbauld, iv. 290.

death, but on February 5, 1771, she is mentioned
in the *Gazetteer* and *New Daily Advertiser* as
denying his connection with a novel called *The
History of Sir William Harrington* said to have
been revised and corrected by him. She died not
long after, in 1773, her end, as we learn incidentally
from Mrs Chapone, having been hastened by the
shock caused by the sudden death of one of her
married daughters while on a visit to Parson's
Green. "The poor mother got up in time to see
her die, and immediately said she had taken her
death-wound, and should not long survive. She
died within a fortnight. Though the circumstance
is so dreadful that one cannot hear of it without
being shocked, one can scarce refrain from smiling
at her will, in which she has left particular direc-
tions to be buried either on a Sunday or a Thurs-
day. These were her lucky days when living, but
I wonder what sort of luck she thought they would
bring her in the grave."[1] This half affectionate,
half patronising, allusion confirms everything else
that we know about Mrs Richardson's character,
and of the estimation in which she was held by her
husband's feminine disciples.

[1] *Posthumous Works of Mrs Chapone*, i. 171. It may be remarked that Mrs Richardson's will, preserved at Somerset House,
contains no allusion to her funeral, beyond the wish that she may be
buried beside her dear husband in St Bride's Church.

CHAPTER III

RICHARDSON'S FRIENDS

IF our information regarding Richardson's early life is scanty, and the existing data concerning his later years give the biographer little opportunity to weave a very exciting story, there is yet plenty of material on which to base an account of the private life of the great apostle of domesticity. For surely no writer ever corresponded with a greater number of friends, and if those friends scarcely vie in notoriety with those whose sayings have been preserved by Boswell, still many of them were celebrities in their own day, and have perhaps been unduly neglected by ours.

The latter part of this statement, however, hardly applies to Aaron Hill, who had probably been acquainted with Richardson for some time previous to the letter of 1736, quoted above, [1] which is the earliest of any in the unpublished correspondence. Hill, though he must be ranked among the literary failures of his age, was a man of some ability and vast energy, who divided his time between theatrical management, dramatic authorship, and commercial and agricultural experiments, which nearly always ended in disaster. Totally destitute

[1] See p. 18.

of any capacity for self-criticism, he had a thorough
confidence in his own powers, and firmly believed
that his name would be still remembered when
posterity had the sense to realise the utter worth-
lessness of the works of Mr Pope. For between
Pope and Hill there existed a bitterness of many
years standing, arising in the first place from a
misreported conversation, and carried on by the
former in the *Treatise on Bathos and the Dunciad*
and by the latter in *The Progress of Wit.* And
though after a time an armistice was made, it is
improbable that complete cordiality was ever restored between them, for after Pope's death Hill
took every opportunity of disparaging him. "Rest
his memory in peace!" he wrote to Richardson in
1744, "it will very rarely be disturbed by that time
he himself is ashes." But his rival's posthumous
fame belying his prophecy, he determined, in 1746,
to open the eyes of the public by publishing a
pamphlet entitled : *Critical Reflections on Propriety
in Writing . . . illustrated by a frankly selected
number of Compared Examples in the opposite Lights
of Excellence and Error from the Works of Mr
Alexander Pope, and other late and still surviving
celebrated English Authors.* This tract was to
leave it "beyond will and testament that Mr Pope
knew nothing as to plan and thought that merited
the name of genius, his merits being confined to
figure and expression." The MS. was submitted
to Richardson, but it does not seem ever to have
been published.

When we first become acquainted with Hill

through the Richardson correspondence he is living at Westminster, but soon afterwards he removes with his three daughters, Urania, Astræa and Minerva, to Plaistowe, bent on a new enterprise which is to make his fortune — no less than the establishment of vine-growing and wine manufacture in England. The enthusiasm that could set on foot such a project at the age of fifty-three, after more than one disappointment in similar schemes, is certainly worthy of all praise. But Plaistowe was damp, and the grapes did not ripen; various ailments attacked the family, and there are obscure allusions to the misconduct of one of its members, probably a son, who married without the approval of his father and afterwards died by his own hand. Want of money compelled Hill to have recourse to his pen and to the sympathy of Richardson, who in 1746 lent him a hundred pounds, and tried to console him by insisting that the unpopularity of his works was mainly due to want of taste among his readers. "I do not think," wrote he, "that were Milton's *Paradise Lost* to be now published as a new work, it would be well received," and he delicately hinted at Hill's exaggerated and bombastic style as one cause of his failure. "Your sentiments, even they will have it, who allow them to be noble, are too munificently adorned, and they want you to descend to their level."

The failure of Hill's health, combined with pecuniary troubles, is probably responsible for the depressed tone of these letters, and for the impatient irritability which they often display. Garrick's delay in producing *Merope*, which Hill had adapted from Voltaire, was attributed by the author to personal dislike, and Richardson once more extended sympathetic reassurance, from his own knowledge of Mr Garrick's difficulties as a theatrical manager. The whole of this correspondence from 1736 to 1750, in which year Hill died, is pathetic reading, for however ridiculous his vanity and egoism may appear, it presents the spectacle of a strong, energetic and assertive nature gradually sinking beneath an accumulation of misfortunes. After his death his works were printed by subscription, and the fact that Richardson's name is down for six sets, testifies to the real regard he had for Hill. Of all the material contained in these volumes only eight lines are now ever remembered or quoted, but these, once written on a window during a tour through Scotland, are not unfrequently found in anthologies of verse.

> " Tender handed stroke a nettle,
>   And it stings you for your pains :
> Grasp it like a man of mettle,
>   And it soft as silk remains.
> 'Tis the same with human natures,
>   Use 'em kindly, they rebel :
> But be rough as nutmeg graters,
>   And the rogues obey you well."

The poetical dedication of the collected edition of Hill's works was addressed by his eldest daughter Urania to the Princess Dowager of Wales, the mother of George III. Urania was fortunately the only one of the girls who made any attempt to justify her name, but as early as 1731 her proud father had sent to Mr Pope a copy of verses written by her four years previously. The great poet had responded by kind messages to the young authoress, and by the present of his version of the *Odyssey*, thus nurturing a talent that had better have been suppressed, since poor Urania's verses surpass those of her father in turgidity and commonplace sentiment. She married, unhappily as it seems, and was either left a widow or deserted by her husband, for in 1755 she wrote to Richardson :—" Cruelty and unkind fortune are not yet grown weary of pursuing me in our affairs, and till they are I can seek out no place of rest or happiness." Richardson tried hard to get employment for her, and sent a glowing testimonial, in which he praises her as "the managing sister of the three." But in 1758 she was once more in trouble, and wrote again to her benefactor, begging him for "a frank—a single frank." Altogether, Hill's family must have made no small demands on his friend's patience. The last mention of Urania is in connection with the MS. of a novel called *Almira*, which she submitted to Richardson for criticism ; but when her adviser ventured to hint at a certain want of delicacy in one of the chapters she wrote a half-hysterical, but wholly pardonable, protest in self-defence. This letter is endorsed in Richardson's handwriting as follows :—

" But surely the unwelcome observations I

F

made show that it was not for want of pains and attention at a time so sad—but I will only say I truly meant service, not criticism. Who but the lady was to see what I wrote?"

The other two sisters, Astræa and Minerva (the latter of whom, it is as well to say, was called Minny by her family) were also ladies of literary tastes, though there is no proof that they ever attempted authorship. They were obliged to rely for their supply of books chiefly on an itinerary bookseller's shop that rumbled through Plaistowe in a wheelbarrow, and it was probably from this source that they obtained the six volumes of *Tom Jones*, published in 1749. Thus, when Richardson desired Hill to let him have the sentiments of the ladies upon it, in the hope that their favourable opinion would induce him to open the volumes, " the rather, as they will be so soon read," they were already well prepared for the task of criticism. But with singular want of insight they took him at his word, and actually forwarded to Fielding's rival the following sensible and temperate, yet withal laudatory appreciation of the new book.

" Having with much ado got over some reluctance that was bred by a familiar coarseness in the title, we went through the whole six volumes; and found much masqued merit in 'em all; a double merit, both of head and heart. Had there been only that of the last sort, you love it, I am sure, too much to leave a doubt of your resolving to examine it. However, if you do, it should be when you can best spare it your attention, else, the author introduces all his sections (and too often interweaves the serious body of his meanings) with long runs of bantering levity, which his good sense may suffer the effect of. It is true he seems to wear this lightness as a grave man sometimes wears a feather, which though he and fashion may consider as an ornament, reflection will condemn as a disguise and covering. . . . Meanwhile it is an honest pleasure which we take in adding that (exclusive of one wild, detached and independent story of a Man of the Hill, that neither brings on anything nor rose from anything that went before it) all the changeful windings of the author's fancy carry on a course of regular design, and end in an extremely moving close, where lines that seemed to wander and run different ways meet, all in an instructive centre.

"The whole piece consists of an inventive race of disappointments and recoveries. It excites curiosity and holds it watchful. It has just and pointed satire; but it is a partial satire, and confined too narrowly. It sacrifices to authority and interest. Its events reward sincerity and punish and expose hypocrisy, show pity and benevolence in amiable lights, and avarice and brutality in very despicable ones. In every part it has humanity for its intention; in too many it seems wantoner that it was meant to be; it has bold shocking pictures, and (I fear) not unresembling ones, in high life and low. And (to conclude this adventurous guesswork from a pair of forward baggages) would everywhere (we think) deserve to please if stript of what the author thought himself most sure to please by.

"And thus, sir, we have told you our sincere opinion of *Tom Jones*. For every woman in the nation owes respect and deference to the parent of *Clarissa* and *Pamela* — we owe 'em both, still more particularly. We also love with daughterly and sisterly affection, and pray daily for, and almost hourly think of, your dear family Clarissas, who encircle you at home, with blessings from a union of three different tendernesses (the parental, conjugal and filial); under social sense of which complete felicity, we beg of heaven to grant you very very *long* enjoyment of it, and of you we beg the happiness of being honoured with the title of your most professed admirers and most humble servants,

"ASTRÆA and MINERVA HILL.[1]"

Richardson's admirers must wish that his answer to this judicious criticism had been suppressed, for literary jealousy, aroused by the eulogies of a rival's work and intensified by the unwilling conviction that they are in the main justifiable, never appeared in a more undisguised and petty form than in his reply. He owns that he has not read *Tom Jones*, but says that he has been told it has a very bad tendency. "And I had reason to think that the author intended for his second view (his first being to fill his pocket by accom-

[1] Forster MS., Miscellaneous Correspondence.

modating it to the reigning taste) in writing it to whiten a vicious character and to make morality bend to his practices. . . . Why did he make his Tom a common—what shall I call it? the lowest of all fellows . . . yet in love with a young creature who was trapesing after him, a fugitive from her father's house? Why did he draw his heroine so fond, so foolish, and so insipid? Indeed he has one excuse, he knows not how to draw a delicate woman—he has not been accustomed to such company—and is too proscribing, too impetuous, too immoral, I will venture to say, to take any other bias than that a perverse and crooked nature has given him, or evil habits, at least, have confirmed in him. Do men expect to gather grapes off thorns, or figs off thistles? But, perhaps, I think the worse of the piece because I know the writer and dislike his principles, both public and private, though I wish well to the man, and love four worthy sisters of his with whom I am acquainted. And indeed should admire him did he make the use of his talents which I wish him to make. For the vein of humour and ridicule which he is master of might, if properly turned, do great service to the cause of virtue."

This and similar ungenerous disparagements of a rival author, under the flimsy disguise of zeal for virtue, have done more harm to Richardson's reputation than the severest criticism ever passed on his books. It is said that Astræa and Minerva wept at this reply, but it is difficult to believe that their tears did not arise rather from shame for a

friend deservedly dear than from mortification at
his reproof.

Considering Richardson's enthusiasm for virtue,
and his strictures on Fielding's private life, it is a
little surprising that he should have remained on
intimate terms with Colley Cibber, a man of un-
doubted moral laxity.   Such a connection throws
much light on Richardson's actual practice, since
it is evident that he not only considered Cibber as
a friend of his own, but also introduced him to his
wife and daughters.   On the other hand, it must
be remembered that Cibber had done more than
anyone else to reform the English stage, and to
restore decency to the plays that were presented
on it.   His delightful autobiography reveals a
man excessively vain but imperturbably good-
humoured ;   every page displays extraordinary
insight into human nature, and his defence of that
philosophy which takes life as it comes, and
extracts from it the highest degree of pleasure
obtainable at the moment, is set forth with so
much verve, so much energetic humour, as to
carry temporary conviction with it.   His intense
enjoyment of life, his *entrain*, the very earnestness
of his frivolity, are curiously fascinating.   And
Cibber had, moreover, many excellent qualities ;
his good humour under the attacks that followed
his appointment as laureate cannot be too highly
praised, and it was only under the sting of almost
unbearable insult that he at last turned to retaliate
on Pope.   But even here his strictures did not
extend to the poet's work, which he honestly

admired, and acknowledged to be superior to his own. It would have been well for Richardson if he also had remembered those words of *The Tatler*, endorsed by Cibber's appreciation : " In all terms of reproof when the sentence appears to arise from personal hatred or passion it is not then made the cause of mankind, but a misunderstanding between two persons." [1]

The few letters from Cibber preserved in Mrs Barbauld's edition of Richardson's correspondence are not very interesting, and extend only from 1748 to 1753, although the acquaintance must have been of much longer duration. Cibber either affected or really felt immense excitement over his friend's novels. Portions of *Sir Charles Grandison* were submitted to him in manuscript ; at other times he formed one of the North End audience and listened to the story from the author's lips. " The delicious meal I made of Miss Byron on Sunday last," he says, not very elegantly, in one place, " has given me an appetite for another slice of her off the spit before she is served up to the public table ; if about five o'clock to-morrow afternoon will not be inconvenient Mrs Brown and I will come and nibble [2] upon a bit more of her." And, again, " the spirited generosity of Sir Charles to the two Danbys and their sister has put me so out of conceit with my own

---

[1] *Tatler*, No. 242. Quoted in *Cibber's Apology*, p. 38.

[2] This is not Cibber's word but, as it conveys the same meaning, I have borrowed it from Mr Leslie Stephen. Introduction to " Richardson's Works," p. xx.

narrow soul, that I cannot be easy for not having been myself the author of your more than mortal history.   By the way, don't I talk nonsense ? But people in rapture never think that common words can express it." [1]

It was probably Colley Cibber who recommended Letitia Pilkington, a well-known literary adventuress of that day, to Richardson.   Born in Dublin, in 1700, she was married when only fifteen to Matthew Pilkington, a clergyman, who also dabbled in literature.   Mrs Pilkington's father had been a college friend of Dr Delany, who interested himself in the young couple, and introduced them to Swift.   "What," said he when they were presented to him, "this poor little child married? God help her, she is early engaged in trouble." Swift's words were prophetic: through his influence Matthew Pilkington obtained an appointment as chaplain to Barber, the Lord Mayor of London, and left his wife behind him in Dublin while he went to perform his new duties.   This separation emphasised an estrangement, which, according to Mrs Pilkington, had originated in her husband's jealousy of her intellectual attainments.   They were never entirely reconciled; Letitia supported herself and her two children by miscellaneous writing, first in Dublin, and afterwards in London, where she fell into such doubtful company that her husband was enabled to divorce her.   She sank from bad to worse, being at least once in prison for debt, and was a

[1] Barbauld, ii. 177.

constant drain on the charity of her benefactors, Delany, Cibber and Richardson. In the second volume of those memoirs which Mrs Delany justly characterised as scandalous, she tells of her first visit to the novelist. " As I had never formed any great idea of a printer by those I had seen in Ireland," she says naïvely, " I was very negligent of my dress, any more than making myself clean ; but was extremely surprised when I was directed to a house of a very grand outward appearance, and had it been a palace, the beneficent master deserved it. I met a very civil reception from him, and he not only made me breakfast, but also dine with him and his agreeable wife and children. After dinner he called me into his study and showed me an order he had received to pay me twelve guineas, which he immediately took out of his escritoire and put into my hand ; but when I went to tell them over, I found that I had fourteen, and, supposing the gentleman had made a mistake, I was for returning two of them, but he with a sweetness and modesty almost peculiar to himself, said he hoped I would not take it ill, that he had presumed to add a trifle to the bounty of my friend. I really was confounded till recollecting that I had read *Pamela*, and been told it was written by one Mr Richardson, I asked him whether he was not the author of it. He said he was the editor : I told him my surprise was now over, as I found he had only given to the incomparable *Pamela* the virtues of his own worthy heart."

This interview must have taken place between
1740, the date of the publication of *Pamela*, and
1743, as in the latter year we find her once more
soliciting Richardson's help. This time it was for
a testimonial as to her character, a request which
must have been somewhat embarrassing to Richardson, especially as she says that she has already
mentioned Mr Cibber as a reference, but "they
had no opinion of him." She repaid her patron's
kindness by poetical addresses even more fulsome
than those of Aaron and Urania Hill, and by
reporting to him the complimentary remarks of
Cibber on *Clarissa Harlowe*. For a time she seems
to have got on very well, but in 1745 she was
again in difficulties, and trying to raise money to
pay her passage back to Ireland. "I hope you
will pardon me a last request," she wrote to
Richardson, "which is that you will oblige me
with a few sheets of gilt paper and a stick of
sealing-wax, in order to write circular letters to
the nobility who have honoured me with their
notice, to raise as much as will carry me to the
land of fogs and fens:—

> "A servile race in folly nurst,
> Who truckle most when treated worst."

It is not quite obvious from the context whether
the writer means to refer this quotation to the
aforesaid nobility or to the Irish nation. But apparently even the gilt-edged paper failed to procure
the necessary supplies, for in December she was
still in England, soliciting help for an unfortunate

daughter whom, as she says, she has less authority to blame than another mother. Richardson and his wife again gave assistance, but in 1746 she wrote once more that she was "quite broke." The allusions in this letter to Cibber and Delany would seem to indicate that Richardson was the most forbearing of her patrons, since the other two had apparently refused to give further aid. She died in 1750.

Dr Delany, who occasionally made Richardson his almoner, is perhaps best remembered as the husband of Mrs Delany, whose voluminous memoirs throw so much light on the social history of the eighteenth century. The story of her forced marriage to Alexander Pendarves, her widowhood, and trying love affair with Lord Baltimore, is well known, and she had probably married the Dean of Down before her acquaintance with Richardson began. Their friendship was based on the admiration she entertained for his work, and she never seems to have regarded him as on altogether equal terms with her. There is always a touch of patronage, a consciousness of superior rank, in her references to "good Mr Richardson," though both she and her sister, Mrs Dewes, were frequent visitors at North End whenever business or pleasure called them to London.

In her early girlhood, when forced by political events to retire into obscurity for a time, Mrs Delany's father, Bernard Granville, had retired to his estate at Buckland, near Broadway, in Gloucestershire, where she made the acquaintance of Sarah Kirkham, the daughter of a neighbouring clergyman.   This was the beginning of a lifelong friendship, which had important results for Sarah Kirkham's children.   She married in 1725 the Rev. John Chapone, Vicar of Stanton, and as her sons and daughters grew up her old friend manifested great interest in them, and, indeed, practically adopted one daughter, Sarah, to whom she frequently refers in her diary.   In 1750 John, the eldest son, coming to London to study law, Mrs Dewes wrote to recommend him to Richardson's notice, and he speedily became intimate with the family at North End.   Kindness shown to her son was a sure way of appealing to his mother's heart, and it was probably in acknowledgment of Richardson's attentions to the young student that Mrs Chapone's correspondence with him began.   She has long, she says, been an admirer of his novels, and goes on to relate how, on the appearance of *Pamela*, her second son, then about twelve years old, was " so utterly possessed by the book that he attempted a sermon upon Mr Williams' text, upon which Pamela tells us that gentleman made an excellent discourse, but gives no particulars of it.   ' The liberal soul shall be made fat,' was the text, on which the boy wrote with a spirit and justness which equally surprised and delighted us all.   This turned his mind into a track of thinking from which I bless God he has made no remarkable deviation since."

Richardson naturally wanted to see this precocious production, but unfortunately it had been so much appreciated by the mice at Stanton that it was no longer in existence. "I ever had a kind of natural aversion to that species of animal," wrote he on hearing of this accident, "I shall now hate them worse than ever." [1]

Mrs Chapone must have been a woman of intellect as well as of heart, for her letters are unusually entertaining. She had a long controversy with Richardson on the subject of the position of women, and pleaded with much force and wit for greater liberty, to which he replied that she must not judge all women by herself, nor think that they were equally fit for power. She retaliated by an amusing letter, in which she supposes herself in the place of her husband, and pretends to adopt the sentiments that Richardson would think suitable to that position. "Were Mr Chapone my wife," she says, "I know you would think it very becoming in me to signify my sovereign will and pleasure to him from time to time as may seem good in my sight. Neither would you in the least doubt my perspicacity and judgment in all courses and over all persons for the well ordering and governance of my private royalty," and she goes on to state the privileges of the husband, as she supposes Richardson to conceive them, supporting her statements by references to *Sir Charles Grandison* and *Paradise Lost*. She concludes by saying that if she were the husband she would point out to Mr Chapone the duty of answering

---

[1] Forster MS., Chapone Correspondence.

Richardson's last letter. "All this I should know and do were I the husband; but as wife, being nothing, I can know nothing, neither have I occasion to know anything; my conscience being provided with a supreme regulator; that is, in cases where I may be allowed to have a regulator; which, according to this sentence of annihilation passed upon wives, must be an extraordinary indulgence. 'They swallowed us up quick when they were wrathfully displeased with us.' This is incorporating with a vengeance! Effectually bringing us to nothing! However, I am just now ordered to emerge into existence, and directed to present Mr Chapone's best compliments, love and thanks to Mr Richardson and his lady for all their goodness to him and his family." [1]

This clever mother had equally clever children, and both John and Sally possessed intellectual gifts beyond the average. Sally was a frequent guest at North End, and once got into serious trouble with her host because she omitted to write to thank him after some weeks spent in his house. But John was especially popular there, and Richardson wrote to congratulate his mother on his "increasing skill in his profession, his sweetness of manners, and his integrity of heart." When Sally was in Richardson's black books, John, who must really have been an excellent fellow, tried to excuse her to his irate friend: "the dear girl does not write to me," he said. This amiability, joined to great earnestness and industry, won for him the affection of another

[1] Forster MS., Chapone Correspondence.

guest at North End, who, indeed, is said to have succumbed to his attractions at their first meeting.

This was Hester Mulso, the only daughter of a Northamptonshire squire, who was accustomed to spend her winters in London, and whose literary tastes had led her to become acquainted with Richardson, with whom she was a great favourite. She was ardent, susceptible, and enthusiastic, and so precocious, that when she was only nine years old she composed a romance, entitled *The Loves of Amoret and Melissa.* Her mother, a spoiled beauty, was jealous of the little girl's ability, and discouraged these essays, but she died just as her daughter was grown up, and Hester then became mistress of her father's house. Amidst her domestic duties she found some time for study, and was unusually well educated for that period, since she knew French, Italian, and some Latin. She had also a beautiful voice, which won for her, from her friend Thomas Edwards, the name of linnet.

It says much for her independence of thought that Hester Mulso, notwithstanding her admiration of Richardson, had the courage to differ with him on some points; she considered that he carried his notions of parental authority too far, and engaged him in a long correspondence on the subject. But though she opposed him herself, she was at some pains to defend him from the strictures of her friend Elizabeth Carter who objected to ·his prolixity on the score that "it was beyond mortal sufferance." "For my own part," says his fair champion, "I should not have quarrelled with

him had there been fourteen volumes of *Clarissa*,
provided they had been equally beautiful with
those we have seen. As to his letters—I do not
allow you to judge of them without having read
them. That they are very long, I confess; nay,
I will even grant that the argument would have
been clearer had they been much shorter; but
there is good sense in every page, wit and humour
in some, entertaining narratives in others." But
Miss Mulso had received an excellent education
in patience in her childhood, when she had
read romances beside which those of Richardson
were mere pamphlets, for she confesses that
she had drudged through *Le Grand Cyrus* in
twelve huge volumes, *Cleopatra* in ten, *Polexandre*,
Ibrahim, *Clélie*, and some others. The combined influence of these romances and of Richardson's novels led her to write for *The Adventurer*,
in 1753, the *Story of Fidelia*, which is supposed
to be the autobiography of a girl who, being the
daughter of a deist, has been taught to deny any
connection between religion and morality. As a
consequence (though the relation between her
advanced religious opinions and her subsequent
misfortunes is not very obvious), she falls a victim
to the wiles of Sir George Freelove who ultimately
forsakes her. She is then rescued, comforted, and
converted by an old clergyman and his wife. The
conception is crude, and the execution leaves one
unconvinced as to the moral that the authoress
intended to draw; but the didactic intention
which afterwards dominated the work of " the

celebrated Mrs Chapone" is here plainly fore-shadowed.

The young authoress, who is said to have already refused an offer of marriage from Gilbert White, of Selborne fame, was more responsive to John Chapone, though want of means for some time prevented any definite engagement. But we are told that even before her lover had made any declaration, Hester, emulating the frankness of Harriet Byron, felt it incumbent upon her to inform her father of the state of her heart. She might probably have made a better match, but she remained faithful for nine long years, till, at last, in December 1760, Mr Mulso arranged his affairs so as to allow of the marriage. Her happiness was short-lived; ten months afterwards her husband contracted a fever of which he died. The blow proved nearly fatal to his widow, but after a long illness she recovered and sought consolation in her old hobbies. Her *Letters on the Improvement of the Mind* (1773) had much influence on feminine education, and won for her the notice of Queen Charlotte; and her correspondence shows that she took a keen interest in contemporary literature. One of her last performances was a rhymed criticism of the sonnets of Bowles, which were dedicated to her cousin by marriage, Dean Ogle of Winchester. She was competent to express an opinion on this subject, for she had herself written one or two very tolerable sonnets; and as the short collection of Bowles had considerable influence

G

on the poetic development of Coleridge, she forms an interesting link between the earlier and later manifestations of the romantic movement.

Mrs Chapone's portrait is preserved for us in the group sketched by Susannah Highmore, to which allusion has already been made. It represents Richardson reading aloud the manuscript of *Sir Charles Grandison* in his "grotto" at North End. The other persons represented in the picture are Thomas and Edward Mulso; Miss Prescott, who married the former; Mr Duncombe, who became the husband of the fair artist, and Miss Highmore herself. She was the daughter of the well-known portrait-painter whose friendship for Richardson is witnessed by the pictures of the novelist and his wife at Stationers' Hall, which are by his hand, and by the illustrations that he designed for *Pamela* and *Clarissa Harlowe*.

To Miss Highmore's love affair, which, owing probably to some parental restrictions, did not run very smoothly, there are many allusions in the correspondence of Richardson from whom, indeed, she seems to have sought and received the sympathy that was denied her at home. The story can be dimly traced in some manuscript verses at South Kensington, in which Corydon (John Duncombe) laments his enforced absence from his mistress, and Stella responds by bidding him

> " To Cam remove
> Try learning's power to cure his love,
> Stella the force of friendship try,
> To good Palemon's grotto fly,
> For all distressed asylum kind,
> Where every sickness of the mind
> Sage Palemon knows how to heal,
> And soothing counsel to reveal.
> Advice in Fancy's garb arrays,
> Instruction with delight conveys,
> Mends every heart that hears his moral page,
> Adapted well to every state and age."

The reference to Richardson in this stanza is probably responsible for the preservation of the verses, but the warm friendship of the novelist for the young couple is abundantly manifested throughout his correspondence. John Duncombe was a man of some talent, and at the age of twenty-five made a hit with his *Feminead* (1754), a poem in defence of learned ladies, which is appropriately addressed to Richardson in these words :—

> " To these weak strains, O thou the sex's friend,
> And constant patron, Richardson, attend !
> Thou who so oft with pleas'd but anxious care
> Hast watched the dawning genius of the fair,
> With wonted smiles wilt hear thy friend display
> The various graces of the female lay,
> Studious from folly's yoke their mind to free,
> And aid the generous cause espoused by thee."

Then follows a long list of illustrious ladies described under fictitious names, among them Miss Carter, Miss Mulso, and Miss Highmore, who is thus characterised :—

" With lovely mien Eugenia now appears,
    The Muses' pupil from her tend'rest years,
    Improving tasks her peaceful hours beguile,
    The sister arts on all her labours smile,
    And while the nine their votary inspire,
    One dips the pencil, and one strings the lyre."

The restrictions that separated the lovers were
at length removed, and after a courtship even
longer than that of Hester Mulso they were
married in April 1763. "A similarity of taste
and love of literature," says a writer in the
Gentleman's Magazine, " had early endeared their
companionship, and a mutual affection was the
natural consequence, which ensured to them
twenty-three years of happiness, rather increased
than diminished by the hand of time."

But of all the members of this little coterie, the
one most worthy of commemoration was Thomas
Edwards, a poet of slender merit, who has missed
the recognition he undoubtedly deserves as one of
the pioneers of the romantic movement in English
literature. Early left by his father's death at the
head of a large family of brothers and sisters,
all of whom he survived, he never married, but
after some time spent in the pursuit of law he
retired to the country where, first at Pitshanger
in Middlesex and afterwards at Turrick in Buck-
inghamshire, he divided his time between agricultural interests and the study of the older English
poets, whom he probably knew better than any
contemporary student. Warburton's slovenly and
dogmatic edition of Shakespeare, which appeared

in 1747, lashed him to a passion quite foreign to his naturally amiable and peaceable disposition, and he chastised what seemed to him almost a sacrilege in an exceedingly brilliant pamphlet, entitled *The Canons of Criticism*. Warburton had said in his preface that he had originally intended to draw up certain canons or rules of criticism, but that he had not done so because they might easily be supplied by the reader from his notes. This gave an opening to Edwards, who, seizing on the many gross blunders which these notes contained, drew up an ironical list of twenty-five canons, illustrating them by quotations from Warburton, together with a glossary exposing the absurdity of many of his interpretations. Warburton never forgave Edwards for this attack, and though he had formerly extended a patronising friendship to Richardson, seems to have included him in his displeasure.[1] Richardson retaliated by urging Edwards to continue the conflict by bringing out a rival edition of the works of Pope, of which Warburton, as his literary executor, had the legitimate monopoly. Edwards, however, refused the task for, as he said, he did not like fighting work unless upon a just and reasonable provocation. Moreover, though he had formerly been on sufficiently intimate terms with Pope to contribute some rare stones to the famous grotto

[1] It appears that Warburton had a further cause for quarrelling with Richardson, inasmuch as he supposed that the latter had " in a new edition of *Clarissa* reflected upon his friend Mr Pope." Barbauld, iii., pp. 60, 61 and 134.

at Twickenham, his regard for the poet was hardly
great enough to induce him to defend his work.
" As to Mr Pope," he says, "though I had some
acquaintance with him and admired him as a
poet, yet I must own I never had any great
opinion of him in any other light ; nor do I see
reason to alter my judgment from what has
appeared of his character since his death. With
all his affectation of humanity and a general
benevolence he was certainly a very ill-natured
man." [1]

Edwards is, however, chiefly notable because he
wrote sonnets at a time when no one else did, and
some years before Warton, to whom the revival
of this form has been attributed. Fifty of these sonnets are printed in the sixth edition of *The Canons
of Criticism*, and among the Richardson MSS.
there are two more, which do not seem ever to have
been published. A few are on the model of Spenser,
the remainder correctly imitated from Italian originals. They display strong family affection, a tender
appreciation for rural beauty, but most prominently
of all, an ardent enthusiasm for Spenser, Shakespeare and ·Milton ; some of them, and these, as
may be supposed, are the very worst, are levelled
at Warburton and Lauder, another sacrilegious
editor, over whose treatment of Milton Edwards becomes almost vituperative. His indignation had
probably some effect in awaking the literary conscience of critics, and his frequent references to the
older poets may have hastened the approaching re-

[1] Barbauld, iii. 43.

action in their favour.   But he himself thought his
efforts futile.   "All I have for it," he complained
to Richardson, "is to write sonnets against these
murderers, which they will mind no more than so
many old ballads."   Richardson, at least, was
always sympathetic, and so were Hester Mulso
and Susannah Highmore, who learnt from him the
trick of sonneteering, and submitted their verses
to his approval.   Great was their distress when in
December 1756 Edwards was taken seriously ill
while on a visit to Parson's Green.   "He got a
bad cold at a friend's house where he stayed a
week on his way to us," wrote Richardson, "and is
so very bad that he cannot be removed.   We do
all we can to comfort him.   My wife and my girls
endear themselves to me and to all the dear man's
friends by their tenderness to him.   While he
laments that he should add to our concern for his
sufferings by dying with us.   Poor man ! he calls
it cruel in himself.   But all we can do to save and
nurse him is too little for our wills."   But all their
solicitude was in vain, and on January, 1757, Richardson wrote again, "a messenger from Parson's
Green just now informs me that good Mr Edwards
commenced immortal this morning at five o'clock." [1]
He deserves to be remembered by all lovers of fine
literature as the gallant champion of Shakespeare
against that most redoubtable of charlatans, William
Warburton.

[1] Forster MS., Scudamore Correspondence.

CHAPTER IV

RICHARDSON'S FRIENDS (*continued*)

OF the later friendships of Richardson's life, by far
the most notable was that with Lady Bradshaigh,
to whom the greater part of his correspondence is
addressed. It was in the interval between the
appearance of the first four and the last three
volumes of *Clarissa Harlowe* that he received
a letter purporting to be sent by a Mrs Balfour
in Devonshire, begging him to falsify the dreadful
rumours she had heard that the novel was to have
a tragic ending. This was the beginning of a correspondence which for nearly two years she carried
on under her fictitious name, and which led to an
intimacy only ended by Richardson's death.

Lady Bradshaigh was the wife of a Lancashire
baronet, whose estate of Haigh was situated near
Wigan. "Here is a noble park," she wrote, "well
watered and wooded, more than ten miles in cir-
cumference. And upon an eminence is placed, in
the centre of serpentine hedges and walks, a beautiful octagon summer-house, inside and out orna-
mented with painting, carving, statues, etc. From
this you have a view of the sea at four miles'
distance, where generally are to be seen, going out
of or entering the harbour of L., ships of consider-

able burden, from all parts of the world."[1]   But in spite of this extensive property, Sir Roger Bradshaigh was by no means a wealthy man.   He was crippled by the necessity of having to pay off the debts of his father, "incurred by a parliamentary mania, though he was not subject to those debts by any law but the law of conscience."   By the help of his wife, however, he managed to keep up an appearance adequate to his rank until these responsibilities were at an end.

Lady Bradshaigh had no children,[2] but her deep affection for her husband, who fifteen years before her acquaintance with Richardson began had married her after a prolonged courtship, is continually manifested throughout her letters ; and her frequent references to the pleasant routine of her home life show that she was not only a bright and well-read woman, but also a kind mistress and a notable housewife.   She did not, indeed, altogether approve of learning in women.   " I hate to hear Latin out of a woman's mouth," she says, "there is something in it to me masculine.   I could fancy such an one weary of the petticoat, and talking over a bottle. . . . Not that I

---

[1] Forster MS., Bradshaigh Correspondence.

[2] A writer in *Notes and Queries*, Aug. 11, 1877, states that Lady Bradshaigh had two daughters, one of whom became the ancestress of the Earls of Balcarres. Through the kindness of Lord Balcarres, and on the authority of Mr W. A. Lindsay, Q.C., I am able to correct this statement.   He informs me that Lady Dorothy Bradshaigh, wife of the fourth baronet, was childless, and that he is descended from Rachel, Lady Bradshaigh, and the previous Sir Roger.

would have it thought unnecessary for a woman
to read, to spell, or to speak English, which has
been pretty much the case hitherto. . . . Thanks
to nature for what we have. You are in the right
to keep us in ignorance. You dare not let us try
what we could do. In that you show your judgment,
which I acknowledge to be much stronger than ours,
by nature ; and that is all you have to boast of, and
a little courage." [1] And Lady Bradshaigh's letters,
entertaining as many of them are, would seem to indicate that, though she had managed to repair youthful deficiencies by industrious reading, her own great
natural ability had received little help from early
education. Her spelling is weak, and her handwriting execrable, and sometimes difficult to decipher.

At the date of her first letter to Richardson,
Lady Bradshaigh was already forty years of age,
so that she can scarcely be classed with the
younger group of his feminine admirers, such as
Hester Mulso and Susannah Highmore. " Middle-
aged, middle-sized, a degree above plump, brown
as an oak wainscot, a good deal of country red in
her cheeks, altogether a plain woman, but nothing
remarkably forbidding," is the lively description of
her own appearance which she sent to Richardson
in exchange for the word portrait already quoted,
and intended to guide her as to his identity should
he meet her accidentally during her visit to London in 1750. Her words are hardly as explicit as
those of her friend, but it was part of her plan to
mystify him and add a touch of romance to the

[1] Barbauld, vi., p. 54.

LADY BRADSHAIGH

approaching meeting by delaying it as long as possible. She had told him that she would attend the park every fine day between the hours of one and two, and this was sufficient to secure Richardson's presence there at the time named. But alas for his expectations! In vain did he peer into every chair that passed him, and eagerly scan the faces of all the ladies in the Mall; in vain he tired his daughter Patty and his friend Miss Collier by making them walk up and down Constitution Hill till they were ready to drop; the lady still eluded his perplexed search. All this time he had no clue to her real name; but going one day to look at Mr Highmore's pictures, she recklessly left her man to chatter with the artist's servant while she interviewed his master. John extracted all the necessary information as to her title, and this, added to her suspicious familiarity with the persons represented in Highmore's painting of the Harlowe family, led him to identify her with Richardson's unknown correspondent. There is no account of the actual meeting, but it took place soon after this, in March 1750.

Lady Bradshaigh's admiration for *Clarissa Harlowe* had been as flattering as the most ambitious author could desire. She entered so thoroughly into the story that she regarded the actors in it as real persons, and took as much interest in their fortunes as in that of living people. Her heart is torn by the sufferings of Clarissa, but "she cannot help being fond of Lovelace," and she intercedes for his conversion with almost passionate ardour.

"Would you have me weep incessantly," she asks
. . . "I long to read it (*i.e.* Vol. V.)—and yet I
dare not." And after she had become acquainted
with the catastrophe she added, "Dear sir, if it
be possible — yet recall the dreadful sentence;
bring it as near as you please, but prevent it. . . .
I opened my letter to add this, and my hand
trembles, for I can scarce hold my pen. I am
as mad as the poor injured Clarissa, and am afraid
I cannot help hating you if you alter not your
scheme"; and she followed this up with another
letter in which she desperately suggested an alternative and happy ending. All her persuasions
were, of course, in vain, and she must eventually
have become reconciled to the catastrophe; but
considering all that she had suffered on Clarissa's
account, it was a little unkind of Richardson to
harrow her by dark menaces as to the fate of Sir
Charles Grandison and Harriet Byron. By the
time he began his third novel he was on intimate
terms with Lady Bradshaigh, who criticised and
discussed the story as it proceeded, and had the
courage to differ with him on the interesting subject
of feminine deportment during courtship. But when
he threatened her with the death of his heroine,
criticism was changed to entreaty. The very idea
depressed her beyond endurance, and she suffered
from it as from a real calamity. "I was forced
to lie down," she says, "and was relieved for a
moment by a flood of tears. May it please the
Almighty to restore my spirits! I was not without some hopes of further relief from your letter,

but alas! I am but more confirmed by it in what I dreaded." And she adds in a postscript, "This letter will weigh heavy with my tears, it has been thoroughly soaked, and I have but one poor consolation left, that if you kill me, it is the way you use all your favourites." Richardson's reply was to send her the seventh volume, in which Sir Charles is restored to Harriet, and her relief at this climax found equally exaggerated expression. "God Almighty bless you, dear sir," she said, "for setting my bursting heart at ease. I wish you had seen me open your letter trembling, laying it down, taking it up again, unresolved whether to look at the beginning or conclusion first. At last I ventured to unfold it partly, and with a side-glance read a few words, which instantly produced the happiest tears I ever shed. O, sir, you would rejoice in the pain you occasioned me, could you but know how I feel. Forgive you? From my heart and soul I thank you."[1] The intense application with which she studied these books is further attested by Richardson's presentation copy of *Clarissa* which contains numerous notes in her hand, forming a commentary on the text. For like the author himself, she seems to have valued the book not so much as an entertaining romance, as a manual and text-book of correct conduct in all the emergencies and circumstances of human life.

After 1754 the correspondence is less interesting, and largely taken up with reciprocal confidences as to the state of the writers' health. The cir-

[1] Forster MS., Bradshaigh Correspondence.

cumstances in which it had originated no longer
existed, for there was no fresh novel to discuss,
and the letters became somewhat less frequent.
They contain, however, some allusions, of which
use has already been made, to Richardson's private
life, and to various philanthropic schemes, the
chief being the Magdalen Charity which had been
founded by a Mr Dingley in 1758 in Prescot Street,
Goodman's Fields.   Lady Bradshaigh ascribes the
inception of this charity to a hint in *Sir Charles
Grandison*, and though Richardson disclaims the
compliment, it is certain that he was greatly interested in the work and assisted its promotion.

As time went on and ill health increased,
Richardson was more and more depressed, and
filled with forebodings as to the fate of those
he would leave behind him; and his family,
anxious to divert his mind, encouraged him in
the idea of publishing his correspondence. He
was never so happy as when he had some literary
work in progress, and it was said by his friends
"that whenever Mr Richardson thought himself
sick, it was because he had not a pen in his hand."
Lady Bradshaigh having been persuaded to consent
to the publication of her share in the correspondence, he began to arrange and annotate it, carefully altering the names of persons and places
to preserve at least the appearance of secrecy.
Some progress had already been made when he
died, and the manuscript correspondence closes
with a letter of condolence addressed by Lady
Bradshaigh to Patty Richardson. A few months

afterwards she contributed some memorial verses, which conclude thus :—

" What time,
What genius can illustrate such a man,
In morals pure, religion most intense,
What more ? A Christian in the noblest sense." [1]

She herself lived for many years afterwards, dying in 1789 at the age of eighty.

Among Richardson's other friends may be mentioned Sarah Fielding and Elizabeth Carter. The former was a sister of the novelist, and two years after the appearance of Joseph Andrews she also tried her hand at a romance and made her début with *The Adventures of David Simple in Search of a Faithful Friend.* It is an exceedingly dull book, boasting of little or no construction, and intended to exemplify the misfortunes and ill-usage which are sure to befall those who judge others by their own high moral standards. David Simple is defrauded of his inheritance by his brother, and after many similar troubles, most of which might have been averted by a little more knowledge of human nature, at last secures a competency and a charming wife. The book had a considerable run, but at the present day it can be regarded only as a literary curiosity. The same holds good of her later works, of which the principal were *The Governess* " designed as a direction for girls to behave to each other and to their teachers " and *The Cry*, written in conjunction with Miss Collier.

[1] Forster MS., Bradshaigh Correspondence.

But Richardson repaid her warm appreciation of his own novels with exaggerated compliments on hers; and, eager as usual to lay hold of any opportunity for disparaging his great rival, wrote: "Well might a critical judge of writing say that your late brother's knowledge of the human heart (fine writer as he was) was not comparable to yours. His was but as the knowledge of the outside of a clockwork machine, while yours was that of all the finer springs and movements of the inside."[1] There is some evidence that Miss Fielding was in bad circumstances, and Richardson may have included her in the assistance that he gave to her friend Miss Collier; at least she was a frequent recipient of his hospitality. This may account for her attachment to her brother's rival, and for the amiability with which she seems to have received his criticisms on Fielding's works. "Poor Fielding," said Richardson to Lady Bradshaigh, "I could not help telling his sister that I was equally and surprised at and concerned for his continued lowness. 'Had your brother,' said I, 'been born in a stable, or been a runner at a sponging-house, we should have thought him a genius and wished he had had the advantage of a liberal education and of being admitted into good company; but it is beyond my conception that a man of family, and who had some learning, and who really is a writer, should descend so excessively low in all his pieces.'"[2] It was perhaps Fielding's familiarity with "high life" that

[1] Barbauld, ii., p. 104.   [2] Barbauld, vi. 154.

made him less eager to depict it than Richardson, who lived only on its outskirts.

A less enthusiastic but yet appreciative friend of Richardson was Elizabeth Carter, one of the most famous of English *bas bleus*. She made an early appearance as a poetess in the columns of the *Gentleman's Magazine*, and in 1738, when she was just twenty-one, Cave published a short collection of her verses in volume form. These productions brought her many friends, among them Mr Johnson, whose name was just beginning to be known in connection with a satire called *London*. But she was more remarkable for her linguistic acquirements than for original work, and is said to have known not only Greek and Latin, but Hebrew, French, Italian, Spanish and German as well. With all these accomplishments she retained to the last a fund of delightful modesty and good sense, and bore with dignified equanimity the unpleasant notoriety that her learning sometimes brought her. But from passages in her letters it is clear that she secretly resented the offensive masculine patronage which women's attainments so often evoke, and perhaps this is one reason why she was not such a wholehearted admirer of Richardson as some of her most intimate friends. Their acquaintance had begun in a somewhat embarrassing manner. Miss Carter had written an *Ode on Wisdom* which had been anonymously circulated in manuscript, and a copy having fallen into the hands of Elizabeth Long, a relation of Richardson, this lady showed

H

it to him as a piece she knew he would admire. He liked it so much that without much further investigation he inserted it in the second volume of *Clarissa Harlowe*, to the just indignation of the author, who sent him a letter of remonstrance. His apology is very characteristic; he explains that he did not make use of the piece for "padding," as he had a redundance of material for the book, and after he had written it "parted with several beautiful transcripts from our best poets which he had inserted in order to enliven a work which was perhaps too solemn; but the ode being shown him as written by a lady, and the intention of his book being to do honour to the sex to the best of his poor abilities, after he had made several inquiries as to the authorship he had ventured to include it in his book." [1]   Mrs Carter was quite satisfied with this apology and remained on good terms with Richardson till the end of his life, though she did not always give unqualified praise to his performances.   She was particularly displeased with his contribution to *The Rambler*. "I cannot see," said she, "how some of his doctrines can be founded on any other supposition than that Providence designed one half of the human species for slaves and helots; one would think the man was in this respect a Mahommedan." [2] Mrs Carter was ten years older than most of Richardson's "daughters," and if he expected her to join in their chorus of undiscriminating flattery,

---

[1] Pennington, *Life of Mrs Carter*, pp. 69, 70.
[2] *Correspondence of Mrs Carter and Miss Talbot.*

she must have felt a little annoyance. She was moreover a warm admirer of Fielding, and shocked Miss Mulso by describing Booth in *Amelia* as "rather frail than wicked." But when after several years of labour she at last produced her version of Epictetus, it was to Richardson's press that she entrusted the work—a work that established her reputation and brought her some measure of independence. And two years later she expressed her sorrow at her friend's death in some neatly turned verses which first appeared in the *Annual Register*, and were reprinted by Mrs Barbauld.

Quite the most charming, because also the most artless of all the letters contained in the Richardson correspondence, are those from the young wife of the German poet Klopstock, who wrote in pretty broken English to express her pleasure at *Clarissa*. The love-story that she tells her unknown friend is a perfect idyll in its way, so evidently is it the spontaneous expression of a heart that can scarcely contain itself for joy. She had conceived a great admiration for *The Messiah*, and on hearing of the author's visit to Hamburg, where she lived, she obtained an introduction to him. The rest must be told in her own words. "After having seen him two hours, I was obliged to pass the evening in a company, which never had been so weary to me. I could not speak, I could not play; I thought I saw nothing but Klopstock. I saw him the next day, and the following, and we were very seriously friends. But on the fourth day he departed. It

was a strong hour, the hour of his departure!
He wrote soon after, and from that time our correspondence began to be a very diligent one. I
sincerely believed my love to be friendship. I
spoke with my friends of nothing but Klopstock,
and showed his letters. They rallied at me, and
said I was in love. I rallied them again, and said
they must have a very friendshipless heart if they
had no idea of friendship to a man as well as to a
woman. Thus it continued eight months, in which
time my friends found as much love in Klopstock's
letters as in me. I perceived it likewise, but I
would not believe it. At the last Klopstock said
plainly that he loved, and I startled as for a wrong
thing. I answered it was no love but friendship,
as it was what I felt for him; we had not seen one
another enough to love (as if love must have more
time than friendship!). This was sincerely my
meaning, and I had this meaning till Klopstock
came again to Hamburg. This he did a year after
we had seen one another for the first time. We
saw, we were friends, we loved; and we believed
that we loved, and a short time after I could even
tell Klopstock that I loved. . . . We married, and
I am the happiest wife in the world. In some few
months it will be four years that I am so happy,
and still I dote on Klopstock as if he was my
bridegroom. If you knew my husband, you would
not wonder. If you knew his poem I could describe him very briefly, in saying he is in all respects what he is as a poet. This I can say with
all wifely modesty."

Other letters in the same strain follow, somewhat ecstatically applauding the condescension of
Mr Richardson in replying to them, and offering
to translate *The Messiah* for his benefit.   She
describes how she and her husband sit together,
she at her needlework, he reading his "young
verses, and suffering her criticisms."   Only one
thing is necessary to complete their joy, and that
is on its way.   "I cannot tell how I rejoice," she
says, "a son of my dear Klopstock!   Oh, when
shall I have him?"   The hope was never realised,
and the correspondence suddenly ends with a
letter from another writer, announcing Mrs Klopstock's death.[1]

This lady was not the only German friend of
Richardson, and one gentleman, a Mr Reich of
Leipzig, visited England purely with the view of
making his acquaintance.   The novelist took him
down to spend Sunday at "Selby House" (as the
home at North End was sometimes called, with a
reference to *Sir Charles Grandison*) and introduced
him to his family.   "It was there," says Reich,
"that I saw beauty without affectation; wit without
vanity; and thought myself transported to an en-
chanted land."   They walked round the garden, and
tasted the fruit; and at last rested in the grotto,
where the visitor's enthusiasm was aroused to such
a degree that he kissed the ink-horn in the arm of
Richardson's chair.   At last, after eight days
spent in England, "it was necessary to quit that
divine man. . . . He embraced me, and a mutual

1 Barbauld, iii. 140-158.

tenderness deprived us of speech. He accompanied me with his eyes as far as he could. I shed tears." [1]

Among Richardson's less intimate friends we must not forget to mention Dr Johnson and Dr Young. Johnson was a much younger man than Richardson, and was still comparatively unknown when *Pamela* appeared. Even in 1747, the year before the publication of *Clarissa Harlowe*, he had only just embarked on the scheme for his great dictionary. The days of his fame were still to come, and Richardson's attitude to him at first was that of a generous and successful man of letters to a younger aspirant for literary fame. We have seen how he interested himself in *The Rambler*, and tried to increase its circulation ; and in 1756 he was able to give a further proof of his friendship by becoming bail for Johnson for a debt, and lending him six guineas to release him from arrest. But at that date their acquaintance was already of some years' standing, since Boswell tells us of a meeting between Hogarth and Johnson in Richardson's house soon after the rebellion of 1745. Hogarth and Richardson had been discussing the case of Dr Cameron, who had been executed for his share in the revolt, and the former had expressed himself somewhat warmly in favour of George II. "While he was talking he perceived a person standing at a window in the room, shaking his head and rolling himself about in a strange ridiculous manner. He concluded that he was an

---

[1] Barbauld, i. 165.

idiot, whom his relations had put under the care of
Mr Richardson, as a very good man.   To his great
surprise, however, this figure stalked forwards to
where he and Mr Richardson were sitting, and all
at once took up the argument, and burst out into
an invective against George II. as one who upon all
occasions was unrelenting and barbarous, mention-
ing many instances; particularly that when an
officer of high rank had been acquitted by a court-
martial, George II. had with his own hand struck
his name off the list.   In short, he displayed
such a power of eloquence that Hogarth looked
at him with astonishment, and actually imagined
that this idiot had been at that moment inspired.
Neither Hogarth nor Johnson were made known
to each other at this interview." [1]

Another interesting glimpse of Johnson as the
guest of Richardson is given by Hester Mulso,
who tells of a delightful party at North End, at
which " Mr Johnson and poor Mrs Williams " were
present.   The latter, as all readers of Boswell will
remember, was a blind lady with literary tastes,
and formed one of that strange company who were
solaced by Johnson's benevolence.   Miss Mulso
was charmed with his behaviour to his protegée,
"which was like that of a fond father to his
daughter.   She seemed much pleased with her
visit; showed very good sense, with a great deal
of modesty and humility, and so much patience
and cheerfulness under her misfortunes that it
doubled my concern for her."   The young lady

[1] Boswell, Ed. Birkbeck Hill, i. 145, 146.

goes on to tell how she had the assurance to dispute with Johnson on the subject of human malignity, which he maintained was natural to mankind, and accused him of having disclosed his opinion in *The Ramblers*. " To which he answered, that if he had betrayed such sentiments, it was not with his design, for that he believed the doctrine of human malevolence, though a true one, is not a useful one, and ought not to be published to the world." [1]

Johnson, on his side, showed his regard for Richardson by hearty appreciation of his writings, which he considered far superior to those of Fielding. " Sir," said he, " there is all the difference in the world between characters of nature and characters of manners, and there is this difference between the characters of Fielding and those of Richardson. Characters of manners are very entertaining, but they are to be understood by a more superficial observer than characters of nature, where a man must dive into the recesses of the human heart." This preference is probably to be ascribed partly to friendship, and partly to the prominence that Richardson gave to the didactic intention, and to his conventional treatment of moral questions.

As time went on, however, the great champion of sincerity, whose favourite exhortation to his disciples was to clear their minds of cant, seems to have become somewhat disgusted with Richardson's mock modesty, and he objected to the preface to

[1] *Posthumous Works of Mrs Chapone*, i. 73.

Sir Charles Grandison on that score. "What is modesty," he said, "if it deserts from truth? Of what use is the disguise by which nothing is concealed?" And after Richardson's death he expressed himself still more strongly. Mrs Piozzi relates how Johnson told her that if Richardson had lived till she had come out her praises would have added three years to his life. "For that fellow merely died for want of change among his flatterers; he perished for want of *more*, like a man obliged to breathe the same air till it is exhausted."[1] And Boswell says that though Johnson expressed a high value for Richardson's talents and virtues, he criticised his love of continual superiority, which made him take care always to be surrounded by women, who listened to him implicitly, and did not venture to contradict his opinions.[2] To which criticism it is not inconceivable that Richardson might have responded with a *tu quoque*.

It was at Richardson's house that Johnson first met Dr Young, who had brought his *Conjectures on Original Composition* to read aloud to the novelist who had accepted the dedication. This was in 1759, but Richardson's own acquaintance with Young was of much longer standing, since their correspondence dates back to 1740. Richardson, as has been seen, was the publisher of the *Night Thoughts*, which appeared between 1742 and 1744, and it is possible that the acquaintance,

[1] *Memoirs of Mrs Piozzi*, i. 311.
[2] Boswell, Ed. Birkbeck Hill, v. 395, 396.

which afterwards ripened into friendship had had
its beginning in business relations.   The correspondence is not very interesting, and on Young's
side, at least, is tinged with much melancholy;
but it contains one criticism on *Clarissa Harlowe*
which is worth preserving.   "Be not concerned
about Lovelace," wrote the poet; "'tis the likeness
and not the morality of a character we care about.
A sign-post angel can by no means come into
competition with the devils of Michael Angelo."[1]
As the utterance of so didactic a poet as Young,
this dictum is not without significance.

Young was probably a frequent visitor at the
office in Salisbury Court as well as at Richardson's
country-house; and there is a tradition that, calling
one day at the former place, he smiled "grimly" upon
a very subordinate person there—a needy Irish-
man, who had just received a welcome appointment
as reader and corrector for the press.   That was
in the days when Oliver Goldsmith was obliged to
carry his hat so as to hide the patch in his coat,
and long before the days of Mr Filby and the
bloom-coloured coat.   When Richardson rejected
the tragedy that his reader begged him to publish,
he little thought that the fame of the despised
playwright would one day rival and surpass his
own.   For at that time Richardson and Young
were two of the most prominent writers of the day,
and were regarded with intense awe by younger
authors.

In spite of Young's melancholy letters and his
frequent references to his approaching end, he

[1] Barbauld, ii. 4.

survived Richardson by some years.   He had
been persuaded by Mrs Montagu to write a poem
to console the widow of Admiral Boscawen on the
loss of her husband, and the first part of *Resigna-*
tion had already been printed by Richardson when
Young received the news of his death.   He took
the opportunity to insert in the second part of
the poem the following tribute to his friend :—

" When Heaven would kindly set us free,
    And earth's enchantment end,
It takes the most effectual way,
    And robs us of a friend.

" But such a friend !   And sigh no more
    'Tis prudent but severe—
Heaven aid my weakness and I drop
    All sorrow—with this tear.

" Perhaps your settled grief to soothe
    I should not vainly strive,
But with soft balm your pain assuage,
    Had he been still alive ;

" Whose frequent aid brought kind relief
    In my distress of thought,
Ting'd with his beams my cloudy page
    And beautified a fault.

" To touch our passions' secret springs
    Was his peculiar care,
And deep his happy genius dived
    In bosoms of the fair.

" Nature, which favours to the few,
    All art beyond, imparts,
To him presented at his birth
    The key of human hearts."

CHAPTER V

THE DEVELOPMENT OF THE NOVEL

BEFORE proceeding to the detailed consideration of Richardson's works, an attempt will be made in this chapter to trace the development of the novel up to 1740, the year of the appearance of *Pamela*, and to estimate and to define the material that Richardson found to his hand. For without some knowledge of his predecessors and their work it will be impossible to determine the extent of his originality or to appreciate the value of his contribution to prose fiction. In order to arrive at an adequate realisation of the service he rendered, one must go back to the beginning, trace the various elements of the novel in their origin and development, and decide for what additions and improvements he was responsible.

"The infancy of the race, like that of the individual," says M. Jusserand, "is lulled by lays and stories"; and, if we except a few isolated and fragmentary charms in verse, our earliest literature is narrative in form. These narratives were at first of mythological or historical origin, the two elements blending, and becoming so much confused that it is almost impossible to separate them, or in such

stories as that of *Beowulf* to decide what is fact
and what is fable. The conversion of England
to Christianity supplied fresh material for the com-
poser; and Cynewulf, the great poet of Northumbria,
found plenty of subjects ready in the Bible and
the lives of saints. After the Norman Conquest,
native legends like those of Guy of Warwick and
Bevis of Hampton still lingered on among the
people, till, caught up by the court poets, they
appeared in a foreign dress, and were then again
translated into the original language. But the
result of the Norman Conquest was to extend
greatly the range of themes. Three great cycles
of romances dominate the literatures of mediæval
Europe—the cycles of Charlemagne, Arthur and
Troy, and in England the most popular of these
was that of Arthur. This is accounted for by the
fact that though he was a British, not an English,
hero, his story was amplified in the Latin chronicles
of monks of Welsh descent, such as Geoffrey of
Monmouth, whose writings formed a storehouse of
material from which the poets drew. The common
characteristic of these narratives, which are sometimes called chivalric romances, is that they all
deal with knightly deeds; the actors are kings,
princes and courtiers; the themes are love and
war. They hardly touch on ordinary everyday
life, but the imagination of the generations of
authors who built them up runs riot in them,
adding one marvellous incident to another and
piling on episode after episode, just as contemporary architects massed together the exuberant

details of those wonderful cathedrals that were centuries in building, and express the spirit, not of a lifetime, but of an age. In the absence of any appeal to, or apparent consciousness of, moral laws, these romances resemble the fairy-tales of children. But as time went on, the earnest religious feeling so prominent in the Christian English literature of pre-conquest times entered into the chivalric romance. The story of King Arthur was spiritualised about the twelfth century by the introduction of the Grail *motif*, and henceforth religion, love and knighthood divided the interest of the story between them.

But side by side with these ponderous romances there sprang up another form of story, the *conte* or *fabliau*. There is far less evidence as to its existence, because these stories, being short, were easily remembered, and were therefore not often preserved in writing. The *conte* differed from the romance in subject matter as well as in form ; it dealt with more commonplace, ordinary things. Much of its material was of eastern origin, but in the course of its transmission from Asia to western Europe, it was entirely remodelled and assimilated to its new environment. The interest is often purely domestic, and the treatment is jocular or satiric ; the didactic intention, though still prominent, being pointed by a jest. The *conte*, however, never became thoroughly naturalised in England, and those that exist in our language are nearly all of French origin. The best examples of short stories of native growth are to be found embedded in religious treatises, especially in the lives of saints.

So far both romance and conte were expressed chiefly in verse; prose was not generally used till the end of the fifteenth century. A prose version of the Arthurian legends was compiled, mainly from French sources, by Sir Thomas Malory in 1469 or 1470, and was printed by Caxton in 1485. Caxton himself translated the *Recuyell of the Histories of Troye*, which had been compiled in 1464 by Raoul Le Fevre, chaplain and secretary to Philip the Good, Duke of Burgundy. His work was carried on by Wynkyn de Worde and William Copland, who, during the reigns of Henry VII., Henry VIII., Edward VI., and Mary, printed version after version of these legends. Lord Berner's *Huon of Bordeaux*, which represented the Charlemagne cycle just as the *Morte d'Arthur* and the *Recuyell of the Histories of Troye* represent the cycles of Arthur and Troy, was printed by Wynkyn de Worde about 1534, and to the same press we owe the *Gesta Romanorum*, a collection of short stories or contes, which had been compiled as early as the fourteenth century, and translated from the Latin original in the reign of Henry VI.

These prose versions mark the culmination of the mediæval romance. With the spread of the new learning it fell into neglect. Scholars who could go to Homer for the story of Troy regarded the popular versions of the story with contempt; acquaintance with the dead languages made men conscious of the true perspective of history and literature; and Virgil, the wizard, was stripped of his magic robe and relegated to his true place as a poet. The decline of the Arthurian legend was still more complete, for in this case there was no classical version of the story to lend it a borrowed dignity. It is remarkable how little this beautiful cycle influenced Elizabethan literature. Shakespeare, who had recourse to all kinds of sources for his plots, did not draw one from Malory, who, in spite of the fact that King Arthur is the hero of *The Faerie Queene*, seems also to have had very little influence on Spenser. And if the Charlemagne romance left a more permanent impression on the literature of the sixteenth century, this was because Ariosto had woven the wonder of his verse about the dying myth, and invested it with fresh charm just as it was falling into decay.

But it is not to be supposed that these romances passed all at once and entirely away. Their immediate influence on literature ceased because at that time the makers of literature were nearly always men of learning. But their popularity among the general public is attested by the number of editions published during the sixteenth and seventeeth centuries. (The last edition of the *Morte d'Arthur* was in 1634.) Passing into chapbooks and broadsides, the stories formed the ware of many a country pedlar, and the influence of such romances as *Bevis of Hampton* has been traced in the *Pilgrim's Progress*.[1] They were

[1] See *Pilgrim's Progress*, Ed. C. H. Firth, Introduction, pp. 31-34.

still read even as late as the eighteenth century as is proved by Fielding's words in the first chapter of *Joseph Andrews*.

"Our own language affords many examples of excellent use and instruction, finely calculated to sow the seeds of virtue in youth, and very easy to be comprehended by persons of moderate capacity, such as the history of John the Great, who, by his brave and heroic actions against men of large and athletic bodies, obtained the glorious appellation of the giant-killer; that of an Earl of Warwick, whose Christian name was Guy; the lives of Argalus and Parthenia, and above all the history of those seven worthy personages, the champions of Christendom. In all these delight is mixed with instruction, and the reader is almost as much improved as entertained."

But this contemptuous mode of reference shows that by this time the romances had sunk to the level of fairy-tales.

The contributions of the middle ages to fiction were thus the chivalric romance, which lingered on in different forms for centuries, and the *conte* or *fabliau*, which had very little influence on English literature. The short story is, in fact, alien to our national genius, and if within the last few years it has attained a certain popularity in our country, this may be attributed partly to French influence, and partly to the exigences of magazine-writing.

During the reign of Elizabeth the novel underwent fresh developments. The mediæval romance had struck one note that was to be dominant in Eng-

I

lish fiction, that of profound earnestness and didacticism; the note that is still heard among the
many voices of our own day, as if the justification
of every novel were its influence on contemporary
morality—the note of Richardson, Fielding and
Smollet; of Dickens, Thackeray, and George Eliot.
The Elizabethan romance struck another, akin to
this, and not less permanent as a national characteristic. "The English," says M. Taine, "are
born psychologists," and this dictum is amply
justified by the two great English romances of the
later sixteenth century, the *Euphues* of John Lyly,
and the *Arcadia* of Sir Philip Sidney. It is true
that the psychology of these books is not to be
found in elaborate characterisation; the men and
women of the *Euphues* are not in the least complex,
and indeed it is somewhat hard to follow with any
interest the fortunes of their loves through the intricacies of Lyly's absurd and memorable manner of
narration. And though Sidney is more successful
in this sphere, and in such characters as Queen
Gynecia, shows a capacity for the portrayal of convincing passion, yet one has only to compare the
wooden and mechanical movements of the heroes
of these romances with those of the free and lively
personages of the contemporary drama to feel the
lack of power. It is rather in the discourses with
which both books are crammed, the long conversations on matters of sentiment, that the psychological interest is to be noticed. Notwithstanding
the artificiality of the pastoral background, Sidney's
shepherd princes display great subtilty and pene-

tration in the discussion of such themes. The same remark applies, though with less force, to the *Euphues*, and the ingenuity which its hero expends on such matters may be compared with that of Richardson in his correspondence on the same subject with Lady Bradshaigh or Miss Mulso, or the interminable letters in *Sir Charles Grandison*, of which it forms the theme.

These romances, however, though they show an advance in this direction, are extremely limited as to their content. The mediæval mind had found an asylum from the fierce struggles of a stormy and insecure life in an ideal world of chivalry and romance ; every hero must be a knight, unconquerable and unafraid. The tradition lingered on through the sixteenth century, and Sidney's characters are not real shepherds but princes in disguise. It would have been impossible for him to treat peasant-life seriously and sympathetically, because he would not have considered the careers of milkmaids and ploughmen sufficiently dignified subjects for romance. The citizen and the peasant had not yet entered into the sphere of the novel, though they are amply represented in the contemporary drama, in such plays as *Arden of Feversham, A Woman Killed with Kindness, Every Man in His Humour, A New Way to Pay Old Debts*, and many others, to say nothing of Shakespeare's immortal rustics and craftsmen. The introduction of low life into fiction was due to less courtly narrators, to men who had dipped deep into life's struggle, and were more familiar with tavern brawls than with court pageants, to such men as Robert Greene, Shakespeare's youthful rival, and his friend Thomas Nash. Greene, having wasted his youth in dissipation, was at length forced to the record of the exploits of thieves and criminals, his companions, as a means of earning a livelihood. But this resort to actual occurrence at once brought the narrative into the domain of real life, and thus one great advance was made. Nash, in his various pamphlets, followed the same method ; they are partly polemical, partly narrative, partly didactic, but they all abound in illustrations drawn from surrounding life and manners. And the only one of his books that can be termed a romance, *The Unfortunate Traveller, or the Life of Jack Wilton,* was an altogether new departure in English fiction. It has been called our first picaresque romance, that is, our first narrative dealing with the fortunes and misfortunes of an adventurer, whose shifts and escapes form the chief subject of entertainment, while the hero himself calls for little admiration or sympathy. Nash takes us into all classes of society, among courtiers, scholars and beggars, and even anticipates Sir Walter Scott by introducing actual historical persons into his story. And, forestalling Defoe, Fielding and Smollet by nearly two centuries, he, first among English novelists, made use of that picturesque detail and local colour, which, so abundant in our poetry (for instance, in *The Canterbury Tales* and *Piers Plowman*), had as yet been almost entirely absent from the romance. But the appearance of this kind of novel, so vivid and so original, must be regarded as premature and sporadic. The latter picaresque romance, exemplified especially by Smollet, was not derived from Nash but from Le Sage, whose *Gil Blas* was not published till 1715. Thus, of the two kinds of romance developed in the reign of Elizabeth, only the first had much influence on the future history of the novel.

The seventeenth century witnessed the growth of this branch of fiction to absurd dimensions. It continued to be altogether divorced from the conditions of familiar life, and the only advance made was in the direction of psychological analysis. Its ideal and aim are summed up in the essay by the Abbé Huet, entitled *L'Origine des Romans,* and prefixed to Madame de la Fayette's novel *Zayde.* He states that the moral intention of a romance is its sole justification ; its principal end being the instruction of the reader, virtue must be rewarded, and vice chastised. But as the mind of man is naturally averse to instruction, and his self-love causes it to rebel against admonition, it must be beguiled by the charm of pleasure, and the severity of precepts must be softened by the delight of illustrations ; its· faults being corrected by their condemnation in another. Thus the entertainment of the reader, instead of being the chief aim, is really subordinate to the principal end, which is the instruction of the mind and the regulation of morals, and novels are more or less correct as they diverge less or more from this definition and this aim. Further, Huet will only admit as " correct "

romances those that represent princes or con-
querors, that paint the life of the aristocratic world
and that can initiate young people of rank into
this world. "Good romances are the dumb instructors who succeed those of the college, and in
a more instructive and persuasive manner than
theirs teach one how to live and how to speak, and
of whom one can say what Horace said of Homer's
Iliad, that it teaches morality more effectually
than the most learned philosopher."[1] This limita-
tion of the actors to high life seems made to fit
the pastoral and heroic romances which reached
their apotheosis in the hands of La Calprenède
and Mdlle. de Scudéry—in such romances as
Cassandre, Le Grand Cyrus, and *Clélie.* None of
these tremendous narratives can boast of any construction ; they are simply aggregations of adventures, and their main interest lies in the long
disquisitions on sentimental themes. Mdlle. de
Scudéry, however, by the introduction of contemporaries under fictitious names, added a new
attraction and at the same time rendered a substantial service, for the very effort of describing
real men and· women, brought the romance down
from the realms of unreality, and gave it an air of
greater probability.

In spite of the immense popularity of these
romances their absurdities were apparent even to
contemporary readers. Parodists, the chief of
whom were Sorel, Scarron, and Furetière, soon
appeared. The first of these, in his preface to *Le*

[1] *Œuvres de Mdme. de la Fayette,* Paris 1812, i. p. 90.

Berger Extravagant, explains that he objects to poetry and romance because they give a false idea of life, and particularly of love. His story is intended to show all the embarrassments awaiting a man sufficiently foolish to take the romantic ideal as a rule for practical life. The hero, like Don Quixote, lives in an imaginary world of his own, and passes for a madman among the sensible and commonplace people who surround him, and play on his hallucinations for their own amusement. The influence of Cervantes is visible in this book, but Sorel has none of the pathetic power of the great Spaniard. The story is simply a gay farce, chiefly noticeable because it attests the extreme popularity of the form it parodied.

Scarron, in *Le Roman Comique*, and Furetière in *Le Roman Bourgeois*, conduct their ridicule in a different manner. They tell the story, one of the adventures of a company of strolling players, the other of simple townspeople. "I am going to tell you simply and faithfully," says Furetière in the first chapter of his book, "the various adventures and love affairs of people who are not heroes nor heroines, who do not conduct armies nor overturn kingdoms, but who are good middle-class people who go their way quietly, of whom some are handsome, others plain; some good, others foolish; and the latter certainly seem to be the more numerous. This will not prevent some people of the highest rank from recognising themselves among them, and from profiting by the illustration of follies which they imagine to be far from them.

To still further avoid the fields worked by others, I design the scene of my story to be moveable, that is to say, sometimes in one part of the town and sometimes in another, and I will begin with the most plebeian, namely the Place Maubert." But the very fact that the adventures of these middle-class people are recounted in a burlesque manner proves that the author did not consider them worthy of any other treatment. He makes fun of the bourgeoisie, satirizes their habits, their small ambitions, their snobbishness, but he is far from exhibiting them as dignified men and women, all, by reason of their common humanity, subject to high as well as to low passions, to good as well as to mean or ridiculous impulses, and therefore fit subjects for serious and sympathetic delineation. His manner is as far as possible removed from that of Richardson, and from his abbey of Chalivoy he regards the lower and middle-classes as one who stands aloof from them, and while thoroughly enjoying their eccentricities and peculiarities lacks the power to penetrate below the surface or to guess at the motives and passions working out of sight.

The view, therefore, that considers this appeal to ordinary life as the point of transition between the heroic romance and the domestic novel is probaby mistaken. The works of the parodists were, in fact, as far removed from real life as the romances they burlesqued. If the romance led one into an ideal world where the trees were always green, the men always brave, and the women always fair, the parody dragged one down into one not less ideal, but less beautiful, where only the mean and sordid aspect of things called for attention. Both are equally unreal, but the former had this in its favour, that it exalted human nature while the burlesque degraded it. As has been justly said by M. Brunetière, " the object of both was to enlarge or to diminish nature, to embellish or disfigure it, to exalt or degrade it, but not at all to represent it as it is, or even as the authors see it." [1]

The required junction between the two kinds of romance must therefore be sought in another direction, and this brings us back to native literary products. The digression into the domain of French literature was necessary, because translations of the French heroic romances abounded in England, and enjoyed almost as great a vogue here as in their mother country, persisting indeed until they were killed by the works of Richardson and Fielding. When Addison represents the spectator as waiting in a lady's library and amusing himself with the inspection of her books, he mentions no fewer than five French romances —*Cassandre, Cleopatra* and *Astræa*; *Le Grand Cyrus,* "with a pin stuck in one of its middle leaves," and *Clélie,* " which opened of itself in the place that describes two lovers in a bower." And not only were these translations popular; they found many English imitators, such as Mackenzie, the author of *Aretina,* and Roger

[1] Brunetière. *Études Critiques, Troisième Série,* p. 69.

Boyle, Earl of Orrery, who in his *Parthenissa*, published in 1634, out-Heroded Herod, as far as prolixity and looseness of construction were concerned. Another imitator was Mrs Manley, who in her *New Atalantis* (also mentioned in the enumeration of the lady's books) followed Mdlle. Scudéry's plan of introducing real people under fictitious names, though her book can hardly claim the moral intention of the French novelist.

Putting aside *The Pilgrim's Progress*, which, owing to its profound allegorical meaning, cannot be classed with other fiction, the seventeenth century produced no great English romance, nor any that had much influence on the development of the novel. But another element, which we should now consider as indispensable in a story as in a play, had meanwhile been slowly maturing—the element of characterisation. By this should be understood not the gradual revelation of a character by means of his own words, which is the dramatic method, but rather that mode of description which enables the reader to realise, by the words of a third person, his appearance, manner and qualities. Collections of what were called *Characters*, on the model of Theophrastus, were enormously read in the seventeenth century, the most famous being those of La Bruyère. But he had been preceded in the same field by Sir Thomas Overbury, John Earle, and Samuel Butler, the author of *Hudibras*. These *Characters* were short descriptions of certain social types, and though the later ones (those of

La Bruyère for instance) undoubtedly refer to actual people, they were in the first instance general rather than particular, and may be compared to a composite photograph of individuals possessing certain characteristics in common. The necessary actuality was given by Addison and Steele in the famous *Tatler* and *Spectator* essays. If Addison had composed some connected narrative of the doings of Sir Roger de Coverley and his friends, and had combined them in the framework of some united action instead of presenting them in isolated episodes, he would have anticipated Richardson and Fielding by a generation, and been our first great novelist. The conception of the Spectator Club satisfies all the requirements of a novel proper except that of construction, and in point of characterisation it is quite equal or even superior to the Pickwick Club. For the grotesque treatment of the later author lends an air of burlesque and unreality to his characters, and the reader, however greatly entertained by them, is left with the impression that this is caricature and not art. But Addison always avoids a farcical treatment, and thus secures the conviction of reality. Sir Roger de Coverley is not caricature but life-like portraiture. We see him going upstairs, talking all the way, and calling all his host's servants by their names ; or patronising the gipsies, and being cheated by them ; or importantly whispering his remarks on the weather to the judge at the county sessions, almost as vividly as if we knew him. But because

his hero fails to look out on us from the framework
of a continuous narrative, Addison cannot strictly
be termed a novelist, and just misses the laurel he
would otherwise deserve.   As it was, he gave
many hints to later writers.   The Tory Foxhunter
(not one of the Spectator Club) has many features
in common with Squire Western in *Tom Jones*,
and Squire Burdock in *Humphrey Clinker*; and
Ryland, into whose mouth Mackenzie put the story
of *The Man of the World*, is obviously modelled
on Will Wimble.

No less remarkable than the fashion of the
character sketch, and equally important in its contribution to the development of the novel, was the
popularity of the memoir.   The later seventeenth
century was the golden age of memoirs, both in
France and in England.   It is hardly necessary
to mention the famous memoirs of St Simon in
the former country, or Burnet's and Clarendon's
histories of contemporary events in the latter,
or Antony Hamilton's *Memoirs of the Comte de
Grammont*, to which both countries may lay claim.
The last named, though nominally a memoir, has
more in common with the novel than the others,
since it does not pretend to give an accurate
account of historical events.   It tells the story of
the gallantries of the Comte de Grammont, an
exile at the court of Charles II., and of his prolonged courtship of the author's sister, "la belle
Hamilton."   But as it was written for no other
end but that of amusement, we may suppose that
the narrative is not always very reliable.   "I have

ventured," says Hamilton, "to alter facts or to invert their order."[1]   But in one point he is a faithful chronicler; there can be little doubt that the hero is a truthful representation of the real Comte de Grammont, and it has been suggested that this fascinating rake appears in the later history of the novel as Robert Lovelace.[2]

The memoirs of real persons being so popular and so much sought after, it is not surprising that certain ingenious men of letters began to manufacture biographies of persons that had never lived, save in the author's imagination. "From writing biographies with real names attached to them," says Professor Minto, in his excellent monograph on Defoe, "it was but a short step to writing biographies with fictitious names"; and, as the chief attraction of the memoir lay in its real or supposed veracity, every care was taken to make the imitation resemble its model in this appearance of truth. The great master in this kind was, as need hardly be remarked, Daniel Defoe. A minute and keen observer, possessing a remarkable capacity for circumstantial invention, he romances with the utmost ingenuity and ingenuousness, and masquerades with admirable effect in the sober garb of a *bonâ fide* historian. His *Memoirs of a Cavalier* actually deceived Sir Walter Scott, while the *Journal of the Plague* has often been taken for the account of an eye-witness. It is this power of circumstantial narration that gives the charm

---

[1] *Mémoires de la Vie du Comte de Grammont,* chap. i.
[2] Le Breton, *Le Roman au dix-septième Siècle,* p. 237.

to *Robinson Crusoe*; its exact and multitudinous details carry conviction with them.

But there was another reason why the form of the memoir should be adopted by writers of fiction. The puritanic prejudice against romances, illustrated by Milton in his condemnation of the *Arcadia*, still dominated the general public, and the reading of fiction was still regarded by the serious as an idle and frivolous amusement. Grandmamma Shirley, who was the chief monitress of the future Lady Grandison, sums up the opinion of the respectable middle-class on the subject when she says :—

"The reading in fashion when I was young was romances. You, my children, have in that respect fallen on happier days. But till I became acquainted with my dear Mrs Eggleton, which was about my sixteenth year, I was overrun with the absurdities of that kind of writing."[1]

It was therefore necessary that the novelist should either disguise his fiction as genuine history, or justify its existence by expressing some moral aim or pretending that it had some hidden meaning. Thus Defoe, besides putting *Robinson Crusoe* into the form of a memoir, further bolstered it up by declaring that it was an allegory of his own life. And still more completely to vindicate his intention, he went out of his way to insert among Crusoe's *Serious Reflections* an earnest protest against the art of fiction, which may fairly be taken to represent the extreme puritanic view on the matter. "This supplying a story by invention,"

[1] *Sir Charles Grandison*, vol. vii., p. 204.

he says, "is certainly a most scandalous crime, and yet very little regarded in that part. It is a sort of lying that makes a great hole in the heart, in which by degrees a habit of lying enters. Such a man comes quickly up to a total disregarding the truth of what he says, looking upon it as a trifle, a thing of no import, whether any story he tells be true or not."[1]

The application to Defoe's own case is obvious enough, and he was certainly an adept in the art of lying. But whatever his practice may have been, he was possessed of a deep religious consciousness. Born of a persecuted sect with a long history of religious experiences, he inherited from his Puritan ancestors the habit of self-examination and analysis, and carried on from Sidney to Richardson the psychological method which has already been noticed as characteristic of the English novel. The sentimental discussions of the *Arcadia* give place in *Robinson Crusoe* to spiritual conflicts in the manner of Bunyan. In *Pamela* both kinds of mental analysis, the religious and the sentimental, are found side by side.

The same reasons for imposing a fictitious narrative on the public as genuine history probably influenced Swift, when he inserted as a frontispiece to *Gulliver's Travels* a portrait pretending to represent the hero, Lemuel Gulliver, of Redriff, or Rotherhithe. But the deception was an innocent

---

[1] Defoe, *Serious Reflections during the Life and Surprising Adventures of Robinson Crusoe*, p. 113.

one, for if any reader ever believed in the actual existence of the Houhynyms or the Yahoos, his credulity and not the guile of the author was responsible. The satirical and political intention of Swift's great work puts it somewhat outside the sphere of the pure romance. But its autobiographical form, like that of *Robinson Crusoe*, may be safely attributed to the popularity of the memoir; nearly all the romances of the time, French as well as English, are presented in this manner.[1]

There was still another literary form that was cultivated with great assiduity in the seventeenth and eighteenth centuries, and contributed in no small degree to the development of the novel. This was the letter. The letters of Mdme. de Sevigné in France, and of the Duchess of Newcastle in England, illustrate the great care and industry with which even familiar and domestic correspondence was conducted in the seventeenth century. During the eighteenth century the collections multiplied to an astonishing degree. Then were composed the brilliant epistles of Horace Walpole, Lord Chesterfield, and the poet Cowper; of Lady Mary Wortley Montagu, and Mrs Delany; of Voltaire and Grimm, to mention only the more famous writers. Letter-writing

---

[1] The most notable example is, of course, *Gil Blas*, which, published in 1715, may have had some influence on Defoe's work. But the quick-witted, light-hearted, and wholly irresponsible rascal of Le Sage has little in common with Defoe's solemn and sententious hero. The resemblance between *Gil Blas* and *Colonel Jack*, which is Defoe's best picaresque novel, is more obvious.

was, in fact, regarded as an art, and letters seem
to have filled in some degree the part played by
the magazine or newspaper of to-day; they were
passed round from house to house, copied and
recopied, and read over and over again on long
winter evenings and in quiet country places, where
any message from the outer world was acceptable.
Contemporary authors refer to letter-writing as if it
were an accomplishment to be acquired like music
or drawing at the present time, and Richardson,
when describing the charms of his heroines, never
fails to mention their epistolary ability. His
young women, too, often compliment their friends
on their letters, or one laments that she cannot
write as elegantly as another. "You, madam,"
says Emily Jervois to Harriet Byron, "are *such* a
writer, and I am such a *poor thing* with my pen.
But I know you will accept the heart. And so
my very diffidence shows pride, since it cannot
be expected from me to be a fine writer ; and yet
this very letter, I foresee, will be the worse for my
diffidence, and not the better. For I don't like
this beginning neither. But come, it shall go."[1]

It is therefore not to the parodist, but to the
essayist, the historian and the letter-writer, that
we must give the credit of bridging over the gulf
between the heroic romance and the novel proper.
And this is especially true in English literature,
since, though imitators of Scarron existed, they
seem to have had little or no influence. The
approach to the novel treating of familiar life was

[1] *Sir Charles Grandison*, iv. 236.

K

made not by grotesque caricature of the pastoral heroic, but by the description of real events by eye-witnesses. This appeal to actual life secured a vividness and picturesqueness that gave an air of realism even to the work of such an idealist as Richardson. And at the same time, the transference of the love interest from remote royalties to English squires and serving-maids brought the novel within range of enjoyment by a much wider public.

CHAPTER VI

" PAMELA "

To the student of contemporary literatures nothing is more striking than the manner in which the same mode of literary expression appears almost simultaneously in different countries and in different languages; as if the mental development of neighbouring nations progressed at the same rate, and brought forth almost identical fruit at the same season. In many cases, of course, one movement is obviously generated by another, and is the result of deliberate imitation. But in others no such connection can be proved, and in spite of many endeavours to show the contrary it is very doubtful whether Richardson, who is one of the most insular of our writers, and the most thoroughly national in his chief characteristics, was in any degree influenced by foreign literature. But it happened that about nine years before the publication of *Pamela* there appeared a French novel, which so closely resembles it in theme and treatment that conjecture has been busy over the possible relationship between the two books.

This was *La Vie de Marianne*, by Marivaux, published in Paris, in two parts, in 1731 and 1734. The author was already well known as a dramatist, and as the writer of two or three novels, the principal of which was *Le Paysan Parvenu*. An English translation of *Marianne* appeared in 1736, so that it is possible that Richardson, who did not know French, was acquainted with the story, which to some extent resembles that of *Pamela*. It is as follows :—

A stage-coach being attacked by robbers, everyone is killed but one person, who escapes, and Marianne, a child of three years old. She is rescued by some soldiers, and taken to the village curé, whose sister brings her up. When she is fifteen, the curé's sister goes to Paris to see a dying relative, and takes with her Marianne, who is to be apprenticed to some useful trade. Disappointed in their expectation of a legacy from the relative, the curé and his sister both die. Marianne is commended to the charge of a good monk, who in his turn appeals to the benevolence of a rich man, named M. de Climal. M. de Climal apprentices her to a linen draper, but falls in love with her at the same time. While Marianne is parrying his attacks, she meets and is wooed by a young man called Valville, who proves to be her patron's nephew. In despair at her difficulties she goes to pray at a convent chapel, where a lady, struck by her beauty, takes compassion on her, and offers to adopt her. The lady is afterwards discovered to be Valville's mother, but such are the fascinations of Marianne that she does not oppose her son's wishes. After some obstacles, including a temporary infidelity on the part of her lover, Marianne is married, and is discovered to be the daughter of a duke.

The chief similarity between the stories is therefore the fact that the heroine of each is a beautiful girl in humble circumstances, who successfully withstands temptation, and has her virtue rewarded. But here the resemblance, as far as plot goes, ends. Pamela is really of low birth, while Marianne is an aristocrat in disguise. Then, again, in point of character, the two heroines are entirely dissimilar. Pamela is a simple little maidservant, showing absurd obsequiousness to the "quality," diffident to the last degree, and, even when horrified by the advances of her master, secretly flattered that he should think her a fit object of pursuit. Marianne has a very good opinion of herself, and accepts the tributes of her admirers as a just homage to her beauty. Marianne is taken almost immediately under the protection of Madame de Miran, who treats her as her own daughter, and carefully preserves her from harm. When, for instance, her lover's cousins carry her off, and try to persuade her to marry a man of low rank, Valville and his mother hurry to her rescue, and prevent the match. But Pamela, through two bulky volumes, has no efficient protectors but her own virtue and good sense. Again, Pamela is thoroughly sincere, and though she is prepared to accept help from her master's chaplain, Mr Williams, she never pretends to love him; she is, throughout, faithful to her persecutor. Marianne, on the other hand, is a thorough coquette, and

when Valville transfers his affections to a new
mistress, she retaliates by listening to the addresses
of another suitor. "Marianne," says M. Larroumet,
in his study of Marivaux, " belongs to a society in
which women are queens by right of their beauty
and their wit, accustomed to adulation both before
and after marriage. Pamela, brought up in dependence and for dependence, regards men as
superior beings, to whom religion, custom and
law give supreme rights. Marianne, deceived by
Valville, confounds him with her indignation; she
crushes the evil designs of M. de Climal by her
scorn. Pamela, subjected to a temptation of the
same kind, cries, with sad astonishment, ' This
gentleman has degraded himself to offer freedoms
to his poor servant.' " [1]

In some respects, however, the two stories have
a good deal in common. In the first place, both
authors made a new departure in choosing as their
theme a love-story of the middle or lower classes.
The novelists of the seventeenth century had confined their attention to princes and princesses;
they liked their literary creations to be of the very
highest rank. As Marivaux himself said, " There
are people whose vanity enters into everything
they do, even into their reading. Give them the
story of the human heart in high life, and it is
an important matter for them; but do not speak
to them of lower conditions of society; they desire
to see only lords, princes, or kings, or at least
people of some distinction. These alone will

[1] Larroumet. *Marivaux, Sa Vie et Ses Œuvres*, Paris 1882, p. 350.

satisfy their fastidious taste. As for the rest of
men, let them exist by all means, but do not let
us talk of them ; these readers will tell you
candidly that nature might have dispensed with
bringing such people into the world, and that the
bourgeoisie do her no credit."[1] And as the taste
of the reader determines the style of the work, it is
greatly to the honour of Marivaux and Richardson
that they had the courage to depart from the
beaten track, and appreciated the possibilities of
untitled humanity as a subject of romance.

Another point of similarity between Marivaux
and Richardson is their manner of narration. It
is true that the form is in one case that of an
autobiography and in the other that of a correspondence, but the autobiography is addressed by
the heroine in her old age to a friend, and has
therefore something of the intimate air peculiar to
a letter. "In relating her adventures," says the
author, " she imagines herself to be with her friend,
talking to her, answering her, and in this way she
instinctively mingles the relation of facts with the
reflections that occur to her in connection with
them." And the plan of Richardson's first novel
is much simpler than that of his later ones, where
multitudes of letters cross and re-cross. Pamela
is almost the only correspondent, and thus tells
her story in much the same way as Marianne tells
hers—with this difference, that Marianne is supposed to draw on her memory, while Pamela writes
while the impression of the events is fresh upon her.

[1] *Œuvres de Marivaux*, Paris 1781, vi. 330.

" The reflections that occur to her." This brings us to another point of contact between the novelists —the habit of subtle self-analysis in which the heroines of both indulge. It is not enough for Pamela or Marianne to commit any action ; they must forthwith examine the reasons that led them to do so, and carefully balancing the motives that impelled them, at last decide whether their proceedings were right or wrong. The interest of both novels lies not in the plot but in the mental conflicts of the characters. But these mental conflicts are conducted with more skill by Richardson than by Marivaux, whose story is, as St Beuve has said, " a skeleton of a romance compared with *Pamela.*" Richardson, indeed, with his simpler education, more limited area and closer acquaintance with the class to which his heroine belonged, was better fitted for the portrayal of the ingenuée than Marivaux, who was a man of the world and a frequenter of salons. In the swift delineation of a character by a few graphic strokes, however, Marivaux shows a skill which is not approached by Richardson. Take, for instance, the description of M. Villot, Marianne's rejected suitor. " Although fairly well built, he seemed then as much as anyone could seem, a mean little fellow of no consequence, whose business was to cringe and flatter, who seemed to have no will of his own, and to whom one could say without offence, ' Retirez-vous.' " The method of the English novelist is entirely different. What Marivaux does with a few bold strokes Richardson accomplishes with a number of minute touches.

On the whole it may be concluded that though Richardson may have seen Marivaux's book, it had very little influence on him. Marivaux's novels were certainly widely read in England, and Fielding, in one of the introductory chapters which precede each book of Joseph Andrews, refers to both *Marianne* and *Le Paysan Parvenu*, though he gives the latter its French name. But Richardson's own account of the genesis of *Pamela* is so simple, and appears so natural, that it would appear wisest to accept it as conclusive. Indeed, if the probability of Marivaux's influence had not been so dogmatically stated by some French, and supported to some extent by some English, critics, it would have been hardly necessary to investigate it.

Richardson's own statement, which is contained in a letter to Aaron Hill, runs thus :—

" I will now write to your question—whether there was any original groundwork of fact for the general foundation of Pamela's story.

" About twenty-five years ago, a gentleman with whom I was intimately acquainted (but who, alas! is no more!) met with such a story as that of *Pamela* in one of the summer tours, which he used to take for his pleasure, accompanied by one servant only. At every inn he put up at it was his way to inquire after curiosities in its neighbourhood, either ancient or modern ; and particularly he asked who was the owner of a fine house, as it seemed to him, beautifully situated, which he had passed by (describing it), within a mile or two of the inn.

"It was a fine house, the landlord said. The owner was Mr B., a gentleman of a large estate in more counties than one. That his and his lady's history engaged the attention of everybody who came that way, and put a stop to all other inquiries, though the house and gardens were well worth seeing. The lady, he said, was one of the greatest beauties in England ; but the qualities of her mind had no equal : beneficent, prudent and equally beloved and admired by high and low. That she had been taken at twelve years of age, for the sweetness of her manners and modesty, and for an understanding above her years, by Mr B.'s mother, a truly worthy lady, to wait on her person. Her parents, ruined by suretiships, were remarkably honest and pious, and had instilled into their daughter's mind the best principles. When their misfortunes happened first they attempted a little school in their village where they were much beloved ; he teaching writing and the first rules of arithmetic to boys ; his wife plain needlework to girls, and to knit and spin ; but that it answered not ; and when the lady took their child, the industrious man earned his bread by day labour and the lowest kinds of husbandry.

"That the girl, improving daily in beauty, modesty, and genteel and good behaviour, by the time she was fifteen, engaged the attention of her lady's son, a young gentleman of free principles.

. . . That she had recourse to many innocent stratagems to escape the snares laid for her . . . . once, however, in despair, having been near drowning; that at last, her noble resistance, watchfulness and excellent qualities subdued him, and he thought fit to make her his wife. That she behaved herself with so much dignity, sweetness and humility, that she made herself beloved of everybody, and even by his relations, who at first despised her; and now had the blessings of rich and poor, and the love of her husband.

" The gentleman who told me this, added, that he had the curiosity to stay in the neighbourhood from Friday to Sunday, that he might see the happy couple at church, from which they never absented themselves; that, in short, he did so see them; that her deportment was all sweetness, ease and dignity mingled; that he never saw a lovelier woman; that her husband was as fine a man, and seemed even proud of his choice, and that she attracted the respects of the persons of rank present, and had the blessings of the poor. The relater of the story told me this with transport.

" This, sir, was the foundation of Pamela's story; but little did I think to make of it a story for the press." [1]

This evidence as to the origin of the tale renders the probability of French influence very doubtful, especially as Richardson followed closely the outline of the romance related above. Even the name of the hero, originally, for obvious reasons,

[1] Barbauld, i. 69.

veiled under an initial, appears in the same form. This fashion of designating characters, possibly set by the writers of sham memoirs to give an air of greater veracity to their fictions, was followed by Richardson in all his novels, and is most irritating and confusing, especially in *Sir Charles Grandison*, which deals with a large number of persons. And its effect on the modern reader is to evoke from the first a spirit of amused criticism. How can anyone be expected to treat "Mr B." with respect or even with seriousness?

To the bare skeleton of his original Richardson added a multitude of details, which invest it with life and energy. Pamela in the first letter is seen lamenting the death of her mistress, yet in the midst of her distress illustrating those qualities of prudence and thrift that Richardson was so anxious to inculcate, by counting up her savings and the presents of her master. In a postscript she indicates that she has attracted his attention, but adds, that though he was formerly supposed to be "wildish," he is now a reformed character. Slowly and gradually the plot unfolds, and each letter betrays more plainly the vulgar, practical little soul of the heroine, and her struggle between gratified vanity and conventional principle. And the convention that Mr B. being a man, and a landowner, and belonging to the upper classes, is therefore her superior, and must be treated with exaggerated respect is quite as strong in Pamela as the convention that at all costs she must preserve her honour. The author, in fact, had to teach his

readers to keep their places as well as to keep
their characters.

It is unnecessary to give all the unpleasant
details of the heroine's persecution. It is enough
to say that she is at last beguiled, under pretence
of a visit to her parents, to a lonely house on her
master's Lincolnshire estate; and is there left in
charge of his housekeeper, Mrs Jewkes. This
lady at first professes great friendship for the girl,
whose point of view may be indicated by the response she makes to these advances. "Once she
offered to kiss me. But I said, 'I don't like this
sort of carriage, Mrs Jewkes; it is not like two
persons of one sex to each other.'" The retort of
her companion is obvious and deserved.

Pamela, indeed, may be virtuous, but she is
anything but pure-minded; and in this lies her
security. Unsuspecting innocence may easily become the prey of vice, but the reader feels that if
Pamela falls, it will be with her eyes open. And
the worst of it is that in spite of her oft-repeated
protestations against her master's wickedness, she
is supposed all the time to have a secret leaning
to him, and dreads nothing more than to incur his
anger. "Oh," she writes, "how I dread the coming
of this angry and incensed master! Yet why is he
angry? Why incensed? I am sure I have done
him no harm! . . . What is the matter that, with
all his ill usage of me, I cannot hate him? To be
sure in this, I am not like other people! He has
certainly done enough to make me hate him; but
yet when I heard of his danger, which was very

great, I could not in my heart forbear rejoicing for
his safety, though his death would set me free.
Ungenerous master! If you knew this, you surely
would not be so much my persecutor! But for
my late good lady's sake, I must wish him well;
and, oh, what an angel would he be in my eyes
yet if he would give over his attempts and
reform!"[1]

It would perhaps be unfair to criticise too closely
the devices by which Richardson prevents his distressed heroine from escaping. It was necessary
here, as in *Clarissa Harlowe*, that the victim
should not get away, and equally necessary, for
the sake of consistency, that she should make an
attempt to do so. A mad bull—the fear of robbers
—a crumbling wall, and a few bruises, are sufficient
to deter Pamela from the attempt; though in her
despair she almost decides on suicide by drowning as an alternative. But the dissuading voice
in this case is that of conscience. Her religion, as
conventional as her morality, restrains her, and
she holds a dialogue with the tempter, which
occupies several pages. At last she emerges
triumphant, and piously resigns herself to her
misfortunes, which she honestly conceives to be
permitted by the Divine Will.

"What then, presumptuous Pamela, dost thou
here?" thought I; "quit with speed these perilous
banks, and fly from these dashing waters, that
seem in their meaning murmurs this still night to
reproach thy rashness! Tempt not God's good-

[1] *Pamela*, i. pp. 237, 238.

ness on the mossy banks, which have been witnesses of thy guilty purpose; and while thou
hast power left thee, avoid the temptation, lest
thy grand enemy, now by divine grace repulsed,
return to the assault with a force that thy weakness may not be able to resist! and lest thou in
one rash moment destroy all the convictions
which now have awed thy rebellious mind into
duty and resignation to the Divine Will!"[1]

Shortly after this episode her master arrives on
the scene, and concealing himself in an anteroom
overhears the chatter of his victim to Mrs Jewkes.
This so softens his heart that he begins to pity the
girl, and from this time Pamela's prospects clear.
It is now only a question between his pride and
his passion; he himself does not know which will
conquer, and frankly tells the now blushing and
yielding maiden of his doubt.

"Ah, sir," said I, "and here my doubt recurs,
that you may thus graciously treat me to take
advantage of my credulity."

"Still perverse and doubting! Cannot you take
me as I am at present? I have told you that I am
now sincere and undesigning, whatever I may be
hereafter." . . .

"If you will be good," said I, "to your poor
servant, and spare her, she cannot say too much!
But if not, she is doubly undone! Undone, indeed!"

"I hope my present temper will hold," replied he.
. . . "And, Pamela, you must pray for the continu-
ance of this temper." . . . His goodness over-

[1] *Pamela*, i. p. 231.

powered all my reserves. I threw myself at his feet and embraced his knees.

"What pleasure, sir, you give me, at these gracious words, is not lent to your poor servant to express! I shall be too much rewarded for all my sufferings if this goodness hold! God grant it may, for your own soul's sake as well as for mine! And oh, how happy should I be if——"

He stopped me and said, "But, my dear girl, what must we do about the world, and the world's censure? Indeed I cannot marry."[1]

Yet, notwithstanding this offensive candour, Pamela's obsequious adoration is undiminished, and she continues to trust herself in her lover's power with the most dangerous confidence; in the hope, that, as he says, "if his mind hold, he will endeavour to defy the world and the world's censures."

At last his pride conquers, and he decides to send Pamela home. But before she has gone many miles, she is recalled by an impetuous letter, declaring that the writer cannot do without her, and begging her to return at once. Her mental conflict at this juncture is admirably described. Her heart leaps at the approaching victory of her love, but she is beset by doubts whether, after all, the cup of happiness that seems within her reach may not at the last moment be dashed from her grasp. "How my exulting heart throbbed, and even upbraided me for so lately reproaching it for giving way to the love of so dear a man! But

---

[1] *Pamela*, i., pp. 293, 294.

take care thou art not too credulous neither, O
fond believer! said I to myself; things that we
wish are apt to gain a too ready credence with us.
Therefore will I not acquit thee yet, O credulous
fluttering throbbing mischief! that art so ready to
believe what thou wishest: and I charge thee to
keep better guard than thou hast lately done, and
tempt me not to follow too implicitly thy flattering
impulses.

"Thus foolishly dialogued I with my heart, and
yet all the time that heart was Pamela."[1]

Her heart having thus turned traitor, she decides,
with somewhat startling temerity, to go back.
But this time her confidence is justified. The
rest of the book describes the interval between
her arrival, and the day that makes her "the
happy, thrice happy, Pamela B.," and is decidedly
less interesting than the earlier portion, where the
reader is still in suspense as to her fate. The hero,
having been compelled to obtain by fair means
what he could not compass by foul, is now treated
as if he were a reformed character, the only faults
of which he is henceforth guilty being a certain
haughtiness of temper and pride of rank, to which
his gushing, humble bride offers no fit antidote.
She is, in fact, so much overpowered by his condescension that she cannot say too much in his
praise, or express too warmly her gratitude for his
hardly complimentary devotion. Both parties are
painfully aware that his union with the "pretty
rustic," as he describes her, in her presence, to his

---

[1] *Pamela*, ii. pp. 44, 45.

L

friends, is a *mésalliance,* and the constant reitera-
tion of his determination to treat her with the
same respect as if she belonged to his own class
is received by her with thankful humility, and by
the reader with growing impatience. And as the
latter finds that the story does not end with the
conventional marriage service, but is prolonged to
tell of Pamela's reception by the neighbouring
gentry, and by her husband's exceedingly vulgar
sister, this impatience is goaded to absolute revolt.
Only the most determined perseverance can achieve
the perusal of these fatuous and tedious pages.

The immense and immediate popularity of the
book led, as already stated, to the production of a
spurious continuation, entitled *Pamela in High
Life.* Richardson, who, like Atticus, could not
bear " a brother near the throne," unwisely resolved
to publish a genuine sequel. But if the interest of
the first part of *Pamela* flags towards the end of
the second volume, that of the second part may be
said to fall still-born. It is not that, as some
critics would have us think, the history of post-
nuptial life cannot be made interesting. Fielding,
in his *Amelia,* gave ample proof to the contrary.
But too many of Pamela's letters after her marriage
are taken up with the merest trivialities, accounts
of visits made and received, with conscientious
catalogues of the compliments exchanged on these
formal and tiresome occasions. Several long epistles
are devoted to an examination of Locke's *Treatise
on Education,* and two more (which are obvious,
though distant, imitations of essays in *The Spec-*

tator) to a criticism of *The Distressed Mother*
and *The Tender Husband*. In fact, the only
interest in the second part of *Pamela* is once more
derived from the errors of Mr B. His wife (who,
when she is no longer a possible victim, seems to
think such errors comparatively venial, and only
natural in so fine a gentleman) gives a full account
of his love affair with the unfortunate Sally
Godfrey; and afterwards, with a frankness somewhat surprising in so discreet a lady, recounts her
own sufferings from an apprehended infidelity on
his part. Altogether the sequel to *Pamela* is
ponderous reading, and hardly possible except for
a student, who may find in it hints that throw
light on the author's artistic development and on
the characterisation of his later novels.

Posterity has not confirmed the contemporary
verdict on *Pamela*, and Mr Leslie Stephen's dictum,
that "it is distinctly the worst of Richardson's
works," probably expresses the opinion of most
people who are acquainted with all his novels.
For the book is vitiated by its wretched morality,
which startles our ethical, no less than our humorous, perceptions. The author's primary object, as
he repeatedly declared, was to write a book for
the guidance of young women in Pamela's position,
and to put it in so attractive a form—

> "That truth embodied in a tale
> Might enter in at lowly doors."

And in an age that taught dogmatically the re-
compense of virtue by means of a material heaven

and the punishment of vice by means of a material hell, the obvious inducement to good conduct was the hope of some substantial reward—not golden harps or glittering crowns in this instance, but the scarely less enviable possession of the jewels that had belonged to Mr B.'s mother. But the common experience of mankind that material reward is rather the exceptional than the inevitable consequence of virtue at once creates in the reader a feeling of antagonism to the author's teaching.

And, again, the genuine character of the heroine's virtue may fairly be called into question. It was long ago remarked by Sir Walter Scott and Mrs Barbauld that Pamela's conduct betrays a lack of delicacy incompatible with the fairest purity. So long as she is merely the frightened maiden, scarcely suspecting her master's real intentions, and childishly gratified by the notice taken of her, she attracts our sympathy. Even when she is fully conscious of her danger, and endeavours by all means to escape it, she is pathetic enough. But no woman will forgive her for what Mrs Barbauld justly defines as the chief blot on the conception—the passion supposed to be aroused in her by her unworthy lover. Her girlish admiration for the fine gentleman, set so far above her by the apparently impenetrable barrier of rank and circumstance, is perfectly natural ; and if he had won her by the ordinary arts of his kind, Pamela's inclination for him might have been more unfortunate for her, but would certainly have seemed

more pardonable and probable. But he assails
her at first with threats, and afterwards with such
coarse ruses as would speedily kill every germ of
affection in the heart of a pure-minded girl; yet
though she is loud in her protests against the
wickedness of her master, it does not arouse in
her the shrinking feeling of disgust that might
be expected. On the contrary, she uses all the
resources of feminine sophistry to persuade herself,
against the evidence of her senses, that he is not
as bad as he appears. Her immediate response
to his entreaty for her return is perilous in the
extreme, but she persuades herself into thinking
that duty requires what inclination prompts. "If
he intends honour to me," she argues, "the least I
can show on my part is that I have gratitude, and
my heart is free, so that I can return love and
duty for it." And so she flies back to the arms
of a man, with whom if she respected herself
she could have no further communication whatever.

And what makes her behaviour particularly repulsive is the conviction it forces upon one that
it is mainly prompted by a disproportionate respect
for her lover's wealth and position. No one can
doubt that if equal insults had been offered her by
a man of her own class she would have rejected
him with scorn. But because Mr B. is a gentleman,
and has a large income, and two or three country
seats, he is to be forgiven what would be unpardonable in a hero of low degree. Richardson's vulgar
exaggeration of class distinctions permeates the

book, and Pamela blissfully crawls to the feet of her master. When he tells her that the happiness of legitimate courtship is greater than any he could have known had he succeeded in his designs on her, she answers humbly :—

"O, sir, expect not words from your poor servant, equal to these gracious professions. Both the means and the will are given you to lay me under an everlasting obligation. How happy shall I be if, though I cannot be worthy of all this goodness and condescension, I can prove myself not entirely unworthy of it! But I can only answer for a grateful heart; and, if I ever give you cause wilfully (and you will generously allow for involuntary imperfections) to be displeased with me, may I be an outcast from your house and favour, as much as if the law had divorced me!"[1]

And all these overwhelming expressions of gratitude are due to the benevolence of a lover who marries her for his own gratification when he cannot obtain what he wants on lower terms!

But putting aside these grave faults of taste and morality, there can be no doubt that the heroine is a masterpiece of characterisation. To this is due the pathetic and moving effect produced by her sufferings; she is so life-like that one feels the same kind of interest in them as in those of a real person. The realisation of a character is the necessary preliminary to the enjoyment of his story, and no history, however exciting, of hair-

---

[1] *Pamela*, ii. p. 65.

breadth escapes or perilous adventure is attractive
to the mature mind unless it is first interested
in the person who encounters these dangers. In
the higher kinds of fiction plot must depend on
character, and that is why Richardson, who had
the most elementary ideas of construction, was so
brilliant a novelist. Pamela is as real to us as
to the ladies who a hundred and fifty years ago
bewailed her woes; by a thousand minute and
graphic touches she is made to stand before us,
waiting with folded hands and downcast eyes the
commands of her lord and master. She is not all
perfection, and has her little vanities; in the midst
of her troubles she carefully details the various
articles of her attire—"two suits of fine Flanders
lac'd headclothes, three pair of fine silk shoes, two
hardly the worse, and just fit for me (for my lady
had a very little foot), and the other with wrought
silver buckles on them ; and several ribbons and
top-knots of all colours; four pair of fine white
cotton stockings and three pair of fine silk ones ;
and two pair of rich stays." And she too has, as
M. Texte has noticed, her own pride of place, for,
when she leaves Squire B.'s house on the intended
visit to her parents, she will not receive any gift
from her inferiors. "They all," she says, "would
have made me little presents ; but I would not take
anything from the lower servants." Then, again,
her mingled superstition and religion, her womanish
dread of cows and robbers, all go to complete the
portrait of a well-behaved little waiting-maid of the
eighteenth century. The picture is wonderfully

convincing; our only complaint is that we can hardly bestow on it the tribute of admiration its painter demands. He continually pauses to cry " How beautiful!" It is difficult to respond with enthusiasm, but of the fidelity and accuracy of the drawing there can be no doubt.

The same verdict can hardly be given on the other characters of the book. Mr B. is not an interesting rake, and his reformation is so sudden and improbable as to give an air of unreality to the whole conception. Richardson was always on delicate ground when he tried to draw a gentleman, and at the time of the composition of his first book he had not seen so much of " high life " as he afterwards did. But Mr B. is certainly one of his most offensive experiments in this direction; even allowing for the grossness of contemporary manners he is unnecessarily objectionable. And in the description of Lady Davers, his sister, the author is involved in still greater difficulties. Her interview with Pamela after the latter's marriage is taken up by a long string of invectives to which no woman of spirit could have listened for a minute. Her manners are those of a Whitechapel termagant rather than of a high-born lady, and in spite of the assurances of one of Richardson's correspondents "that he could find him half-a-dozen Lady Davers (her wit excepted) among his quality acquaintance," it is as evident that she is drawn from imagination as that Pamela is the result of actual experience. Lady Davers, it may be noticed in passing, is the first crude sketch of the character after-

wards toned down in Anna Howe and Charlotte
Grandison.

The character of Pamela's father, Goodman
Andrewes, has been highly praised by Scott, who
says that the description of his interview with the
squire, "when he inquires after the fate of his
daughter, would have immortalised Richardson
had he never wrote another line." But even Scott
notices his want of spirit and independence. To a
reader of the present day these faults are so glaring
as to quite obscure what other merits the passage
may boast.

Of the other minor characters, the most successful are Mr Williams, the clergyman, and Mrs
Jewkes. It is impossible to help feeling some
sympathy for the former, who is so badly treated
by the heroine when she has no further need of
his help. But as she, recalling the risks he has
run for her sake, piously remarks, " Providence
would perhaps make it up to Mr Williams!" As
for Mrs Jewkes, the author exhausted his power of
detailed description in making her as hideous and
repulsive as he could. "She is a broad squat,
pursy, fat thing, quite ugly, if anything human can
be so called ; about forty years old. She has a
huge hand, and an arm as thick—I never saw
such a thick arm in my life. Her nose is flat and
crooked, and her brows grow down over her eyes ;
a dead, spiteful, grey, goggling eye ; and her face
is flat and broad ; and as to colour, looks as if it
had been pickled a month in saltpetre. I daresay
she drinks. She has a hoarse, manlike voice, and

is as thick as she's long."[1]   Nothing could be
more graphic, and from the point of view of
morality, it was no doubt necessary that personified
vice should be thus unmercifully pictured ; though,
unfortunately for youth and inexperience, the devil
does not always appear in so unmistakable a form.
Pamela is not for a moment deceived as to the
woman's real character, and the astonishing part
of it all is that she makes no more desperate effort
to escape, and actually extends her favour to the
wretched creature, when, in the security of the
married state, she can afford to be quixotically
generous.   The effect of this angelic sweetness
is such that in the second part of the book Mrs
Jewkes turns from the error of her ways and is
immediately seized with a mortal illness, during
which she receives every attention at the hands of
her forgiving mistress.

Such, then, is the story of Pamela, a book the
defects of which can scarcely be over-stated ;
whose warped morality, glaring want of taste, and
improbability of incident, would seem sufficient to
obscure all the merit that cannot be denied to it.
It is only when we remember that both plan and
subject matter were entirely original, and that the
sentiment and treatment correspond to the ordinary
tone of lower middle-class feeling at the time, that
we can comprehend or sympathise with the immense
enthusiasm it excited.   It inaugurated a new school
of fiction, and if its permanent popularity in England
was somewhat impaired by the speedy publication

[1] *Pamela*, i. p. 146.

of Fielding's parody, its effect on the literary development of France and Germany, where many imitations were produced, was of the greatest importance. But the consideration of Richardson's influence on the continent must be reserved for another chapter.

CHAPTER VII

" CLARISSA HARLOWE "

EVERYONE knows the famous passage in Trevelyan's *Life of Macaulay*, which tells how the tedium of a rainy season in the Neilgherries was beguiled by the reading of *Clarissa Harlowe* ; how, in Thackeray's graphic words, "the whole station was in a passion of excitement about Miss Harlowe, and her misfortunes, and her scoundrelly Lovelace. The Governor's wife seized the book ; the Secretary waited for it ; the Chief Justice could not read for tears." And all this emotion was occasioned by a story that had long before obtained the position of a classic, yet was as little known to the general public as classics too often are.

Clarissa had already for many years been out of fashion ; the novels of Fielding, Sterne and Smollet, of Miss Burney, Sir Walter Scott, Miss Edgeworth and Miss Austen, had pushed her story into obscure corners of library shelves ; the excitement and enthusiasm occasioned at its first appearance had been quite forgotten ; it had been almost relegated to its present position as a literary curiosity ; when, after half a century of oblivion, as if raised from the dead, the heroine appeared once

172

more to vindicate the fame of her creator and the plaudits of her first admirers. To the grandchildren of the men and women of Macaulay's generation she is almost unknown ; her story is a long one, and, in its original form, not very accessible. It may therefore be permitted to tell the tale of the "divine Clarissa" once again; briefly, of course, but with more circumstance than most modern historians of literature have thought necessary.

Clarissa Harlowe, a young lady of great beauty and merit, is the youngest child of James Harlowe, Esq., of Harlowe Place. She is the soul of purity, amiability and honour, a chief favourite with all the elders of the family, including her two uncles Antony and John. The whole family is exceedingly wealthy, and Clarissa has inherited as her exclusive property the estate of her paternal grandfather. But the ruling passion of all the Harlowes, with the exception of the heroine, is avarice, and though Clarissa relinquishes the entire management of her fortune to her father, it exposes her to the intense rivalry and jealousy of her brother James and her sister Arabella. Arabella, just before the time at which the story begins, has been sought in marriage by Robert Lovelace, a gentleman of very good family and reported to be quite irresistible. So he proves to her, but unfortunately soon discovers that he has been mistaken in the name of the lady recommended to his attention. He had meant to pay his addresses to Clarissa, and finds himself

involved with her sister.   He, however, holds to his
proposal, but puts it in such a way that Arabella is
obliged to refuse him ; whereupon he transfers his
attentions to Clarissa.   She receives them coldly ;
not that Lovelace is not in person, family and
accomplishments all that could be desired, but
because she has heard reports injurious to his character.   The loss of her admirer enrages Arabella
beyond measure, and she makes common cause
with her brother against their sister.   The one
idea of the former being family aggrandisement,
he wishes to force Clarissa into a marriage with
a Mr Solmes, whose estate adjoins that of Mr
Harlowe, and may some day be exchanged for one
of his own in Scotland.   Thus both brother and
sister are interested in opposing the alliance with
Lovelace ; they meet him with insults and affronts,
till at last a challenge is given and a duel fought
in which James Harlowe is wounded.   Clarissa,
meanwhile, has been placed in the painful position
of trying to conciliate both parties.   She is not
in the least in love with Lovelace, but his threats
that, if she reduces him to despair, her brother will
suffer for it, persuade her into continuing her
correspondence with him.   By degrees the whole
family is drawn into the league against her, and
her gentle determination to refuse a man from
whom she feels a positive revulsion only increases
their desire to make her submit.   In the struggle,
the second distinguishing characteristic of the
family, its obstinate strength of will, is shown in
full relief; but herein Clarissa proves herself a

worthy daughter of her house; she remains absolutely inflexible. Lovelace, who is perfectly aware of her indifference to him, now, with diabolical selfishness, plans a means of compelling her to fly to his protection; by the aid of his agent, Joseph Leman, who is a servant of Mr Harlowe, he fans the anger of the brother and sister and keeps everyone in a state of suspense as to what his next move will be. Clarissa is confined to her room, but she finds means of corresponding with her friend Anna Howe, and, still hoping to avert a catastrophe, with Lovelace; while at the same time she offers to give up all thought of his suit if only she may be freed from the addresses of Solmes. But no offer that she can make meets with any approval, and her misery is increased by a multitude of petty persecutions; her own maid is sent away and her sister's servant appointed to attend on her, and the influence of all the family friends is engaged on behalf of Solmes. And on the other hand she is subject to Lovelace's continual protestations of devotion and sympathy, till the contrast between his conduct and that of her relations almost inclines her to lend him a favourable ear. At last she is persuaded to submit to an interview with Solmes, but as she remains invincible she is informed that a day has been fixed for her marriage with him, and that it is to be celebrated at her Uncle Antony's lonely country-house, where no help can reach her. Thus driven to bay, she determines to accept Lovelace's offer and to seek the protec-

tion of his aunts; but directly she has written the
letter making the appointment her heart misgives
her, and she revokes it in another. This Lovelace
is careful not to remove, and, thinking that he has
not seen it, she goes in her indoor dress to tell
him that she has changed her mind. A long
conversation follows in which Lovelace uses all
his eloquence to persuade her to fly with him,
but she remains quite unmoved, and is just reach-
ing for the key of the gate to return to the house
when Leman, who has been lying in wait for that
purpose, raises a cry which convinces her that she
is discovered. Half beside herself with fear, and
too much agitated to notice that there is only one
pursuer, she allows Lovelace to drag her away to
a coach waiting in the lane, and protected by
armed horsemen.

Lovelace's intentions, though still hidden from
his victim, are now quite evident to the reader.
His proposals had at first been honourable, but
her indifference and haughty reception of his
advances have piqued his pride; he is concerned
to keep up his character as a lady-killer, and
though he loves Clarissa as much as his selfish
nature will allow, he has resolved to make her a
sacrifice to his vanity. She is no sooner within
his power than she is conscious of an almost imperceptible change in his manner to her. "He
looks with more meaning, I verily think, than he
used to look; yet not more serious; not less gay
—I don't know how he looks. But with more
confidence a great deal than formerly; and yet

he never wanted that." In her ignorance and
conscious innocence the poor girl thinks that she
is still free to accept or reject him as she will;
and, fearing to take the irrevocable step which
will finally separate her from her family, she
refuses to identify herself with his by seeking its
protection. That, after all, is a matter of little
moment, since he never intends that she shall
have the opportunity for doing so; but by urging
it on her, and then submitting to her refusal, he
is able to assume an air of injured generosity. He
places her in lodgings near St Albans, and in spite
of her entreaties for him to leave her, contrives to
remain at her side until she is at length convinced
that the only thing left to her is a speedy marriage
with him. This he repeatedly urges, but manages
the occasion so artfully that all her pride and
delicacy revolt from the proposal, and prevent her
from consenting to it; while he is careful to affect
a humble submission to her wishes, and to avoid
pressing the matter. This conduct puzzles and
vexes his victim, who, hitherto so much sought
and admired, cannot at first realise the depth of
her humiliation. "Would he have had me catch
at his first, his very first word? I was silent, too
—and do not the bold sex take that for a sign of
favour? Then so lately in my father's house!
Having also declared to him in my letters, before
I had your advice, that I would not think of
marriage till he had passed through a state of
probation, as I may call it. How was it possible I
could encourage with very ready signs of approba-

tion such an early proposal, especially after the free treatment he had provoked from me? If I were to die, I could not."[1]

Lovelace has no intention of remaining at St Albans; it is but a resting-place on the way to the city which at that time offered so great a security for evil deeds, and so little chance of escape for an ignorant victim. He is therefore highly pleased when Clarissa herself proposes to go there. He pretends to commission a friend to get rooms for her, and to leave Clarissa free to choose between several that are described. She settles, as he has designed, on some kept by a widow named Sinclair, who is employed by him, and thus enters as if willingly into the trap prepared for her. Thus they arrive in London, and from this moment poor Clarissa's fate is sealed. Up till now her charm of person and character has on several occasions so far prevailed with her lover as to render momentarily sincere his protestations as to his honourable intentions. From this moment, his victim entirely in his power, he knows no compassion. The duel is between Clarissa's will and his own, between her pride and his vanity, but the odds are so desperately against her that there can be no doubt as to its issue.

He continues, however, to keep up the fiction of matrimonial projects, deluding Clarissa with discussions about the house he will take her to, and with other plans as to the future. " He now does nothing but talk of the ceremony," she writes,

---

[1] *Clarissa Harlowe*, ii. p. 334.

"but not indeed of the day. I do not want him to urge that—but I wonder he does not." But even now she cannot make up her mind to believe him utterly vile, especially when he actually accompanies her to church, and there behaves in the most exemplary manner. "Have been at church, Jack," he informs his friend Belford. "Behaved admirably well too! My charmer is pleased with me now; for I was exceedingly attentive to the discourse, and very ready in the auditor's part of the service. Eyes did not much wander. How could they when the loveliest object, infinitely the loveliest, in the whole church was in my view?" This behaviour so delights the guileless girl that in her next letter to Anna Howe she acknowledges the impression he has made. "Indeed, my dear," she says, "I think I could prefer him to all the men I ever knew, were he to be always what he has been to-day." But she is soon put out of humour with "him, with herself, and all the world," for an evening spent in the society of his friends thoroughly disgusts her; notwithstanding which she makes a conquest of one of them, the above-mentioned Belford, who from this time is her devoted partisan. She becomes more and more uneasy, but her modesty and pride combine to prevent her from urging on the final arrangements for her marriage. Even when Lovelace has the settlements drawn up, and affects to lament the delay caused by the absence of his uncle, who is to be present at the ceremony, she will do nothing to hasten matters.

"'Would to heaven, my dearest life,' added he, 'that, without complimenting anybody, to-morrow might be the happiest day of my life! What say you, my angel?' with a trembling impatience that seemed not affected. 'What say you to for to-morrow?'

"It was likely, my dear, I could say much to it, or name another day with such an hinted delay from him.

"I was silent.

"'Next day, madam, if not to-morrow?'

"Had he given me time to answer, it could not have been in the affirmative you must think. But in the same breath he went on—'Or the day after that?' And taking both my hands in his he stared me into a half confusion. Would you have had patience with him, my dear?

"'No, no,' I said, as calmly as possible. 'You cannot think that I should imagine there can be reason for such a hurry. It will be most agreeable for my lord to be present.'

"'I am all obedience and resignation,' returned the wretch, with a self-pluming air, as if he had acquiesced to a proposal made by me, and had complimented me with a great piece of self-denial.

"Is it not plain, my dear, that he designs to vex and tease me? Proud yet mean and foolish man if so! But you say all punctilio is at an end with me. Why, why will he take pains to make a heart wrap itself up in reserves that wishes only, and that for his sake as well as my own, to observe due decorum?"[1]

[1] *Clarissa Harlowe*, iii. p. 319.

Thus the time drags on, Lovelace still devising
fresh reasons for delay, and fresh schemes for the
ruin of his victim, who by her own sweet innocence
and purity constantly evades him. At last she
manages, with the help of Miss Howe, to mature
a scheme for escape. But Lovelace defeats this
project by introducing to her a Captain Tomlinson,
who professes to be an intimate friend of Clarissa's
uncle, John Harlowe, and commissioned by him to
bring about a general reconciliation, provided he
can be convinced that she is actually married.
Lovelace's behaviour on this occasion is so unexceptionable, and Clarissa is so much delighted
by the prospect of reconciliation, that she shows
unmistakable signs of softening, until he attempts,
by a false alarm of fire, to take advantage of her.
Then, thoroughly convinced of his baseness, she
determines to stay not a day longer in the house,
and the next day effects her escape to Hampstead.
Meanwhile he manages to intercept a letter from
Miss Howe, who has been making investigations
on her friend's behalf, and substitutes for it one of
his own manufacture, so skilfully forging the writing
that Clarissa is quite deceived. He soon traces
her to her place of refuge, and still supported by
her uncle's supposed agent, again urges marriage.
She refuses to give him an answer till she has
heard from Miss Howe, and this letter, containing
the plans for Clarissa's rescue, and further warnings as to the supposed mediator, Lovelace also
manages to intercept. He assures her that his
aunt, Lady Betty, and his cousin, Charlotte Mon-

tague, will themselves wait on her and escort her to
his uncle's house, where the marriage may be celebrated ; and, as a further proof that he is in earnest,
actually procures the license for it. He then
causes two women to personate the ladies, and an
amusing account is given of the manner in which
he coaches them for their parts. Clarissa, imagining
that she is on her way to Montague House, is thus
beguiled back to London.

The next morning finds her out of her mind,
while Lovelace himself is for the moment awed
into distress and remorse. After all, he is genuinely
in love with Clarissa, and dare hardly think of
what he has done. "I could be very grave," he
says, "were I to give way to it. The devil take
me for a fool! What's the matter with me, I
wonder! I must breathe a fresher air for a few
days." And again, "Cæsar never knew what it
was to be hipped, I will call it, till he came to be
where Pompey was; that is to say till he arrived
at the height of his ambition; nor did thy Lovelace know what it was to be gloomy, till he had
completed his wishes." [1]

In the midst of her distress, poor Clarissa's
mania for writing remains as strong as ever, and
incoherent fragments, in which she appeals first to
her friend, then to her family, and again to Lovelace, are given. Half conscious of her own mental
disturbance, she entreats piteously for compassion
and deliverance. "I shall never be what I was.
My head is gone. I have wept away all my brain,

[1] *Clarissa Harlowe*, v. p. 52.

I believe, for I can weep no more. Indeed I have
had my full share, so it is no matter." By degrees,
however, she recovers her senses, but indignantly
refuses the reparation that Lovelace is now anxious
to make. She again and again attempts to make
her escape, and there is no finer scene in the book,
nor indeed in the whole eighteenth century novel,
than that in which she confronts her persecutors,
and indignantly repudiates the idea of a marriage
with her lover.

"She would have spoken but could not," writes
he, "looking down my guilt into confusion. A
mouse might have been heard passing over the
floor; her own light feet and rustling silks could
not have prevented it; for she seemed to tread air,
and to be all soul. She passed to the door, and
back towards me, two or three times, before speech
could get the better of indignation; and at last,
after twice or thrice hemming, to recover her
articulate voice :—

"'O thou contemptible and abandoned Lovelace,
thinkest thou that I see not through this poor
villainous plot of thine, and of these thy wicked
accomplices?

.   .   .   .   .   .

And ye, vile women, know that I am not married.
Ruined as I am by your help, I bless God I am
not married to this miscreant. And I have friends
who will demand my honour at your hands! And
to whose authority I will apply, for none has this
man over me. Look to it then, what further insults

you offer me, or incite him to offer me. I am a
person, though thus vilely betrayed, of rank and
fortune. I never will be his; and, to your utter
ruin, will find friends to pursue you. And, now I
have the full proof of your detestable wickedness,
will have no mercy on you!'

" They could not laugh at the poor figure I
made. Lord, how each devil, conscious-stricken,
trembled!

·   ·   ·   ·   ·   ·

" Then, taking one of the lights, she turned from
us; and away she went, unmolested. Not a soul
was able to molest her." [1]

Lovelace now retires to his uncle's seat, whence
he sends repeated letters to Clarissa, begging for
her consent to a speedy marriage. But she is
inexorable, and never ceases to search for a means
of escape. At last, in spite of all his precautions
to prevent it, she succeeds in getting away and in
finding an asylum in the house of a mercer of
Covent Garden. Here, by correspondence with
Lady Betty Lawrence, she becomes acquainted with
the plot of which she has been the victim. All
her lover's schemes lie open before her, and, as she
writes to her foster mother, it is apparent to her
that Lovelace, whose errors have generally been
supposed to be due to the careless impulses of
youth, " has acted upon a regular and preconceived
plan of villainy." But her troubles are not yet at
an end. Her retreat is discovered by the woman

[1] *Clarissa Harlowe*, v. p. 162.

she has left, who arrests her for debt. Lovelace, on hearing the news, at once begs his friend Belford to fly to her assistance ; she is restored to her own lodgings, and from this time, Belford, whose friendship for Lovelace has hitherto prevented him from taking more active measures on her behalf, becomes her guardian and champion. Clarissa is now beset with entreaties from Anna Howe to marry Lovelace, but she remains firm in her resolution, and will have no further communication whatever with him. At the same time she seeks earnestly, though ineffectually, for a reconciliation with her family ; but her relations still refuse belief in her innocence, or in the tidings of her failing health. Day by day she grows weaker and weaker, and her malady is not lessened by the constant apprehension that Lovelace will renew his persecutions. In the meantime her cousin Morden, who is also her guardian, returns, too late to be of any use, for it is now clear that Clarissa can live but a few weeks. And so she fades away, every stage in her decline being faithfully reported to Lovelace, who, when at length the fatal blow does fall, is driven beside himself with agony and remorse. Only for a time, however ; on his recovery he affects his former gay and irresponsible behaviour, and departs on a foreign tour, realising that for him there is no mean between actual melancholia and apparent frivolity. "Adieu, dear Belford," said he. "Whatever airs I give myself, this charming creature has fast hold of me here" (clapping his hand upon his heart), "and I must either appear what you see me, or be what I so lately was."

As soon as remorse is unavailing, Clarissa's relations are filled with horror at what they have done, and a large part of the last volume is occupied by their repentant letters, the writers of which vie with each other in bearing testimony to the virtues of the dead lady. Finally, Colonel Morden also sets out for the continent, nursing schemes of revenge against Lovelace should chance bring them together. And the latter, who scorns to fly a foe, and, moreover, only longs for some termination to his own mental sufferings, contrives that the meeting shall take place. A duel is the inevitable result. Lovelace is mortally wounded, and dies in agony, exclaiming, " Let this expiate ! "

This is the brief outline of a story whose effect on the contemporary public can hardly be over-estimated. It speaks well for Richardson's independence of judgment that he remained insusceptible to the flattering entreaties of the multitudinous correspondents, who, during its publication, begged him to give the book a happy ending ; his genius refused to be misled, and he conducted the tale to its inevitable close as remorselessly as Sophocles himself might have done. He saw that the moral as well as the artistic effect would be irretrievably spoiled if he allowed Clarissa to be one whit more tolerant of her vicious lover.

Yet the action is so skilfully conducted that the tragic ending is not plainly foreseen till after the central catastrophe. Expectations of a change in Clarissa's fortune are continually raised; Lovelace may reform, the heroine may escape, or be reconciled with and rescued by her family. These expectations it is the work of succeeding letters to efface; there is a constant alternation of hope and disappointment, which feeds suspense, and keeps alive the interest. Even after Clarissa's escape there is just the possibility that she may relent and marry her repentant lover; the last hope of a happy ending fades only with her breath. And this long drawn-out tragedy could not be portrayed by any other means than by those ponderous letters, that no one who has really become interested in the story will think tedious. For they exactly represent the manner in which the great, pathetic crises of life approach;—the passionate clinging to the last shreds of hope, the momentary despair that vanishes at the least whisper of better tidings, the fierce revolt or dumb acquiescence of the sufferer, the unrelieved gloom that follows the worst and final blow of fate.

In other respects, however, the plot is open to serious criticism. It is full of improbabilities and weak connections, which are apparent to the most careless reader. Clarissa is described as being a favourite daughter, who has hitherto met with every indulgence from an adoring family. The motive that sets them all against her is painfully inadequate; for why should she, who has been regarded as a special favourite by her father and mother, be sacrificed to the wishes of her brother?

Again, she is described as a woman of such exceptionable capacity that she has undertaken the
whole management of the domestic affairs of her
parents' house; yet when she is thrown on her
own resources she exhibits very little enterprise.
Her attempts at escape are but feebly conceived;
when every possible motive urges immediate flight,
she delays and deliberates, hoping for another
loophole, some external assistance that never
comes. It was, of course, impossible that it
should, for the exigences of the story require her
prolonged confinement; yet that a woman of such
independent character should show so little re-
source is extremely improbable, and, so far, a
defect in construction. When she does escape
for a time, she actually takes refuge at Hampstead,
the place of all others to be avoided, since she has
once been there with Lovelace. How much better
would it have been, if, as Scott suggests, she had
thrown herself on the protection of that very
magistrate, who was at once Richardson's parodist
and rival. Her case would certainly have evoked
all the sympathy and chivalry of Henry Fielding.

Further, the complicated schemes of Lovelace
could never have been seriously devised or executed.
In the first place, such a crime as his was at that
time punishable by death; that he should not
only have dared it, but should also have taken so
many people into his confidence, is quite incredible.
His plans required the utmost secrecy, yet he
expatiates on them in the frankest fashion to his
friend Belford, and to a host of other correspon-

dents, including a treacherous servant who might
well be liable to a bribe. And when his conduct,
though not all the circumstances of it, is notorious
in the circle to which both he and Clarissa belong,
he is represented as attending a ball, and being
graciously received by most of the ladies present.
Society in the eighteenth century was sufficiently
corrupt, but it is difficult to believe it was as
corrupt as this. And, again, as has been often
remarked, it is quite inconceivable that Belford,
who, except for the incidental sowing of wild oats,
is represented throughout in the most amiable
light, should not have interfered sooner to check
the diabolical schemes of Lovelace. The friends
of both parties are, indeed, chiefly useful as the
recipients of letters. Anna Howe, in spite of her
protestations, does singularly little for Clarissa's
assistance, even though she has a willing agent
in the person of her lover Hickman. Instead of
marrying him, and obtaining the right to act
independently of her mother, who is under the
Harlowe influence, she coquets and delays, and
will not wed him till Clarissa is happy, thus losing
her one chance of giving any effectual aid. The
same dilatoriness is characteristic of Colonel
Morden, who is a whole fortnight in England
before visiting his ward ; though, to be sure, he
is represented as being occupied with her affairs.
It may be argued that all these delays were
necessary to the author's purpose, but that they
appear so wanton and improbable is due to clumsy
workmanship. In the old romances that Richard-

son's novel was to supersede, such carelessness of detail was more pardonable. Where everything was supposed to be enacted in a realm that existed only in the imagination of the author, fancy was free to take her wildest flights. But when Richardson applies the same license to a story of contemporary life, the incongruities are too startling to be easily excusable. Clarissa and all the other actors in the story are so real to the reader, that when he finds them behaving in a manner that no rational person would consider possible, a feeling of impatient irritation with them, with the author, and the entire story, possesses his mind.

But all these defects are forgotten when the attention is concentrated on Clarissa's character. No heroine who has existed merely on the printed page has ever had a more charming or convincing personality; she is even more life-like than Pamela, and far more admirable. For though her creator evidently meant to draw a paragon, and exhausts his power of description in portraying her perfections, yet her action is not always free from censure, and her attraction consists quite as much in her innocent mistakes as in her fortitude and high ideals. Her weaknesses, however, are communicated to the reader chiefly by her own self-betrayal, by her vacillations when she should have been decided, by her determined action when she should have remained in suspense. From the letters of her friends one would gather that she is "all perfection." A marvel of beauty in both face and figure, she is further endowed with such instinctive elegance that she sets the fashion to the county. She is educated far beyond the average woman of her time, and is quite equal to keeping the household accounts, for, as we are particularly told, she is "a perfect mistress of the four principal rules of arithmetic." Besides being thus accomplished in mathematics, she can sing charmingly, talk with sense and wit, and is well read in the English, French and Italian poets, and in the Latin classics (in translations). She has also a good idea of drawing, though, from want of practice, she does not excel in the "executive part" ("she could not in everything excel," adds Anna Howe, as if reluctant to admit any imperfection in her beloved friend). Added to this, she is an adept in all the peculiarly feminine arts, in housekeeping, dairy-management, and needlework. She is extremely methodical and regulates her day according to a laborious system, which, if ever practicable, must have been extremely inconvenient. "For rest she allotted six hours only," and from this time she would often steal an hour to add to the three which she devoted to study and writing. Two hours she gave to domestic duties, five to sewing, drawing and music, and the visits of the clergy (for whom she has a proverbially feminine regard); three hours to breakfast, dinner and conversation, one to visiting the poor, and the remaining four hours to supper and social duties. After all this, it is a relief to hear that "this method, which to others will appear perplexing and unnecessary, her early hours and custom had made easy and

pleasant to her." But a method so cut and dried
betrays itself at once as the invention of a middle-
aged man of business, rather than that of a charming, and (as we are repeatedly told) unaffected, girl.
It indicates the least attractive traits in her character, her tendency to priggishness and didacticism,
and prepares us for the adages we must be prepared
to hear "flowing through teeth of ivory and lips of
coral." For Clarissa, like her creator, is possessed
with the importance of her mission as a social reformer. When more frivolous damsels gathered
round the card-table or indulged in the spice of
scandal, "she often insensibly diverted the company
from them by starting some entertaining subject,
when she could do it without incurring the imputation of particularity." She is in fact, like a good
many earnest people, inclined to take herself too
seriously; yet, though she has no pity on herself,
she shows infinite compassion for the frailties of her
friends.

For, after all, she is a very womanly woman; a
woman of strong and tender attachments, loyal to
the limit of endurance, and holding out hands of
futile entreaty to an obdurate and implacable family.
Her heart bleeds at her mother's displeasure. "I
had rather all the world should be angry with me
than my mamma!" she writes, and in spite of that
mother's weakness in her daughter's defence, she
cannot be induced to blame her; even of her
father she will hear no ill. "If then you would
avoid my highest displeasure, you must spare my
mother; and surely, you will allow me, with her

to pity as well as to love and honour my father."
She has the natural feminine partiality for the
weaker side, and as soon as Lovelace is exposed
to the ill-will of her brother and sister, he becomes
doubly attractive to her; all her friends, to use
Anna Howe's words, "by fighting against him,
with most impolitic violence fight for him." And
so the slight inclination develops into what may
almost be called an attachment — what decent
conduct on the part of Lovelace would have
ripened into steady love. People blamed the
author for a certain frigidity in his heroine, and
wished that he had made her more ardent.
Richardson, however, did not approve of passion,
or rather he had no conception of the chastening
and cleansing effect that passion may have. To
him it was a bad thing, to be rigorously suppressed.
"He taught the passions," said Johnson, "to move
at the command of virtue." It would be juster to
say that he suppressed the passions to make way for
a conventional virtue which consists more in the
insusceptibility to temptation than in the conquest
of it. The one passion of Clarissa is for purity;
her inclination for Lovelace is hardly strong
enough to be dignified by the name of love.
Richardson did not realise that by this very
suppression of passion he endangered his moral
effect. For if Clarissa were thoroughly in love
with Lovelace, though it is difficult to realise how
her love could have survived his conduct, she
might take some credit for repelling his advances.
But if she is not thoroughly in love, she is under

N

no temptation to yield; if she is in no danger
from the solicitations of her own heart, there is
little merit in rebuffing those of her lover. And
Clarissa always keeps herself well in hand. She
will not confess to more than a "conditional
liking" for Lovelace, even when she shows a
suspicious jealousy of a peasant girl, at whose
home he is lodging. She cannot believe any
good of the poor little thing (though in this
matter, for once, her lover is innocent). "Would
a girl," she asks, "modest as simple, above
seventeen, be set singing at the pleasure of such
a man as that?" And when Lovelace catches
cold through waiting for her letters in an
adjoining copse, she exclaims impatiently, "A
sycophant creature! With his hoarsenesses, got
perhaps in a midnight revel, singing to his wild
note-singer, and only increased in the coppice!"
But this warmth may be partly accounted for by
the fact that Clarissa is altogether unused to any
rivalry. She is so well used to flattery and admiration, that without having her mental balance
at all upset by it, she is filled with a serene sense
of superiority to ordinary human nature; even
after she has placed herself in the power of
Lovelace, she treats him with the air of a princess,
and realises only by slow degrees that she has
forfeited her claim to be regarded as a model of
propriety and decorum. In this lies her tragedy;
in the gradual breaking of the proud spirit, which
had moved with such complacent self-confidence
among its fellows. Not that Clarissa ever con-

fuses the points at issue; in the depth of her misery she knows that the moral victory is all her own. "I had given Mr Lovelace no reason to think me a weak creature," she repeatedly writes, after the blow has fallen. But she knows too, that nothing can restore her to her former position; how can she ever again go among the village maidens, exhorting them to virtue, and warning them of the perils of life's voyage? "One of my delights," she says, "was to enter the cots of my poorer neighbours, to leave lessons for the boys and cautions for the elder girls. And how should I be able, unconscious, and without pain, to say to the latter, 'Fly the delusions of men,' who had been supposed to have run away with one of them?" No, she who once made it her pride to be an example to her sex, must now be content to be a warning; henceforth she can hope for very little influence or consideration. "People in calamity," she has learnt by bitter experience, "have very little weight in anything or with anybody."

Closely allied to Clarissa's pride is her obstinacy, which appears sometimes as fortitude, and sometimes as mere tenacity. "I have something in me of my father's family as well as of my mother's," she says once, and the same strength of will that makes her relations persist in their persecution of her enables her to withstand all the blandishments of Lovelace and the persuasions of Anna Howe. "My will," she exclaims proudly, "is unviolated! No credulity, no weakness, no

want of vigilance, have I to reproach myself with."
She adheres inflexibly to every resolution, and
once an idea has entered her mind nothing can
dispossess her of it. She is full of pious super-
stitions, and the consciousness of her father's
curse is not the least of her afflictions; all her
calamities, she is ready to think, are due to this.
Her views are narrow, her horizon very limited,
but she feels intensely, if not passionately, and
she clings with incredible fidelity to relations who
have exiled her from their hearts.

" Above all," says M. Texte, " she has the sentiment of respectability." She has no sympathy
with anything that is not perfectly proper according to the conventions of her age. She never
descends sufficiently to understand thoroughly;
her attitude to the poor is one of lofty patronage;
her consciousness of class distinctions is too plainly
evident. " These are not people," she says once,
" I should choose to be intimate with, or whose
ways I can like, although for the station they are
in they may go through the world with tolerable
credit." And when she presents a servant with
a cast-off dress, she adds, " The sleeves and the
robings and facings must be altered for your wear,
being, I believe, above your station." She is
indeed painfully aware of the advantages derived
from wealth and position. " His fortunes in possession are handsome, in expectation, splendid,"
she says in discussing the attractions of Lovelace;
and the sense of her own advantages in these
particulars makes it difficult for her to doubt her

lover's honourable intentions. She knows he has
deceived others; "yet," she says, "I did not
mistrust his honour to me neither; nor his love;
because nobody thought me unworthy of the
latter, and my fortune was not to be despised."
Clarissa is quite aware that her person is not her
only attraction, and a love-match, unsanctioned
by an adequate income, would probably have
appeared to her the height of folly; she moves
and lives and breathes in an atmosphere of convention—social, moral and religious.

And it is on this very fact that the salutary moral
effect of the book depends. Clarissa, the slave of
convention, suddenly revolts against its tyranny,
and vindicates her claim to liberty. All possible
inducements urge her to marry Lovelace. She
knows that if she does so she will be warmly
welcomed by his family and reconciled to her own.
The disgrace will be forgotten, and the circumstances of the courtship will be viewed in no more
serious light than a youthful escapade, a romantic
episode, to be passed on to unborn generations as
part of the family history. With their beauty and
position, the couple may make a social sensation;
Clarissa may look forward to being a leader of
fashion, or what would suit her better, the queen
of a *salon*. All these dazzling prospects she re-
solutely puts away. To her the real shame consists
in having any connection with one so vile; she will
not even take his name to cover her humiliation.
Her innate purity vanquishes the conventions of
her breeding, and she welcomes death itself rather

than submit to their rule.   In the first consciousness of her degradation she longs only for the
eternal silence, and in her mad ravings there is
something of the tragic horror familiar to us in
the plays of Webster.   " Make sure work, I pray
thee.   Dig a hole deep enough to cram in and
conceal this unhappy body ; for, depend upon it,
that some of those who will not stir to protect me
living, will move heaven and earth to avenge me
dead."   But with restored reason her fortitude
returns, and she views her approaching end with
fine serenity.   She knows now the worst that life
can bring ; the " slings and arrows of outrageous
fortune " can terrify her no longer, and she is
encompassed with a pathetic sanctity that is infinitely touching.   It may be urged that her agony
is too long drawn out, and that the reader might
have been spared the long correspondence of her
friends after the catastrophe.   But even this is
not inappropriate, since it exhibits that natural
and ever-recurring phase of human experience,
the remorse that comes too late to repair the ill
that has been done.   "L'inutilité même," says
M. Villemain, of these letters, " en fait la
pathétique."

The character of Lovelace is more difficult to
analyse.   This is due to the fact that Richardson
knew very little of the typical aristocratic rake ;
his life, passed in warehouses and round the tea-
table, gave him small opportunity for close observation of the species.   Sometimes, coming home
at night to his quiet country-house, he may have

been disturbed by a party of those young roisterers, who, in the exuberance of animal spirits tolerated by the age, seem to have found supreme pleasure in ill-treating innocent pedestrians and setting the decrepit watchmen at defiance, but he can have had little social knowledge of them. It must not be forgotten, however, that he was intimate with Colley Cibber and other men of the world; and he himself explicitly states that the character of Lovelace was drawn from life. "I am a good deal warped," he says, in a letter to Aaron Hill, dated January 26, 1747, "by the character of a gentleman I had in my eye, when I drew both him and Mr B. in *Pamela.* The best of that gentleman in the latter; the worst of him for Lovelace, made still worse by mingling the worst of two other characters, that were as well known to me, of that gentleman's acquaintance, and this made me say in my last that I aimed at an uncommon, though I supposed a not quite unnatural character"; and again, on January 5, 1747, "I had not in my aim to write after anything I had ever read or heard talked of; though I had in my mind's eye something I had seen years ago."[1] These allusions may refer to the Duke of Wharton, but if so, the hint thus given must have been greatly elaborated and expanded. Lovelace does not convey the impression of having been drawn from life, though as the story proceeds one is constantly amazed at the fascination exercised by this extraordinary and impossible hero.

[1] Forster MS., Hill Correspondence.

The task of his creation was indeed a formidable
one, especially for a person of Richardson's narrow
views and strong prejudices. To fulfil his rôle of
moralist he was obliged to render vice as ugly as
possible, yet in order to beguile so blameless a
maiden as Clarissa, it must have an attractive
exterior. Lovelace is therefore a bundle of
contradictions, of conflicting qualities, that could
not possibly co-exist in the same person. His
villainy as regards women requires that the rest
of his character should show a corresponding de-
pravity. Yet in every other relation of life he is
represented as not only decent, but even admirable.
He is a loyal friend and a generous landlord; his
own servants adore him, and his liberality and
graciousness win the devotion even of those at
Harlowe Place. " He was ever a favourite with
our domestics," writes Clarissa, "and having always something facetious to say to each had made
them all of his party." Then he has few of the
ordinary characteristics of the rake; his dissipation
is confined to one point; he does not game, does
not drink, is even economical and temperate.
Richardson himself, in an unpublished letter of
October 3, 1748, is at pains to point out his good
qualities. " Have you," says he, " read Lovelace's
bad and not his good? Or does the abhorrence
which you have for that bad make you forget
that he has any good? Is he not generous? Is
he not with respect to *meum* and *teum* matters just?
Is he not ingenious? Does he not on all occasions
exalt the lady at his expense? Has he not there-

fore many sparks of goodness in his heart, though, with regard to the sex, he sticks at nothing?"[1] He is, moreover, a man of education, and is full of literary allusions; indeed, his frequent citations border on pedantry. He is brimming over with wit and spirit, and goes through the world with such combined grace and recklessness as make him a most charming comrade. And, "gay and lively as he is," says Clarissa, "he has not the look of an impudent man." His appearance is, in fact, all that can be desired. "So little of the fop, yet so elegant and rich in his dress; his person so specious, his air so intrepid; so much meaning and penetration in his face, so much gaiety, yet so little of the monkey; though a travelled gentleman, yet no affectation; no mere toupet man, but all manly; and his courage and wit, the one so well known, the other so dreaded." Truly as dazzling a monster as ever fascinated a poor maiden to her undoing. Then he is quite unexceptionable in the matter of creed, and (though he sets it at defiance) is careful to recognise the existence of a moral law. "For libertine as I am thought to be," he says once, "I never will attempt to bring down the measures of right and wrong to the standard of my actions." He is plausible enough to others; but, until remorse overtakes him, he does not attempt to justify his crimes to himself. His independence of morality is a matter of deliberation, and only one illustration of his inordinate vanity; for it is due to his desire for

[1] Forster MS.

singularity, to his distaste for being classed with the common herd.

Vanity is, in truth, his ruling passion. He is no sensualist; and in undertaking the chase, the enjoyment of the prey is his least consideration. He has been so long regarded as irresistible that he cannot bear defeat, and the possibility of failure piques his pride and puts him on his mettle; he summons all his resources to ensure victory. But, like all bad men, he has no understanding of a good woman; he constantly miscalculates, and is driven to the poorest and commonest expedients to attain his end. Yet the mental exercise afforded by his project is not the least part in its delight, for his intellectual activity finds delightful employment in continual scheming, and in the invention of plots that are never brought to maturity. "Had I been a military hero," he writes, "I should have made gunpowder useless; for I should have blown up all my adversaries by dint of stratagem, turning their own devices upon them." This estimate of his own powers is supported by Belford's testimony: "A man born for intrigue, full of invention, intrepid, remorseless, able patiently to watch for thy opportunity; not hurried, as most men, by gusts of violent passion." He is, in short, an example of the intellectual, as opposed to the sensual, villain; all the more formidable because of his perfect self-control. He is essentially cruel, delighting in torture, and in the wretched fluttering of his victim in her cage; he is so entirely master of the situation that he can take his time over her release. "Marriage," he cries, "will always be in my power."

But this is just where he is mistaken. The perseverance with which he follows up his project is met by an equal perseverance in resistance from Clarissa, and his will clashes ineffectually with hers. He has found his match, and in his shameful triumph his admiration for her is stronger than ever; she has henceforth no real need of any external aid, for her persecutor has become her champion. His indignation flares up when Hickman hints at her misfortune. "You may tell Miss Howe from me," he exclaims, "that neither she nor any other woman in the world can be more virtuous than Miss Harlowe is to this hour, as to her own mind." The irony of the situation is that he has put the woman he loves and wishes to marry in such a position as to render necessary his protestations in her support.

There is, of course, much that is absurd in this conception, much that must strike any reader with a sense of humour as irresistibly comic. But to appreciate the intention of the author and to reconstruct Lovelace according to his idea, we must put aside these considerations and try to take him seriously. Much of what strikes us as incongruous and ridiculous was imperceptible to contemporary readers, and Richardson's lady correspondents certainly thought the hero sufficiently life-like. They had wept at Clarissa's death, but fresh tears were shed over the last words of Lovelace. Of him, as of so many others

in fiction and reality, it might be said that
"nothing in his life became him like the leaving
of it." Even a modern reader, made callous by a
hundred such imaginary scenes, must be touched
by this tragic close to a gay career.

Concerning the other characters in the book
there is much less to be said. Richardson seems
purposely to have isolated his principals as much
as possible, so that the unequal contest between
them may be more vividly realised. Anna Howe
and Belford, who are their chief correspondents,
exist mainly for that purpose.

The former, however, has a very distinct personality. She is supposed to be almost as admirable
as her friend, her chief failing being a tendency
to flippancy and too great vivacity of spirits. Although a loyal friend, she is a thorough coquette
and a born tease. She does not readily submit to
the parental rule or to masculine domination ; she
is a woman of independent character, fretting at
the shackles imposed on her by her sex. And
any approach to liberty, unconnected with matrimony, being at that time impossible for a girl of
her class, she accepts the addresses of Hickman, a
man of irreproachable fame, but lacking spirit and
virility. He is her slave, and she treats him as if
he existed merely for her pleasure, now encourag-
ing, and now repulsing him ; even after he is her
acknowledged lover she still keeps him in suspense
as to her real intentions towards him. Naturally
enough, his devotion to her makes her think meanly
of his capacity. " Poor man," she says, " he has

not much penetration. If he had, he would not think so well of me as he does." And so, though she is supposed to have a real regard for him, she treats him with an open scorn that in actual life would certainly alienate the most attached lover. She is in fact outrageously rude. But this defect she has in common with the other reputedly witty women of Richardson's novels, with Lady Davers and Charlotte Grandison. Still, her letters are decidedly amusing, and her accounts of her difficulties with her mother and of the latter's courtship by Anthony Harlowe serve to relieve the strain of some of the most tragic moments in the story.

The more important of the remaining personages may be considered in a group, for they all belong to the family of Harlowe. They stand out before us in a series of extraordinarily vivid portraits, like family pictures in the gallery of some ancient house. They all, with the exception of Mrs Harlowe, exhibit in varying degrees the same characteristics of avarice and obstinacy; and, indeed, the opening chapters of the book would lead one to expect a sermon on avarice rather than on chastity. The extraordinary extent to which these people are dominated by their greed reminds one of some of Balzac's studies, of Père Grandet, for instance, or the heirs of Dr Mirouet, though they betray a brutality which was perhaps possible only in English country gentlemen of the early eighteenth century. The bad qualities of the elder generation, of John, Anthony, and James Harlowe, seem to have culminated in the son of the last.

He is a stupid egoist, seeing only the goal before him, and quite oblivious of attending circumstances; and, making for it by mere force, defiant of obstacles and insensible to compassion, he carries with him by sheer strength of will his father and his uncles, in whom wider experience might have produced greater toleration. But the truth is that the whole family has been too successful; their wills have never been crossed, and the slightest suspicion of rebellion produces in them a fury of opposition. Clarissa ventures to protest against her father's tyranny, whereupon his gout flies to his stomach, and this infirmity is tearfully advanced by Mrs Harlowe as a reason for her daughter's submission. "He has pleaded, poor man," says she, "that his frequent gouty paroxysms (every fit more threatening than the former) give him no extraordinary prospects either of happiness or of long days, and he hopes that you, who have been supposed to have contributed to the lengthening of your grandfather's life, will not, by your disobedience, shorten your father's." He is a petty despot, ruling his timid subjects according to no law but his own whims, and exaggerating the theory of parental prerogative to absurd dimensions. He applies to his children the law that contemporary politicians applied to the colonies, that they exist only for the good of those who called them into existence. The idea of such relations has undergone a complete change since the eighteenth century, and what may appear impossible at the present time is perfectly credible of Richardson's generation. He himself, as has been seen, demanded excessive respect from his daughters, and, while he treated their contemporaries with sentimental deference, never abated one tittle from the reverence that he, as a parent, expected. And matrimonial arrangements were then considered as less the concern of the lady than of her parents; though nominally free to choose, the ultimate disposal of her hand lay in her father's pleasure. Forced marriages were not uncommon, and thus, in his determination to marry Clarissa, with or without her consent, to Mr Solmes, her father was not exceeding what the opinion of the time allowed to be his just privilege.

In uniting to this overbearing tyrant a woman like Mrs Harlowe, Richardson showed much penetration. She is a sweet amiable soul, torn between maternal solicitude and marital duty; she, too, considers obedience as an obligation; her spirit has been broken by years of submission, and she sacrifices her daughter because she is too weak to think or to act independently. Her timorous policy is well summed up in the words of Anna Howe: "You pity her mother! So do not I. I pity no mother that puts it out of her power to show maternal love and humanity in order to patch up for herself a precarious and sorry quiet which every blast of wind shall disturb."

But if the story of Clarissa still lives, it is not by virtue of any of the subordinate characters, but by reason of the one matchless central figure, who stands unrivalled among the other inventions of her creator. And, as long as the English language is spoken or its literature read, the " divine Clarissa " will hold her own among the noblest of its ideal women, with Imogen, and Portia, and Cordelia. Torn from the proud pedestal of maidenhood, dragged in an unclean company through foul and miry ways, a sacrifice to vanity rather than to lust, she loses none of her charm or potency. For through her there speaks the authentic voice of the best women of all ages, who refuse to disassociate love and respect from the most sacred of human relationships, or to subject themselves to the humiliation of a union unsanctioned by these motives.

CHAPTER VIII

"SIR CHARLES GRANDISON"

" IT is the longest of novels and one of the best."
So wrote the late Dr Jowett of *Sir Charles
Grandison*. But there are probably few readers of
his delightful letters who have time or inclination
to test the value of this judgment by independent
investigation, since the perusal of the book is the
work not of hours, nor of days, but literally of
weeks. And to appreciate it properly one must
choose the time and place; one would not think
of taking one of the seven volumes as a companion
on a railway journey. It is a book for a long
vacation, because it cannot be read hurriedly, and
for its enjoyment requires the consciousness of
prolonged leisure. And it is a book for the
country, or at least for some decayed provincial
town, where the illusion produced by the author's
skill is not liable to frequent interruption by the
prosaic accidents of a busy life. But perhaps the
ideal place to read it in would be some old retired
garden, whose trim cut yews and mossy red brick
walls are eloquent of the pride and foresight of
departed men; or, better still, an oak-lined chamber
whose charms should vie with those of the " cedar
parlour " at Selby House.

The story, like those of *Pamela* and *Clarissa Harlowe*, is told by means of letters, the principal correspondents being "young ladies of polite education and lively spirits." Of these the chief are the heroine, Miss Harriet Byron, and her cousin, Miss Lucy Selby. Harriet, left an orphan in babyhood, has been brought up by her grandparents, Mr and Mrs Shirley, who have made it their first concern to pack her pretty head with maxims on conduct and morals, with the somewhat improbable result of turning her out a paragon of mingled discretion and sensibility. When the story opens, her grandfather is dead, and she is living with her uncle, Mr Selby; and in spite of her moderate fortune (she has only fifteen thousand pounds, the interest of which, as Macaulay calculates, must have been quite exhausted by her postal expenses) she is persecuted by the addresses of neighbouring gentlemen. The book artfully opens with a letter from her cousin relating the despair of three of these suitors when they hear of Miss Byron's proposed visit to London. Close upon this follows one from one of the rejected swains, called Greville, who describes her charms in glowing terms, and declares that she alone has converted him to a belief in feminine goodness. "O, madam, women *have* souls. I now am convinced they have. I dare own to your ladyship that I once doubted it. . . . And have I not seen her dance? Have I not heard her sing? But, indeed, mind and body, she is all harmony!"

No sooner has Miss Byron arrived in London

than she makes a profound sensation. Fresh
wooers appear, among them a young gentleman
named Fowler. His suit is warmly supported by
his uncle, a Welsh baronet, who, in accordance
with the extraordinary lack of reticence characteristic of most of the persons in this book, presses
the matter on the lady in the midst of a roomful
of company. While the matter is still progressing
there enters a fifth admirer, Sir Hargrave Pollexfen,
universally considered a desirable *parti* on account
of his long rent-roll and handsome person. He
is so confident of success that Harriet has some
difficulty in persuading him that her refusal is
seriously meant.

" I thank you, sir, for your good opinion of me,
but I cannot encourage your addresses."

" You cannot, madam, encourage my addresses !
And express yourself so seriously ! Good heaven !"
(He stood silent a minute or two, looking upon me
and upon himself, as if he had said, Foolish girl !
Knows she whom she refuses ?) " I have been
assured, madam," recovering a little from his
surprise, "that your affections are not engaged.
But surely it must be a mistake ; some happy
man——"

" Is it," interrupted I, "a necessary consequence
that the woman who cannot receive the addresses
of Sir Hargrave Pollexfen must be engaged ? "

" Why, madam, as to that I know not what to
say ; but a man of my fortune, and I hope not
absolutely disagreeable either in person or temper ;
of *some* rank in life ; what, madam, if you are

as much in earnest as you seem, can be your objection ? "[1]

But in spite of the apparent absurdity of her rejection, Harriet persists in it, and by her obstinacy drives Sir Hargrave to desperation. He manages to insinuate into her service a footman named Wilson, and with his assistance carries her off from a masquerade to a house at Paddington (then quite in the country), where he endeavours to force her to marry him. In her struggle to escape she is hurt, and this frightens him so much that he defers the rite, and attempts to take her in a chariot and six, with an armed escort, to his country-house.

And now the time is ripe for the appearance of the hero of the story. Harriet Byron is being driven along, wrapped in a long cloak, a handkerchief tied round her mouth, and held fast in her lover's arms, when in a narrow place where there is no room to pass their coach is met by another. She manages to disengage one hand and to scream for assistance, at which the gentleman in the strange coach bars the way and begins to inquire into the matter. Sir Hargrave draws, but the lady is rescued, and placed in the carriage of her deliverer. He proves to be Sir Charles Grandison, lately arrived in England after a prolonged tour on the continent, and now on his way to join his sisters at Colnebrook. Thither he insists on taking Harriet, and she, nothing loth, consents; for her heart, hitherto invincible, has been taken a willing captive by his charms, which she thus describes :—

[1] *Sir Charles Grandison*, i. 113.

" This grandeur in his person and air is accompanied with so much ease and freedom of manner as engages one's love with one's reverence. His good breeding renders him very accessible. . . Well might his sister tell Mrs Reeves that whenever he married he would break half a score of hearts. Upon my word, Lucy, he has too many personal advantages for a woman who loved him with peculiarity to be easy with, whatever may be his virtue from the foible our sex in general love to indulge for a handsome man. For, O my dear, women's eyes are sad giddy things, and will run away with their sense, with their understandings, beyond the power of being overtaken either by—Stop, thief! or hue and cry. I know that here you will bid me take care not to increase the number of the giddy. And so I will, my Lucy." [1]

A challenge is the natural consequence of the encounter between the two baronets, and the fear lest her rescuer may suffer for her sake raises Harriet's newly kindled passion to fever pitch. Sir Charles, however, whose principles are opposed to duelling, manages to evade the necessity of fighting by disarming his adversary in the nick of time (a useful accomplishment, by which in the course of the story he twice confounds his rivals). This feat he follows up by a long discourse on the history and philosophy of duelling, and having quite won over his opponent, gracefully retires from the scene, victor in argument as well as in

[1] *Sir Charles Grandison*, i. 255.

arms. "Sir Hargrave seemed greatly disturbed and dejected. He could not, he said, support himself under the consciousness of his own inferiority. But what could I do? said he. The devil could not have made him fight. Plague take him! he put me out of my play."

All this time Sir Charles, though professing the greatest admiration for Miss Byron, has given no sign of desiring a deeper interest with her, and her difficulties are increased by a new suitor, whom her family combine in recommending to her acceptance. The Earl of D. has twelve thousand a year, and is in every other respect highly eligible, but Harriet's affections are by this time far too deeply engaged for her to dream of any man but one. "Every child in love matters," says her grandmother, "would find you out," and straightway implores her to overcome this laudable affection. "The more desirable the object, the nobler the conquest of the passion, if it is to be overcome." But with a singular lack of delicacy, Mrs Shirley deems it necessary to inform the earl's mother that Harriet's heart is already won; for, as the identity of the happy man must be obvious to all his acquaintance, she imagines that this avowal will lead to an inquiry into Sir Charles' engagements and thus, by one means or another, put an end to Harriet's suspense.

At this juncture the heroine makes another visit to Colnebrook, where she is received with open arms by Sir Charles' sisters, Lady L. and Charlotte Grandison, though their brother cruelly takes the opportunity for important business at Canterbury. A close intimacy between the ladies follows, and Harriet—and alas! the reader also —is informed of all the family history of the Grandisons, of the matrimonial differences of their father and mother, and of the love-story of Lady L., in which narrative Sir Charles constantly plays an amiable and attractive part. At last he returns to Colnebrook, and the sun shines once more. "My philosophy is quite gone," says Harriet, "I must take sanctuary, and that very soon, at Selby House." But the object of her adoration seems as far as ever from a declaration. He busies himself with everybody's affairs but his own, helps to release Charlotte from a girlish entanglement, and hurries on the negotiations for her marriage with Lord G.; performs the duties of executor to a deceased friend, and arranges the complicated affairs of his ward, Emily Jervois (who is another of his victims). But at last, on the pretext of obtaining Harriet's suffrage for Charlotte's suitor, he invites her to a private interview, during which he takes her into his confidence on the subject of his own embarrassments. During his residence abroad he was enabled to perform a signal service to Jeronymo della Poretta, the youngest son of a noble Italian house, and this led to an acquaintance with the whole family. They received him on the most cordial terms, and even allowed him to teach English to their only daughter, Clementina. The inevitable consequence followed, though Sir Charles, feeling, as he says, that "to have recommended myself to the young lady's favour, though by looks and assiduities, would have been an infamous breach of the trust they all reposed in me," had made no sign of love. Thereupon Clementina fell into a deep melancholy, which was increased by his departure, and she was at last induced to reveal her affection. The family had then made proposals to him, but the terms were such as precluded acceptance. "For I was to make a formal renunciation of my religion, and to settle in Italy; only once in two or three years was allowed, if I pleased, for two or three months to go to England; and as a visit of curiosity, once in her life, if their daughter desired it, to carry her thither, for a time to be limited by them." His proposed compromise being rejected, Sir Charles took a final leave, and this drove Clementina to actual madness. Now, in their distress, her parents had summoned him once more to their palace, in order to enter on a further discussion of the matter

"And now, madam," said he, in conclusion, and he was going to take my hand, but with an air as if he thought the freedom would be too great—a tenderness *so* speaking in his eyes, a respectfulness *so* solemn in his countenance—he just touched it, and withdrew his hand. "What shall I say? I cannot tell what I should say. But you, I see, can pity me—you can pity the noble Clementina. Honour forbids me! Yet honour bids me. Yet I cannot be unjust, ungenerous, selfish!"

He arose from his seat: "Allow me, madam, to

thank you for the favour of your ear. Pardon me
for the trouble I see I have given to a heart that
is capable of a sympathy so tender."

And, bowing low, he withdrew with precipitation, as if he would not let me see his emotion.[1]

This interview throws Harriet into a state of
the utmost suspense and agitation. Sir Charles'
confusion is plainly caused by the conflict between
his love for her and his obligations to Clementina ;
yet never has her own case seemed more hopeless.
For the summons from the haughty Italian family
indicates that they are prepared to waive their
objections, and Sir Charles thinks his honour
engaged to meet them half way. He therefore
prepares for another visit to Italy, but in the
interval before his departure he is fully occupied
with the affairs of various friends, and with the
somewhat delicate task of rebuffing the attentions
of another Italian lady, who has sought him out
in England. At last, however, he departs, leaving
at least three aching hearts behind him. " Lady
Olivia," writes Harriet, " was the most thoughtful
at dinner-time ; yet poor Emily ! Ah, the poor
Emily ! She went out four or five times to weep ;
though only I perceived it."

Meanwhile Harriet has been made more fully
acquainted with Sir Charles' difficulties by means
of copies of the correspondence with his former
tutor, Dr Bartleet, during his first Italian visit ;
and she is now kept informed of his movements
by similar means ; for her lover is almost as

[1] *Sir Charles Grandison*, iii. 194, 195.

industrious a writer as herself, and relates everything that passes with a minuteness worthy of
so conscientious a person. Even contemporary
readers dared to hint "that some thought the
Italian scenes tedious repetition," and certainly
many of these pages might have been omitted without much loss. One becomes desperately tired
of all these conferences, carried on with as much
solemnity as if they related to an act of parlia-
ment, and attended by all the uncles, aunts and
cousins of the poor mad lady. But the suspense
is well sustained, and things are beginning to look
somewhat dark for Harriet. Her rival's family
agree to Sir Charles' terms, and matters are
almost concluded, when suddenly Clementina's
conscience conveniently asserts itself, and she
decides that it is impossible for her to marry
a heretic; Sir Charles entreats her to reconsider
her decision, but her resolution remains unshaken;
she only desires to be allowed to enter a convent,
and urges him to marry an Englishwoman. And
so, with the greatest apparent reluctance, he departs, leaving her to struggle for the peace which
his return home brings to the tortured heart of
Miss Byron.

For, as Sir Charles is nothing if not businesslike,
and has fully determined to marry as soon as he
can decide which of the two ladies has the greater
claim on him, he loses no time in paying his addresses to Harriet, thereby raising her to the
seventh heaven of delight, and filling her admirers with despair. One of them, the before-

mentioned Greville, attempts to fight his rival, who disarms him with his usual dexterity; the others, recognising the superior excellence of the successful wooer, acquiesce in the lady's choice. The greater part of two volumes is taken up with an account of the engagement, which only lasts six weeks, and with references to the domestic affairs of Lady L. and Lady G. At last, nearly at the close of the seventh volume, when the reader is beginning to wonder how long these "femalities" (the author's own word) will be dragged out, Clementina reappears on the scene. In order to avoid an unwelcome proposal of marriage, she has taken refuge in England, and calls her old lover to her aid. With magnificent, if somewhat improbable generosity, Harriet extends a warm welcome to her and to her family, who in full force follow the fugitive to these shores. She is reconciled to them and the story closes with her reluctant consent to perhaps allow, at some distant period, the addresses of the Count of Belvedere, and the departure of the visitors from England.

The story of *Sir Charles Grandison*, like all the other works of its author, is distinctly a story with a purpose, and is told with the definite intention of presenting to the world a character of ideal human goodness. "He is," says his creator, "in the general tenor of his principles and conduct (though exerted in peculiarities of circumstances that cannot always be accommodated to particular imitation), proposed for an example." And Richardson

defends his intention by a quotation from Tillotson.
"There is no manner of inconvenience in having
a pattern propounded to us of so great perfection,
as is above our reach to attain to. . . . The ex-
cellency of the pattern, as it leaves room for
continual improvement, so it kindles ambition, and
makes men strain and contend to the utmost to do
better. And though he can never hope to equal the
example before him, yet he will endeavour to come
as near it as he can. So that a perfect pattern is
no hindrance, but an advantage rather, to our
improvement in any kind."

Now, avoiding any discussion as to the legitimacy
of giving so great a prominence in a work of fiction
to the didactic aim, the question arises whether
Richardson has been successful in presenting such
an example as he intended. Is the character of
Sir Charles likely to stir anyone to imitation, or
to inspire young men, for whose edification it was
mainly conceived, with a desire for virtue?

On a first consideration one might be inclined
to answer in the negative. Sir Charles, say the
critics, is a compound of every excellence, but he
does not live, and if he did he would be an exceedingly unpleasant person. Sir Walter Scott
applies to him the quotation: "The faultless
monster whom the world ne'er saw," and Mr Leslie
Stephen, though less severe in his condemnation,
characterises him as "a prig of the first water. . .
self-conscious to the last degree." This verdict
would apply more or less to all Richardson's
characters, and was indeed unavoidable in the

creations of so absurdly self-conscious a man as he. Sir Charles is self-conscious in the same manner as Pamela or Clarissa, or his ante-type, Lovelace. Self-consciousness is an almost necessary accompaniment of the analytic mind, and in Richardson it amounted to a disease.

Admitting this drawback, it is perhaps worth while to enter upon a somewhat detailed examination of Grandison's character, and determine whether he is altogether so unnatural and disagreeable a person as has been stated. His first drawback is that he is too fortunate; he is rich, handsome, charming in speech and manner; by the mere influence of his personality subduing his foes, and turning their enmity into reverent admiration. His friends never weary in their chorus of approbation, till at last the perpetual iteration of his virtues has an effect contrary to what was intended, and a feeling of actual antagonism is provoked; so much praise has the result of prejudicing the hearer against its subject. One feels that it is an infringement on the right of independent judgment, and this is perhaps one reason why Sir Charles has had so many adverse critics. His popularity with his acquaintances damages his popularity with the reader.

Yet, it must be admitted that his conduct is quite unexceptionable. He is courteous, if slightly patronising, to the objects of his benevolence; he is compassionate and charitable even to those who have wronged him. He is always actively pursuing the good of his fellow-creatures, and like a good magician in a fairy-tale he conjures up a wife for that old reprobate, Lord W.; starts a crowd of deserving young people in life; arranges marriages, reconciles families, procures justice for distressed gentlewomen, manages admirably two estates of his own, and the large fortune of his ward. And all this at twenty-six years of age! One cannot help wondering whence he obtained his experience and knowledge of the world.

He is indeed much too old for his years, and his attitude to all those under his protection is that of a man superior by age and experience as well as by condition and natural talent. He treats his ward, who, according to the ideas of contemporary society, is a grown up young lady, as if he were her father. "Sir Charles was then engaged in talk with his Emily; she before him; he standing in an easy, genteel attitude, leaning against the wainscot, listening smiling to her prattle with looks of indulgent love, as a father might do to a child he was proud of." He regards Harriet "with a benign aspect"; there is no question of reciprocal shy glances, of mute confession on either side—she adores, and he smiles graciously upon her. He is moreover always ready to improve the occasion, and alters the words of *Alexander's Feast* to support his theory as to the sinfulness of fighting,

> "Happy, happy, happy pair,
> None but the *good* deserve the fair."

Yet, notwithstanding these drawbacks, no one

can lay the book down without feeling that he has
been in the company of a high-minded, if somewhat ridiculous, man.   The whole question of the
value of the conception hinges, not on Sir Charles'
manners, nor even on his philanthropic leanings,
but on his relations with women, and especially
with the two who win his affection, namely Harriet
and Clementina.   For Richardson considered that
the crucial test of a man's character was his conduct towards the other sex.   He disapproved of
the moral license of the age, and since his rival
Fielding had presented more than one hero who
was far from immaculate in this respect, he determined to portray one who should be absolutely
blameless ; who, being placed in circumstances of
great delicacy and perplexity, should behave in a
manner to which not the nicest sense of honour
could take exception.   And Sir Charles' love affairs
are conducted with great sagacity and penetration.   Grandison is not, any more than Richardson
himself, a man of strong and absorbing passions ;
he is a sentimentalist, and it is the sentimentalist,
rather than the man of strong passion, who
becomes involved in affairs of this nature ; with
the best intentions in the world he finds himself
in the position of a common flirt.   Now when Sir
Charles first knew of Clementina's attachment to
him he was flattered by it into an answering regard ; he was not deeply in love, but what man
could resist the plainly expressed affection of a
beautiful and amiable girl ?   Besides, he has been
daily thrown into her society, and propinquity is

a great match-maker. But when his suit to her has apparently failed, and under peculiarly romantic circumstances he meets Miss Byron, he wavers in his adherence. Miss Byron is equally beautiful, equally amiable; she has, moreover, the advantage of being a Protestant and an Englishwoman. If no Clementina existed, Harriet would certainly have his heart. "From the first," he says, in relating his story to her, "I called Miss Byron sister, but she is more to me than the dearest sister." Further than this he dare not go, for, as he says afterwards :—

"The farewell interview (*i.e.* with Clementina) denied her, demonstrated, I thought, so firm an affection for me, at the same time that she was to me what I may truly call a first love ; that though the difficulties in my way seemed insuperable, I thought it became me, in honour, in gratitude, to hold myself in suspense and not to make my address to any other woman until the fate of the dear Clementina was determined." But when he returns to Italy, and falls once more under the old charm, he is apparently quite sincere in his renewed addresses, though he is not undisturbed by the thought of what his proposed marriage may mean to Harriet. "The two noblest minded women in the world," he writes to Jeronymo, "when I went over to Italy, held almost an equal place in my heart. But when the dear Clementina began to show signs of recovery . . . and when I further experienced the condescending goodness of your whole family, all united in my favour, I had not a wish but for your Clementina."

This "divided love," as Richardson called it, evoked a good deal of censure from some of his correspondents. "You have made me bounce off my chair," wrote Lady Bradshaigh, "with reading that two good girls were in love with your hero, and that he was fond of both. I have such despicable notions of a divided love that I cannot have an idea how a worthy object can entertain such a thought." And again, "I cannot think such a man as Sir Charles Grandison can think her (Clementina) a desirable wife, though compassion and gratitude forces (*sic*) him to be earnest in his suit; too earnest, surely. I think he says 'his future peace depends upon his success,' calls her the best of women, the noblest of her sex; so has he said of Harriet, whom he must now look upon in an inferior light. I know not how to solve the difficulties; he cannot be a good man and insincere.[1]" Richardson in his reply defends himself by asserting that such a state of indecision is not at all uncommon among men, however unnatural it may appear to women, and hints that a man may be equally in love with two women at the same time, and that a mere accident may affect his final decision. But in this difficult circumstance, when the average man would give way to the impulse of the hour, and declare his affection for her who has most influence at the moment, Sir Charles remembers his prior engagement. He is not really

[1] Forster MS., Bradshaigh Correspondence.

P

bound in any way to Clementina; he has every excuse for breaking with her family, but his "honour forbids him." The explanatory scene with Harriet before his second Italian journey is truly affecting. Behind all the starched phrases, the madams and sirs, the elaborate bows and stately courtesies, one hears the throb of perplexed human hearts, beating in suspense and anxiety. The stiff phraseology and ceremonious bearing of the lovers ought not to blind us, and probably did not blind contemporary readers, to the sincerity of the passion. Their very restraint intensifies the pathos; it is true that Harriet weeps, but Sir Charles is prevented by the nature of the case from offering any tender consolation; he can use no term of endearment, nor venture on the slightest caress. So they part, the one to find speedy consolation elsewhere, the other to await in sick suspense the issue of her drama.

Richardson's evident purpose is to convince the romantic heart of youth that its wounds are not incurable. "The disappointed heart, not given up to unmanly despair, in a world so subject to disappointments, will catch at the nearest good to that which it has lost," writes Sir Charles. The author firmly believes that the married state is the most desirable for all women and for most men, and since few people are so fortunate as to attain a union with that other who seems most desirable to them, young persons must be brought up to believe that no passion is so strong as to be invincible. A moderate amount of felicity is within the reach of

1. MR RICHARDSON IN HIS USUAL
   MORNING-DRESS
2. MR MULSO
3. MR EDWARD MULSO
4. MISS MULSO, AFTERWARDS MRS CHAPONE
5. MISS PRESCOTT, AFTERWARDS MRS MULSO
6. THE REV. MR DUNCOMBE
7. MISS HIGHMORE, AFTERWARDS MRS DUNCOMBE

everyone; it is unreasonable to expect anything
more. No one will dispute the common sense of this
position, but it is open to objection. Richardson
does not sufficiently take into account the elevating
and purifying effect of a passion that is not con-
quered, but remaining faithful to its first object
will stoop to no compromise, and prefers lifelong
solitude to a marriage that does not satisfy its
ideal; and secondly, he takes no account of the
multitude of unhappy unions that were assuredly
not less common in his day than in ours. Nor is he
quite consistent. We are led to suppose that had
not Clementina's religious scruples released her
suitor no amount of prudence or common sense
would have consoled Harriet or led her to accept
the proposals of the Earl of D., who was plainly
"the next good to that she had lost." And though
Richardson maintains his theory with regard to
Clementina, and allows it to be concluded that,
having resigned Sir Charles, she will console herself with the Count of Belvedere; yet this is only
another instance of the manner in which he spoils
his artistic effect by the intrusion of his moral
purpose. The dignity of Clementina demands
that she should listen to no other proposals. The
strength of her love unhinges her mind, and since
all deep feeling commands respect, the involuntary
exhibition of hers is not felt to be repellent. But
if its force is such as to overcome her reason, it
should also be such as to secure its permanence;
"it were better to die, and soon," or at least to
seek an asylum behind quiet convent doors, than

thus to waver in fidelity. As it is, one is forced
to the conclusion that her madness is due not so
much to the strength of her passion, as to the
weakness of her mind.

Neither of the two heroines of *Sir Charles
Grandison* is in fact very attractive. Of the two
most critics have preferred Clementina, perhaps
because one's sympathies are apt to go with the
loser, and because her madness is really pathetic.
Warton actually preferred it to that of Ophelia,
but this must have been a concession to the prevailing fashion, for the few distracted snatches of
song in *Hamlet*, being used with more restraint,
give a far more poignant impression than Clementina's endless ravings. Richardson never knew
when to stop, and so prolongs these scenes that
he converts our pity to impatience, and poor
Clementina would receive more compassion if she
were less long-winded. And when the sweet
enthusiast, having taken a solemn farewell of her
rejected suitor in Italy, actually seeks his help
and protection in England, one begins to doubt the
much vaunted delicacy of her mind. If she was
still in love with Sir Charles it was unpardonable ;
if she was not, any woman of nice feeling would
have known to what imputation this reckless
conduct laid her open. To bring Clementina to
England was quite to destroy the effect produced
by her tragic resignation ; on her lover's departure from Italy she should have passed altogether
from the scene ; the author spoils all by being
too explicit.

But probably Richardson intended this action only as another tribute to the fascinations of his hero. If so, he made a grave mistake. The devotion of all these ladies makes the object of their affection slightly ridiculous; a man in such a position cannot fail to lose some dignity in the eyes of his fellows. And as Sir Walter Scott justly remarks, with regard to Harriet Byron, "Most readers have felt that this conduct, . . . though designed to elevate the hero, has the contrary effect of degrading the character of the heroine." Sir Charles is not a coxcomb, but in real life he must have inevitably become one, while most men would be tempted to regard lightly a prize so easily won as either Clementina or Harriet.

It is not that one would support the cruel and unnatural convention that a woman must not give her heart till it is asked for—a convention established by generations who considered passivity to be the whole duty of woman, and any attempt on her part at initiative as a treason against her sex. Harriet could not have been blamed for falling a victim to the irresistible attractions of Sir Charles, nor even for confiding her passion to her cousin Lucy. Richardson, who was learned in feminine psychology as few men have been, knew that the convention of modest inaction was responsible, not only for many of the sorrows, but also for much of the dissimulation of women. He understood the bad effect of constant self-repression, and of the continual effort to conceal legitimate emotion; and since, in his opinion, perfect sincerity was the most

charming of feminine graces, his ideal heroine must
not stoop to the slightest disguise. And, unable
to distinguish between the reserve dictated by
ordinary prudence, and a deliberate attempt to
give a false impression, he endowed Harriet with
an expansiveness which the most independent and
liberal critic must find offensive. The case could
not be better put than it was by Lady Bradshaigh
when she wrote that this frankness "will for ever
remain a blemish on the character . . . of Harriet
Byron . . . . I should have admired her more
had she suffered in silence, nothing should have
drawn her to an acknowledgment but Sir Charles'
addresses; it is not affected reserve, or too close a
way of thinking that I am recommending, but there
is a modest prudence which I think ought to tie
a woman's tongue in this delicate circumstance."[1]

Another blemish which a modern reader will
find in Harriet's character is her preoccupation
with the question of matrimony. It absorbs her
whole attention, and, in spite of her numerous
admirers, she is always on the look-out for more.
She regards every man she meets as a probable
suitor; immediately after her rescue by Sir Charles
she begins to speculate on his possible behaviour
to a possible wife. His sister complains of his
reticence. "Very likely," writes Harriet, "he
would be as reserved to his wife." She cannot
imagine what are his engagements, and why he
is so backward in paying her his addresses; and
when Mrs Reeves suggests that "had he any such

[1] Forster MS., Bradshaigh Correspondence.

thought he would be under difficulties to break his mind, lest such a declaration should be thought to lessen the merit of his protection," she eagerly seizes on the suggestion. "A good thought, my Lucy, of Mrs Reeves," she says, "and who knows, my Lucy, but there may be some foundation for it?" Her passion is patent to everyone, though the object of it is supposed to be miraculously blind to it. "You ladies must have seen that Miss Byron has a more than grateful regard for your brother," says Dr Bartleet, and Lady Olivia observes that "her eyes, by their officious withdrawing from his, and by the consciousness that glowed in her face whenever he addressed her, betrayed at least to a jealous eye more than she would wish to have seen." In letters that are read not only by her cousin, her grandmother, her uncle and aunt, but by her other relations of various degrees of consanguinity, she describes Grandison in the following glowing terms :—

"Oh, my aunt, be so good as to let the servants prepare my apartment at Selby House. There is no living within the blazing glory of this man! But for one's comfort he appears to have one fault, and he owns it. . . . This fault is pride. Do you mind what a stress he lays now and then on the family name? 'Dignity,' says he, 'that becomes my sisters!' Proud mortal! O, my Lucy, he is proud, too proud, I doubt, as well as too considerable in his fortunes. What would I say? Yet I know who would study to make him the happiest of men."[1]

[1] *Sir Charles Grandison*, ii. 239.

At this point there is nothing for it but to lay the book down in disgust, and not to resume the reading till the disagreeable impression has passed off.

It is impossible to feel much sympathy for such a heroine, even when Sir Charles goes away, and her cheek grows pale and thin, and everyone knows the reason, and condoles with her upon it. When the letter announcing the near union of Sir Charles and Clementina is received, its contents are communicated to no less than nine people, who discuss it together, and announce the news to her in full assembly. "I see," said she, "by the compassionate looks of everyone, that something is the matter. . . . Well, my friends, you are all grieved for me because the man is Sir Charles Grandison. And so, doctor, he is actually married? God Almighty," piously bending one knee, "make him and his Clementina happy!" Most women in such circumstances would feel openly expressed sympathy to be the extremity of torture, but Harriet parades her resignation and invites compliments upon it.

If, however, one can pardon her for this exaggerated candour, one may find a good deal that is interesting in this study of the workings of a woman's heart. The secret agitations, the alternations of hope and despair, of depression and gaiety; all those things, which, by a supreme effort, are generally kept hidden from the world, are here laid bare to the reader. "Let me ask you, my Lucy," she says, "you have passed the fiery ordeal, Did you ever find in yourself a kind of impatience,

next to petulance; and in your heart (only for
fear of exposing yourself) that you were ready to
quarrel, or be short, with anybody that came upon
you of a sudden, yet have no business of consequence to engage either your fingers or your
thoughts?"[1] The letters are full of passages like
this, showing subtle insight and sympathetic understanding of the growth of passion; and since their
existence is dependent on the objectionable candour
which Richardson intended as an additional attraction to his heroine, this drawback must be forgiven
for their sake.

The minor characters in *Sir Charles Grandison*
are more numerous and better drawn than those
of the other novels. It is a long step from Lady
Davers to Charlotte Grandison, though both belong
to the same genus, and the latter is only the
finished portrait of which the former is the rough
sketch. Yet even Charlotte is by no means an
ideal gentlewoman, and contemporary readers
found much to criticise in her conduct. "His
Anna Howe and Charlotte Grandison," said Lady
Mary Wortley Montagu, "are recommended as
patterns of charming pleasantry, and applauded
by his saint-like dames, who mistake pert folly
for wit and humour, and impudence and ill nature
for spirit and fire. Charlotte behaves like a
humorsome child, and should have been used
as one, and well whipped in the presence of
her friendly confidante, Harriet." And, indeed,
Charlotte's practical jokes and open contempt of

[1] *Sir Charles Grandison*, ii. 101.

the man whom she is nevertheless willing to marry are certainly somewhat incomprehensible, even taking into consideration the fact that she was by no means anxious for matrimony, but was forced into that state by the officious benevolence of her philanthropic brother.

Nevertheless, Charlotte's entertaining letters, and especially those in which she relates her matrimonial experiences, add much to the liveliness of the book, and help to relieve the suspense caused by the uncertainty of her brother's matrimonial projects. Take, for instance, the following passage :—

"My Lord sent up his compliments, and desired to know if he might attend me. I was in my dressing-room. He was not always so polite. . . . Up he came, one leg dragged after the other, not alert as he used to be on admission to his Charlotte. The last eight stairs his steps sounded : I, go, up, with, an, heavy, heart. He entered ; bowed : 'Were the words yours ? You would be glad to see me, madam !'

"'They were, my lord.'

"'Would to God you said truth !'

"'I did, I am glad to see you. I wanted to talk to you—about this Northamptonshire visit.'

"'Are you in earnest, madam, to make that visit ?'

"'I am. Miss Byron is not well. Emily pines to see her as much as I. You have no objection ?'

"He was silent.

"'Do you set out to-morrow, sir, for Windsor and Oxford?'

"He sighed. 'I think so, madam.'

"'Shall you visit Lord W.?'

"'I shall.'

"'And complain to him of me, my lord?' He shook his grave head as if there were wisdom in it. Be quiet, Harriet—not good all at once—that would be not to hold it.

"'No, madam, I have done complaining to anybody. You will one day see that you have not acted generously by the man who loves you as his own soul.'

"This, and his eyes glistening, moved me: 'Have we not been *both* wrong, my lord?'

"'Perhaps we have, madam, but here is the difference: I have been wrong with a *right intention*; you have been wrong and *studied* to be so.'

"'Prettily said. Repeat it, my lord. How was it?' And I took his hand and looked very graciously.

"'I cannot bear these airs of contempt.'

"'If you call them so, you are wrong, my lord, though perhaps *intending* to be *right.*'

"He did not see how good I was disposed to be; as I said, a change all at once would have been unnatural.

"'Very well, madam!' and turned from me with an air, half grieved, half angry.

"'Only answer me, my lord. Are you willing I should go to Northamptonshire?'

"'If you choose to go, I have no objection. Miss Byron is an angel.'

"'Now don't be perverse, Lord G. Don't praise Miss Byron at the expense of somebody else.'

"'Would to heaven, madam——'

"'I wish so too.' And I put my hand before his mouth—so kindly!

"He held it there with both his, and kissed it. I was not offended. 'But do you actually set out for Windsor and Oxford to-morrow, my lord?'

"'Not, madam, if you have any commands for me.'

"'Why, now, that's well said. Has your lordship anything to propose to me?'

"'I could not be so welcome to you, as your escort, as I am sure I should be to Miss Byron and her friends as her guest?'

"'You could not? How can you say so, my lord? You would do me both honour and pleasure.'

"'What would I give, that you mean what you say!'

"'I do mean it, my lord. My hand upon it.' I held out my hand for his. He snatched it, and I thought would have devoured it."[1]

But this dialogue takes place when Charlotte has been married some months, and is becoming reconciled to the assiduities of her husband. While he is still her lover she can hardly endure his devotion. "I shall hate this man," she says, "he does nothing but hop, skip, and jump dance about

[1] *Sir Charles Grandison*, vol. v. pp. 59-61.

me, grin, and make mouths." Poor Charlotte! It must be confessed that it was somewhat hard for a lady with her keen sense of humour to fall to the lot of a man who is clearly intended to be somewhat ridiculous—a humble, deferential creature, with a passion for collecting moths and old china.

On the whole, she is a likeable character, and in spite of her pride of place and her attitude to the ungenteel, ("One married lady was there," she says once, "the wife of Sir—Somebody—I am very bad at remembering the names of city knights), she has a good heart, and plenty of sympathy to spare for her friends. Even Aunt Nell, who has committed the unpardonable sin of remaining single, is kindly described by her, though her foibles are not spared. "Aunt Nell was all joy and gladness. She was in raptures last night, it seems, at her nephew's first arrival. . . . The good old soul imagines she is of importance to him, in the direction of family matters, now I have left him. *I*, Harriet! there's self-importance! But, good creatures, these old virgins! they do *so* love to be thought useful. Well, and is not that a good sign on Aunt Nell's part? Does it not look as if she would have been a useful creature in the days of nightrail and notableness, had she been a wife in good time? I always think, when I see those badgerly virgins fond of a parrot, a squirrel, a monkey, or a lapdog, that their imagination makes out husband and children in the animals—Poor things. . . .

"I wished her in Yorkshire fifty times, as we sat at breakfast; for when I wanted to ask my brother twenty thousand questions, and to set him on talking, we were entertained with her dreams of the night before his arrival and last night. Seas crossed, rivers forded—dangers escaped by the help of angels and saints, were the reveries of the former night; and of the last, the music of the spheres, heaven, and joy, and festivity. The plump creature loves good cheer, Harriet. In short, hardly a word could we say, but what put her upon recollecting a part of one of her dreams. Yet some excuse lies good, for an old soul, whose whole life has been but one dream, a little fal-lal-ishly varied." [1]

Charlotte Grandison, as may be seen from the above extract, has plenty of common sense, and sometimes shows greater penetration than her angelic brother or "his Harriet." "I never was fond of matches between sober young women and battered old rakes," is her comment on the marriage arranged by Sir Charles for his uncle, Lord W. And again, with a cynicism born of her own discontent with matrimony, she says, "Married people by frequent absences may have a little chance for happiness." And in the face of the immense time spent in confabulation by the rest of the characters, it is refreshing to come across her comment on consultations: "I never knew consultations of any kind turn to account. It is only a parcel of people getting together, pro-

[1] *Sir Charles Grandison*, v. pp. 273, 274.

posing doubts and puzzling one another, and ending as they began, if not worse."

Of the other minor characters, Emily Jervois
has her attractions, though, at times, she is, as
Lady Bradshaigh remarked, rather too old for her
years, and at others her ingenuousness is a little
forced. "What a pleasure, yet what a pain, is
there in sighing when I think of him! Yet I
know I am an innocent girl," she says; and it
strikes one as a little odd that an innocent girl
should think anything at all about her innocence.
Young ladies grew up sooner in the eighteenth
century than they do at the present time, but the
best thing for Emily would have been to go back
to boarding-school, and to be kept well-employed
till her too fascinating guardian was well within
the matrimonial pale.

Other interesting persons are Uncle Selby, who
is always putting his niece to the blush by his
blunt observations on her delicate position, Grandmother Shirley, whose favourite literature is of
a somewhat sombre character ("I was reading
Sherlock upon death," she writes, "with that
cheerfulness with which I always meditate the
subject"), and Beauchamp, the hero's bosom
friend, with whom Emily afterwards consoles
herself. There are many more characters in *Sir
Charles Grandison* than in either *Pamela* or
Clarissa Harlowe—no fewer than fifty, including,
according to the author's own curious classification, "men, women and Italians."

It must not be supposed, however, that every

one of these individuals has much importance in the development of the plot. Many of them are introduced simply to illustrate the benevolence of the hero, and as subjects towards whom he may exercise his charity. The chief justification for the existence of others, Lucy Selby and Dr Bartleet, for instance, is that they are convenient receptacles for the confidences of Sir Charles and Harriet. But the very number of personages irrelevant to the plot helps to lend an air of reality to the whole. For in actual life all men and women are surrounded by, and even brought into constant communication with, people who have no shadow of influence on the evolution of their histories; and though the skilled novelist, fearful of overcrowding his scene, is accustomed to eliminate such characters, their introduction, if one can pardon the digressions that they necessitate, is a distinct advantage to Richardson. He rambles garrulously on, bringing one after another on the scene, and then carelessly dismissing them from it; they appear and vanish with as little apparent reason as the crowds who pass us in our own lives. Every day brings a fresh figure into the pageant of our world; but of all those with whom accident or intention makes us acquainted, how few touch our hearts or affect our destiny!

But, notwithstanding the number of characters, the plot of *Sir Charles Grandison* is more skilfully constructed than those of Richardson's previous novels. The reader is made acquainted with Harriet, and prejudiced in her favour, long before there is any mention of Clementina, and the rival claims of the two heroines are admirably balanced throughout. The interest of the first five volumes is skilfully sustained. They fall into two well-marked portions, each ending in a crisis, one being the interview between Sir Charles and Harriet, during which he confesses to her his embarrassments; the other, the final result of his second Italian journey. In the former the suspense hinges on the reader's ignorance of the hero's engagements, in the latter on the question as to whether he will or will not marry Clementina after all. But with the decision of this momentous question the book should have closed. The greater part of the sixth, and the whole of the seventh, volume are quite superfluous, because the fate of the lovers is decided, and perfect felicity knows no suspense.

CHAPTER IX

THE ART OF RICHARDSON

THE study of literary form is the last subject to which a writer, who, as it were, becomes an author by accident, gives much attention. He is so much preoccupied with what he has to say, with the narrative of the thoughts or actions of his characters, or with the information that he wishes to place before the reader, that the idea of presenting it in a highly finished manner does not occur to him. The feeling for form does not always accompany the impulse towards creation; indeed, one might almost argue that they are in a measure contradictory, or at least mutually limiting, the least inventive writers often being the greatest masters of style, while those who are more original and imaginative treat the matter with indifference. To pay equal attention to both branches of the work, to the subject matter and the mode of its presentment, seems possible only to the greatest genius.

Now to Richardson his subject matter was everything, and he probably never gave a moment to the consideration of form. Writing letters one day, he suddenly discovered that he was writing a

story. Accident, and not choice, determined the
form of his romances, and the contemporary fashion
for memoirs and correspondence ensured its popularity. It was not till he had won a decided
success that he paused to inquire into the theory
of his method, and formulated his results in the
preface to *Clarissa Harlowe*.

Richardson's manner of narration, although in
some ways extremely clumsy, is not without its
advantages, and contributed in no small degree to
the life-like impression produced by his work. For,
next to actual conversation, letters are the most
luminous means of communication between man
and man; although, even here, the physical action
involved by writing may induce a certain amount
of self-consciousness and a consequent effort after
concealment, yet in the correspondence of intimate
friends the heart is laid bare as it can be in no
other way save by the fugitive, unrecorded gestures
and words of personal intercourse. By means of
these letters the reader is brought into immediate
contact with the characters of the story. He
does not seem to be listening to what the author
says about them, or to become acquainted with
them through the description of a third person.
The method has something in common with the
dramatic; we form our conception of the actors
by means of their own confidences.

Another advantage of this method is, that since
the letter is supposed to be written during the
progress of the events it relates, before the issue is
known to those who are writing, the sentiment of

suspense can be conveyed more vividly than by any other means. When the narrator tells his story after many years one may suppose the keen emotions of the time to have subsided ; or when the tale is told by a third person, although he may be supposed to be omniscient, and to have a divine intuition into the feelings of the actors in it, yet the very fact that he tells it as a spectator detracts from the intensity of the effect. The most poignant and pathetic expression of passion must take a lyrical, that is, a personal form. Richardson, indeed, was quite conscious of this himself. " Much more lively and affecting," says he in the preface to *Clarissa*, " must be the style of those who write in the height of a *present* distress, the mind tortured by the pangs of uncertainty (the events then hidden in the womb of fate), than the dry narrative unanimated style of a person relating difficulties and dangers surmounted, the relater perfectly at ease, and if himself unmoved by his own story, then not likely greatly to affect the reader." The inward searchings and painful agonies of souls wandering in mazes, whose secret is not yet manifest, could find no more satisfactory expression than these leisurely and voluminous epistles.

Then, again, the method allows for the introduction of a large number of persons on the scene, and gives opportunity for thorough acquaintance with each. They do not stand aside to let the principal persons pass, nor is their individuality concealed by the domination of the others. Each, as he writes, holds the stage for the time ; our attention is concentrated on him ; we learn to know him even by his comments on the chief characters. And we see the events narrated not from one, but from many points of view; just as in actual life our ears are filled with the comments of a hundred spectators on a single incident. Moreover, since they write while the impression is still fresh, what can be more natural than that they should give us thousands of minute details, unimportant in themselves, yet, by force of accumulation, conveying the conviction that things must have happened exactly so, and not otherwise? Harriet Byron returns to Selby House, but simply to relate that fact is insufficient. She must describe circumstantially how she was greeted by each member of the family, what each said to her, and the number of kisses given and received. These things are evidently so interesting to the writer that the reader learns to treat them with equal gravity, and actually finds himself becoming absorbed by them. These ghosts in powder and patches, in wigs and hoops, silk stockings and stiff brocade, are after all animated by the same small delights and trivial vexations as play so large a part in our own lives. We are akin to them not only in titanic conflicts, in moments of supreme passion, but also in these common-place, everyday emotions, that pass and leave no apparent trace.

On the other hand, this method has obvious disadvantages. The events of a day are chronicled by half-a-dozen witnesses, hence this incredible languor in the progress of the narrative ; it is as if a boat had been launched in a quiet lake, and the crew had waited for every ripple to subside before progressing an inch. In the important crises of life action proceeds rapidly; so rapidly, indeed, that the momentous deed is done almost before we are aware. And according to the actual time supposed to elapse during the events recorded in Richardson's novels, they also occupy but a brief interval. But, owing to the scale on which it is all told, one feels as if they were spread over many years; Clarissa's hesitation to seek the protection of Lovelace appears the conflict, not of days, but of months. Life was more leisurely in the eighteenth century, and most of Richardson's readers do not seem to have objected to this delay. "You have formed a style," wrote one of his admirers, "in which prolixity becomes a virtue." But the present generation scarcely knows how to saunter, and the divine Clarissa has been known to have not only a soothing, but even a soporific effect.

But perhaps the most striking disadvantage of the epistolary method is the effect it must have on the construction of the plot. It is almost impossible to conceive a symmetrical, proportionate plot conducted in this manner. For since no character in the story can be ubiquitous or omniscient, the attempt to trace how a certain event or action must needs put into motion other events and actions, as its inevitable consequence, is rendered extremely difficult. The information that the writer possesses concerning events that happened in his absence, must necessarily be second-hand; and, moreover, the proper sequence is hard to follow. We are made familiar with a fact before we are acquainted with its cause, and the result is either some confusion, or an elaborate and ill-placed exposition of the situation. But the method exactly suited Richardson, because he obviously composed without any preconceived plan, and at the first setting off had no clear conception of either character or action. "I am a very irregular writer," he told Lady Bradshaigh, "can form no plan, nor write after what I have preconceived. Many of my friends wonder at this, but so it is. I have not therefore that encouragement to proceed which those have, who, forming an agreeable plan, write within its circle, and go on step by step with delight, knowing what they drive at." This accounts for the laborious nature of the earlier chapters of his novels, where he himself has evidently no thorough grip of the story; but as he proceeds, the idea becomes clearer; he is so much interested in his characters that they evolve as if spontaneously; the vague and unsatisfactory outline is gradually sharpened and defined by myriad minute touches. Yet even when the characterisation is firm and sure, his plots are as loose and ill-constructed as it is possible for plots to be. He was a master of situation, but these situations are brought about by a series of events so absurd and improbable as to tax the patience of the reader to its utmost limit. The situation of Clarissa, ensnared and struggling, could not be better conceived or described ; yet one is haunted by the sense that it could never have been thus indefinitely prolonged. In real life she would certainly have escaped, or her friends would have come to her rescue. Her own behaviour is perfectly natural, it is the necessary exposition of her character, but the circumstances that demand it are forced and artificial. Richardson, in fact, proceeds exactly in the same manner as did his predecessors in fiction ; he rambles on from one event to another, without troubling much about their coherence. If he brings his characters into a narrow pass whence egress is difficult, he has only to invent some fresh improbability, and the way is clear. Nothing could be more unlikely than that Clarissa should seek refuge at Hampstead, but she has to be taken there in order to be discovered.

Nor is he always very original in the mechanism he employs. Elopements and abductions were the favourite *motifs* of the old heroic romances. " J'ai vu des gens," says Furetière, "qui pour marquer l'endroit où ils en étaient d'une histoire, disaient, ' J'en suis au huitième enlèvement' au lieu de dire ' J'en suis au huitième tome.' " [1] In each of Richardson's novels there is an abduction, successful or abortive ; athwart the clatter of teacups and the tinkle of the harpsichord, one hears the thud of galloping hoofs, the sudden report of a pistol. It is true that in Richardson's day these things still happened. Gentlemen had not yet left

[1] Furetière. *Le Roman Bourgeois*, pp. 174, 175.

off wearing swords, and society, like the novel that
represented it, was in a state of transition; in both
there may be traced a vestige of barbarism.   But
these time-worn expedients seem little suitable to
a story that is in many ways so modern; they
remind one of rusty armour hung on the staircase
of a semi-detached villa.

As has been already remarked, the plot of
Sir Charles Grandison is more elaborate than
those of *Pamela* and *Clarissa Harlowe*.   The
double interest is, on the whole, skilfully managed,
and though the approach of the hero is too long
delayed, the scene of his appearance is admirably
conducted; the author becomes, for once, actually
dramatic.   It is unfortunately, only for a moment;
the reader is almost immediately lost in a labyrinth
of episodes.   "Oh, the endless love-making," said
Dr Jowett, "not of one or two people, but
of at least fifty!"   *Sir Charles Grandison* contains sufficient material for at least half-a-dozen
novels of moderate size; for, in the manner of
Le Sage, Richardson cannot introduce a fresh
character without relating his history from his
cradle.   Thus the entire stories of the married
life of Sir Charles Grandison's father and mother,
of Lady L.'s courtship and marriage, of Beauchamp,
Emily Jervois, the Danbys, and Lord W., are
given; they have little or no bearing on the plot,
and are there simply because of the inexhaustible
fertility of the author's invention.   "Des sept
volumes il en faudrait faire trois," wrote Lord
Chesterfield.   The truth is, they might very well

be extended to a dozen others, each containing a complete novel, while all that is essential to the story of Sir Charles, and Harriet, and Clementina, might be compressed into two. This episodical habit mars nearly all the novels of the eighteenth century. Even Fielding, that master of construction, is not free from it; witness the story of the Old Man of the Hill in *Tom Jones;* while the less skilful craftsmen, such as Henry Brooke, are its absolute slaves. *The Fool of Quality*, a novel praised by John Wesley and Charles Kingsley for its high moral tone, contains no less than eight episodes, connected by the merest thread of continuous narrative. The result is a book that is now practically unreadable; for, in spite of the recommendations of professed moralists, lack of interest cannot be atoned for by any amount of high feeling.

Fortunately for Richardson his episodes have sufficient intrinsic interest to extenuate their introduction, and if they did not interrupt the narrative they would be entirely acceptable. What if they concern people who have only the remotest connection with the story? But these people live and move before us, and have an independent attraction that is all their own. Take, for instance, the description of Mr Singleton, in *Sir Charles Grandison*, who just moves across the scene for an instant, and never reappears. "He smiled and looked delighted with all he saw and heard. Once, indeed, he tried to speak; his mouth actually opened to give passage to his words, as sometimes seems to be his way before the words are quite ready. But he sat down, satisfied with the effort." The words convey the impression of actuality; Mr Singleton was certainly someone whom Richardson had himself known. His books are full of such graphic descriptions, and it is this naturalistic treatment that has led so many critics to class him among our greatest realists. One cannot help feeling as if one had been present at these scenes, so vividly are every gesture and movement described. Clarissa is trying to repel the attentions of an unwelcome suitor; her mother and sister are present at the interview. "The man stalked in. His usual walk is by pauses, as if he were telling his steps; and first paid his clumsy respects to my mother, then to my sister, next to me, as if I were already his wife, and therefore to be last in his notice; and, sitting down by me, told us in general what weather it was . . . then addressing himself to me: 'And how do you find it, miss?' was his question, and would have taken my hand.

"I withdrew it, I believe with disdain enough. My mother frowned, my sister bit her lip.

"My mother coloured and looked at him, at my sister, at me. My sister's eyes were opener and bigger than I ever saw them before.

"The man understood me. He hemmed and removed from one chair to another.

"I went on supplicating for my mother's favourable report. . . .

"'Is the girl mad?' said my mother, interrupting me.

"My sister, with the affectation of a whisper to my mother : 'This is—this is spite, madam, because you commanded her to stay.'

"I only looked at her, and turning to my mother : 'Permit me, madam,' said I, 'to repeat my request. If I lose my mamma's favour I am lost forever.'

"Mr Solmes removed to his first seat, and fell to gnawing the head of his hazel, a carved head, almost as ugly as his own. . . .

"My sister rose, with a face all over scarlet, and stepping to the table where lay a fan, she took it up, and fanned herself violently." [1]

All this could not be better, and the passages quoted are only typical of many others equally vivid. Richardson is indeed inexorable ; he never flinches from any stroke that will add to his design ; some of his descriptions might have been taken from the pages of a modern Russian or Norwegian novelist. The illness of Jeronymo, Clementina's brother, is minutely related, and a painstaking account of the improved treatment of the English doctor follows. It is neither very pleasant nor very instructive reading, but it is an admirable illustration of the realistic manner. When Clarissa is discovered by Belford in the Sheriff's house no touch is omitted that may serve to bring the scene in greater relief before our eyes.

"A horrid hole of a house in an alley they call

[1] *Clarissa Harlowe*," i. 138.

a court; stairs wretchedly narrow, even to the first floor rooms. And into a den they led me, with broken walls which had been papered, as I saw by a multitude of tacks and some torn bits held on by the rusty heads.

"The floor indeed was clean, but the ceiling was smoked with a variety of figures and initials of names that had been the woful employment of wretches who had no other way to amuse themselves.

"A bed at one corner, with coarse curtains tacked up at the feet to the ceiling, because the curtain-rings were broken off, but a coverlid upon it with a cleanish look, though plaguily in tatters, and the corners tied up in tassels, that the rents might go no farther.

"The windows dark and double-barred, the tops boarded up to save mending; and only a little four-paned hole of a casement to let in air; more, however, coming in at broken panes than could come in at that.

"Four old turkey-worked chairs, bursten-bottomed, the stuffing staring out.

"An old tottering, worm-eaten table that had more nails bestowed in mending it to make it stand than the table cost fifty years ago when new.

"On the mantlepiece was an iron shove-up candle-stick with a lighted candle in it, twinkle, twinkle, twinkle; four of them, I suppose, for a penny.

"Near that, on the same shelf, was an old look-ing-glass, cracked through the middle, breaking out into a thousand points; the crack given it, perhaps, in a rage by some poor creature to whom it gave the representation of his heart's woes in his face." [1]

Well may M. Texte say, in speaking of such passages as these, " Si le réalisme est l'art de donner l'impression de la vie, Richardson est le plus grand de réalistes."

But the truth is that, notwithstanding his method, no greater mistake can be made than to class Richardson as a pure realist. His form is realistic, but in intention and conception he is an idealist. In Pamela he attempted to depict an ideal serving-maid, in Clarissa an ideal gentlewoman, in Sir Charles Grandison an ideal gentleman. And though objections may be raised to this designation of characters whose faults are often very patent to the reader, yet such faults are due rather to the inherent imperfections in the writer's ideal than to any intention on his part to leaven their virtues by a few natural weaknesses. "No man," says Professor Raleigh, with reference to the character of Sir Charles Grandison, "can build higher than he knows," and it was inevitable that these persons should reflect to some extent the failings of their creator, and especially his inordinate self-consciousness. But such faults as they have, Richardson would have been the last to perceive, and, as a moral reformer, his chief endeavour was to furnish an example for the age, which we have seen he explicitly declared he had done in Sir Charles. This intense earnestness had the effect of giving

<hr />

[1] *Clarissa Harlowe*, v. pp. 335, 336.

additional life to the creatures of his fancy, the vigour of their author passing into their very substance, and vivifying everything they are supposed to do or say. For these children of his brain were no imaginary beings to him, but suffering, and striving, and victorious champions, lifting the ensign of virtue above the dark confusion of struggling humanity. The illusion was nourished by the profound gravity with which he and his friends discussed the conduct and fortunes of his heroines. Clarissa might well have been one of that little circle of young ladies who discussed her griefs so sympathetically; and, indeed, there is some evidence to indicate that Hester Mulso and Harriet Byron were near relations.[1] So thin a partition divided those ardent worshippers of Richardson from the children of his imagination, that they might not have been greatly surprised if Harriet Byron or Anna Howe had suddenly walked in among them and taken their seats on those exceedingly uncomfortable chairs depicted in Miss Highmore's drawing of the summer-house.

In this way Richardson's enthusiasm for virtue actually added to the artistic effect of his work, besides supplying him with a reasonable pretext for so frivolous a pursuit as novel-writing. For he never quite freed himself from the puritanical prejudice against fiction; and he would have had his books classed, not with *Robinson Crusoe*, or *Oroonoko*, or *Moll Flanders*, but with works

---

[1] It may be noticed as not without significance that the home of both these ladies was in Northamptonshire.

of devotion, such as Taylor's *Holy Living and Dying*, with the *Practice of Piety*, and Nelson's *Fasts and Festivals*; "not as being worthy of such company, but that they may have a chance of being dipt into thirty years hence; . . . they will not be found unworthy of such a chance, since they appear in the humble guise of novel only by way of accommodation to the manners and taste of an age overwhelmed with luxury, and abandoned to sound and senselessness." Such being his view, it is not surprising that his amiable characters are at so much pains to rebuke offenders and formulate moral laws for the benefit of all their acquaintance, or that even his bad ones, Lovelace included, should indulge in a vast amount of serious reflection. The smallest detail is made the subject of a contest between right and wrong, and a spiritual conflict accompanies the decision of questions usually referred to etiquette or convenience.

But Richardson's morality, obtruded alike by lovely maidens, gallant gentlemen, serving-women and old ladies, though sound and sensible in the main, is not always above criticism. After all, he was a typical member of the more serious section of middle-class society of the early part of the eighteenth century. Upright, rigid, narrow and earnest, he was ruled by contemporary convention ; it was only when by force of genius he broke through that convention, as in the culmination of Clarissa's story, that he rose above the average morality of his class. Sufficient stress has already been laid on the contemptible treatment of the

vital motive in *Pamela*, whereby a certificate of
marriage is transformed into a certificate of good
character for one of the most vicious heroes ever
conceived or presented.   But in the other novels
persons supposed to possess the greatest refinement and delicacy of feeling stoop to actions that
are little short of dishonourable.   Sir Charles
Grandison arranges for Clementina's mother to
listen, unknown to her, to a conversation which
she supposes to be private ; shortly afterwards,
Father Marescotti, whose only fault is supposed
to be religious zeal, is also guilty of eavesdropping.
Charlotte Grandison, having picked up a confi-
dential letter from her brother to Dr Bartleet,
takes it to Harriet and tries to persuade her to
read it ; and Harriet is actually represented as
having some difficulty in resisting the temptation.
These are grave faults of taste, at least, and an
enemy might call them by a worse name.

But if one must not always expect to find great
refinement in Richardson's ideal of conduct, he at
least provided his readers, and especially his lady
readers, with good working-day maxims, admirably
adapted to guide through the social labyrinth a
young woman of sensibility, who aimed also at the
strictest propriety.   " In a collection of the sentiments contained in the three histories, it will be
seen that there are not many of the material
articles that may be of use for the conduct of life and
manners, unattended to in one or other of them,"
he wrote to Mr Hildesley.   And though the sale
of this collection was not excessive, there is no

R

doubt that the author's habit of moralisation did commend his books to contemporary readers. It was mainly on this score that Johnson, in the same spirit as he condemned Gray's Bard (because it does not advance any political or moral truth), preferred him to Fielding; himself delighting in moral aphorism, he had much sympathy with Richardson's love of didacticism. "Why, sir," he said, "if you were to read Richardson for the story, your impatience would be so much fretted that you would hang yourself. You must read him for the sentiment, and consider the story only as giving rise to the sentiment."[1] And Richardson's sentiments, if sometimes trite and obvious are, on the other hand, often trenchant and amusing; often full of quick insight into hidden motives. "Hope is the cordial that keeps life from stagnating." "What once a woman hopes in love matters she always hopes, while there is room for hope." "Some persons have meanness in their very pride." "If our hearts do not harden and contract, as we experience ill-treatment from the world, we shall be on very unequal terms with it." "To endeavour to force a free mind is to dishonour it." "To borrow of relations is to subject oneself to an inquisition into one's life and actions." "Women love those best who give them most pain." Such passages as these justify Chesterfield's observation that though Richardson "grossly mistakes the modes, he never mistakes nature."

With all his insight, however, he is far from

[1] Boswell, *Life of Johnson*, Ed. Birkbeck Hill, ii. 175.

taking an altogether tolerant view of the foibles of
his fellow men. His books are full of humorous
description, but it is to be noticed that he seldom
applies such description to his virtuous characters ;
he never meant to induce a smile at the expense
of Sir Charles Grandison. He cannot illustrate
the pleasant follies of a man without making him
slightly contemptible, as in the case of Lord G. or
Uncle Selby. He has little of that large, loving
sympathy with the frailty of human nature, observ-
able in the greatest humorists, in Shakespeare
Fielding, Sterne, and Goldsmith. Falstaff and
Partridge and Uncle Toby and Dr Primrose
would have been impossible to him. Thus his
humour never trembles on the verge of pathos
and in his very laughter a sneer is latent. But,
to tell the truth, Richardson never does laugh
quite heartily ; he had a young lady's horror of
anything approaching farce, and for his comic
effects he depends much more on the minute
relation of gesture, dress and manner, than
on the action or language of his characters.
The element of malignity, which has been de-
noted as one of the ingredients of amusement,
is indispensable to his humour ; and he might
have been a successful satirist had he not been
impeded by the constant affectation of benevolence. And when he forsakes description and
attempts humorous dialogue, he is far less successful. His " raillying " is decidedly ponderous ;
his repartee is weighted with lead ; he has no
facility in innuendo. And that this heaviness is

not the result of contemporary formality or a ceremonious habit of phraseology, any scene from *The School for Scandal* will show.

On the other hand, Richardson is often, unintentionally, extremely funny. His unconscious humour is in fact so prominent that it has prevented many critics from treating him with a proper amount of gravity; though unless his work be regarded seriously, it is impossible to estimate it fairly. He was so much preoccupied with his moral intention that he had seldom leisure to consider whether its presentment was not a little quaint; thus in Pamela's extraordinary parody of the hundred and seventeenth psalm, which is more amusing than most intentional parodies, he saw only a beautiful illustration of his heroine's piety and devotion. The temptation of a quotation cannot be resisted :—

> "When sad I sat in Brandon Hall,
> All guarded round about,
> And thought of ev'ry absent friend,
> The tears for grief burst out.
>
> "My joys and hopes all overthrown,
> My heart strings almost broke,
> Unfit my mind for melody,
> Much more to bear a joke.
>
> "Then she to whom I pris'ner was
> Said to me tauntingly,
> Now cheer your heart and sing a song,
> And tune your mind to joy.

.   .   .   .

> " Remember, Lord, this Mrs Jewkes,
> When with a mighty sound,
> She cries, Down with her chastity,
> Down to the very ground ! " [1]

And again, a comic effect is often produced by the same kind of self-consciousness in his characters as so frequently raises a smile in Richardson's private letters. Clementina, in order to set the crown on her magnanimous action, and to reassure Harriet Byron by an explicit renunciation of Sir Charles, does so in the following effusion, appropriately arranged (since it marks the burial of her love) in " the lapidary style."

> Best of Men ⎫
>   ⎬ Be ye one.
> Best of Women ⎭
> Clementina wishes it.
> Grandison, Lady, will make you happy,
> Be it your study to make him so !
> Happy as Clementina would have made him
> Had not obstacles invincible intervened.
> This will lessen her regrets :
> For
> His Felicity, Temporal and Eternal
> Was ever the wish next her heart.
> GOD be merciful to you both
> And lead you into His paths :
> Then will everlasting happiness be your portion.
> Be it the portion of Clementina—
> Pray for her !—
> That after this transitory life is over
> She may partake of Heavenly Bliss :
> And
> (Not a stranger to you, Lady, HERE)
> Rejoice with you both HEREAFTER.

---

[1] *Pamela,* i. 184.

"Generous, noble creature!" is her friends' comment on this production. "Does it not show a raised imagination, especially in the disposition of the lines?"[1] Literary fatuity could scarcely go further.

If we examine into the cause of the ridiculous impression made by the passages quoted above, and by many others in Richardson's novels, we shall probably conclude that it is due to a suggestion of pose, of insincerity in those whose griefs find such expression. An undemonstrative race is accustomed to view with suspicion any great exhibition of feeling, and to consider that the sorrow which easily finds a voice is not yet unendurable. The sufferer seems to look round him with some complacency, exclaiming, "What a beautiful and pathetic figure I am! And how much compassion do I deserve!" And the appeal for sympathy frustrates its object. To Richardson's contemporaries, however, much of what seems mere bathos to us was truly touching, and the legitimate expression of a breaking heart. Many such outbursts, which we consider puerile and out of · taste, would not have been found objectionable by a generation which, after a long period of emotional repression, was quite ready to run to the other extreme of exaggerated sensibility.

Richardson's pathetic power, however, lies after all not in these lyrical laments, but in his situations. Pamela, so long as her innocence blinds her to her peril ; Clarissa, proud and inflexible in the depth

[1] *Sir Charles Grandison*, vi. 242, 243.

of her humiliation ; Harriet waiting in miserable
suspense for the delivery of the letter that will
decide her fate ; Clementina, torn between divine
and earthly love—all these are infinitely touching.
They might lament for ever, and their lamentations
would leave us cold; we could gaze unmoved upon
their tears. It is the suffering so wantonly imposed upon them, the bitter strife with destiny,
their love and longing, their disappointments
and their joys, that appeal to the reader's own experience and compel his sympathy. The triumph
of Clarissa over innumerable hearts is due, not to
the eloquence of her complaint, though that is
great, but to the pathos of her position, fallen
from her high estate, yet unsubdued, and standing
in austere beauty upon the ruin of her life, to
vindicate the mastery of spirit over flesh.

To the smaller details of his art, it need hardly
be said, Richardson paid no attention whatever.
He has no style at all ; he wrote just as he talked,
and as he composed those innumerable epistles on
which we have drawn so largely. His sentences
are often quite invertebrate, and innocent of anything that could do duty for a predicate, the finite
verb being replaced by a participle or adjective.
He never troubles about the symmetry of his
paragraphs, and he never wastes time in compres-
sing into ten words what is easier to say in twenty.
There is no nice choice of epithet, nor fastidious
rejection of the trite or homely ; if he had been
more careful he could never have been so prolix.

And there is not in his books what has often
redeemed the style of writers no less homely in
their way, that appeal to, and constant illustration
by means of natural beauty, which elevate the
novels of a writer so much inferior to him as Mrs
Radcliffe.   The description of Grandison Hall
sounds like a passage from an auctioneer's cata-
logue.   When Sir Charles crosses Mount Cenis
on his second Italian journey, his travelling
companion speaks of Savoy as "one of the worst
countries under heaven, clothed in snow and
disfigured by hurricanes. . . .   Every object which
here presents itself is excessively miserable."[1]
With this may be compared the well-known passage in Gray's journal, describing the journey to
Geneva.   "You here meet with all the beauties
so savage and horrid a place can present you with ;
rocks of various and uncouth figures, cascades pour-
ing down an immense height out of hanging groves
of pine-trees, and the solemn sound of the stream
that roars below, all combine to form one of the
most poetical scenes imaginable."[2]   But in his appreciation of savage beauty, Gray was at least a
generation in advance of his age, and it was a
Frenchman and not an Englishman who first
introduced "the pathetic fallacy" into the novel.
It is strange that the very scenery that Richardson
depreciated should have been chosen as the setting
of *La Nouvelle Héloise.*

[1] *Sir Charles Grandison*, iv. p. 274.
[2] Gray's *Works*, Ed. Gosse, i. p. 244.

CHAPTER X

THE INFLUENCE OF RICHARDSON

THIRTY years after the appearance of *Clarissa Harlowe*, Mrs Chapone, being obliged to accompany an aunt on a long and tedious journey, took with her, to beguile the way, a copy of *Pamela*. " I must own," she wrote, " that it appeared somewhat different from what I thought of it thirty years ago ; yet I still see in each of Richardson's works amazing genius, unpolished indeed either by learning or knowledge of polite life, but making its way to the heart by strokes of nature that would have been lost, or at least weakened, by the restraints of critical elegance. It is only from the ignorant that we can have anything original ; every master copies from those that are of established authority, and does not look at the natural object." [1]

This moderate eulogy from one who had been one of the most enthusiastic of Richardson's early admirers indicates the change that had taken place in the general estimation of his work. Richardson had set the fashion to so many other writers of greater genius, or at least in greater sympathy

[1] *Posthumous Works of Mrs Chapone*, i. 175.

with the national feeling, that his fame had been overshadowed by theirs. The cult of Richardson was a fashion, and as such was bound, sooner or later, to disappear. Yet though he passed out of vogue with the general public, traces of his influence abound in many of the novels published in England during the fifty years that succeeded his death, and he may be said to have founded one very definite school of novelists.

It was in 1749 that Lady Bradshaigh wrote to Richardson to ask him the meaning of the word *sentimental*, so much used by the polite, both in town and country. "Everything clever and agreeable is comprehended in that word, but (I) am convinced a wrong interpretation is given, because it is impossible everything clever and agreeable can be so common as this word. I am frequently astonished to hear such a one is a sentimental man; we were at a sentimental party; I have been taking a sentimental walk."[1] Gradually the meaning got narrowed down to imply an excess of feeling, emotional susceptibility; and it is in this sense of the word that it may be said that the sentimental school of novelists originated with Richardson.

Frequent stress has already been laid on the prominence given in his books to emotional indulgence. The degree of sensibility attained by his characters is the touchstone of their value as men and women. Clarissa, when she feels most bitterly against her sister, says that "poor Bella

[1] Barbauld, iv. 282.

has not a feeling heart," which is a terrible indictment of her whole character. And this exaltation of feeling above all the other ingredients of which our complex human nature is composed led to an objectionable freedom in its expression, a tendency to "gush," which in the long run weakened the very quality of which it was intended as a witness. For when a man's moral worth was determined by his capacity of response to impressions of pity and terror, there was a great temptation to affect feeling which did not exist, but, by the general consensus of opinion, ought to have been present. People acquired the habit of expressing more than they felt, and even genuine emotion, instead of being transformed into a moral force, was dissipated in loquacious utterance.

The leading member of this school was, of course, Sterne, whose *Tristram Shandy* first appeared in 1759. Not that Richardson would not have earnestly deprecated any connection between his own books and those of a writer of whom he said, "One extenuating circumstance attends his works; they are too gross to be inflaming." But the fact remains that it was he who had made popular the novel of sentiment, and had prepared the way for that luxurious indulgence in emotion which has been well termed a "sensuous debauch." It would be unjust to say that Sterne's effects are always, or generally, forced; he was, on the contrary, capable of very deep and genuine feeling, and a pathos much more delicately balanced than that of Richardson; but, having once discovered the popularity that might ensue from this ability to extort tears from his readers, he cultivated his sensibility as a kind of literary speculation.

And if this is true of Sterne, it is much more true of the other members of his school, of Henry Mackenzie and Henry Brooke. The *Man of Feeling* (1771) is nothing but a study in emotion and simply describes a few scenes in the life of a hero whose facile tears are constantly evoked by accidents obviously devised for that purpose. His visit to London in search of a government appointment, his brief stay there, his disappointment and death, compose all the story ; there is no character-drawing, no humour, no plot; everything that we are accustomed to look for in a work of fiction is devoured and swallowed up by this leviathan of sentimentality.

But the worst offender of all was Henry Brooke, whose *Fool of Quality* has already been condemned for its loose construction. The hero is a gentle-man of rank who is kidnapped in boyhood by his own uncle, a character as virtuous, but hardly as interesting, as Sir Charles Grandison. He brings up his nephew in his own likeness, and little Harry is practically the same person at an earlier period of life, only that his idiosyncracies, being exempli-fied in a child, appear more incongruous and im-probable. He is distinguished by an affectation of unaffectation, a studied simplicity, and a sus-ceptibility that finds vent in tears on the slightest provocation. " I love to weep, I joy to grieve ; it is my happiness to have my heart broken in pieces," says, quite seriously, another of Brooke's characters; and this utterance may not unfairly be taken to represent the attitude of his school.

Both Mackenzie and Brooke show the influence of Richardson in another way; they are deeply preoccupied with the question of education, which forms so prominent a topic in the second part of *Pamela*; but as their novels were issued after the publication of Rousseau's *Emile* (1762), it is possible that they may owe something to him also.

But the sentimentalists were not the only writers who were profoundly affected by the example of Richardson. His novels, as has been seen, appealed particularly to women; not only because he possessed so much knowledge of feminine psychology, but also because he limited himself to topics which were well within the comprehension of an ordinary woman of the eighteenth century. It is extraordinary how few references his books contain to home or foreign politics, and in this respect he may be justly contrasted with Fielding, who, in *Amelia* especially, devoted himself with so much zeal to the satirical exposure of crying evils. Richardson's novels were essentially novels for the parlour, and this applies particularly to *Sir Charles Grandison*, which, as Miss Burney has told us, was a great favourite with her in her girlhood. It treats of those topics which are most familiar to women, and which will never lose their attraction as themes for the lady novelist. It has been said that Sir Charles is "a lady's hero," and perhaps this is the reason that he was one of Miss Burney's early idols, until a cynical young gentleman dashed her enthusiasm by declaring that he was too perfect to exist. As time went on, her admiration diminished ; she had too keen a sense of humour not to see the ridiculous side of Richardson's books, and when a friend expressed the opinion that Sir Charles might do very well for a guardian, or the trustee of an estate, but not for a lover, she only made the half satirical reply, " Not even when he bends his head ? "

The early study of Richardson has, however, left its traces on her work. Her manner of building up a character by means of a number of minute touches, the spiritual conflict of her heroines, especially of Cecilia, in her novel of that name, and her spirited accounts of social functions, are much in his manner. Evelina's account of her impressions of London society, for instance, may be well compared with those of Harriet Byron. Cecilia's intense earnestness, and the plans she makes for improving her mind while staying at the Harrells, remind one of Clarissa Harlowe, with whom she has another point in common, for, like her, she is driven out of her mind by her misfortunes. And though Miss Burney related her other novels in the third person, *Evelina* is told by the heroine herself in the form of letters, thus following closely the method of *Pamela*.

Miss Burney's mantle fell on Miss Austen, and a study of the literary relations of these two women would be extremely interesting. There is of course no comparison between their respective power; Miss Austen, besides being a great humorist and social satirist, is a thorough artist, and is as unselfconscious as the greatest artists always are; while Miss Burney is continually obtruding her own personality in the shape of excellent but rather wearisome moral axioms. But both work in the same field, that of the society novel, and both have the same Richardsonian delight in detail, and the careful analysis of thought and feeling. But while Miss Burney has a large share of sensibility, Miss Austen's delicate reserve relegates passion to the background, and sometimes even makes her appear a little hard. It will be remembered how she directed her gentle satire at the sentimental heroine, as represented by Marianne Dashwood, just as she ridiculed her romantic sister in *North anger Abbey*. Yet, notwithstanding the absence of sentimentality in her own books, she was a great admirer of Richardson. "Her knowledge of his works," says Mr Austen Leigh, "was such as no one is likely again to acquire. . . . Every circumstance narrated in *Sir Charles Grandison*, all that was ever said or done in the cedar parlour was familiar to her; and the wedding days of Lady L. and Lady G. were as well remembered as if they had been living friends."[1]

But, after all, Richardson's influence in England was small compared with what it was on the continent. In France, especially, the greatest

[1] Austen Leigh, *Memoirs of Jane Austen*, p. 84.

enthusiasm prevailed, and continued for many years, among such diverse admirers as Diderot, Rousseau, La Harpe, George Sand, Balzac, and Alfred de Musset, whose verdict on *Clarissa Harlowe* as " le premier roman du monde " is well known. His early popularity there was no doubt partly due to his extraordinary good fortune in his translator, Prevost, himself a novelist of great power, who in *Manon Lescaut* achieved a more artistic result than Richardson ever attained. Prevost took great liberties with his original ; he abridged and omitted and softened whatever he supposed would be obnoxious to his countrymen ; he left out, for instance, the account of Mrs Sinclair's death in *Clarissa Harlowe*. " Ce tableau," he said, " est purement anglais, c'est à dire, revêtu de couleurs si fortes et malheureusement si contraires au goût de notre nation, que tous nos adoucissements ne les rendraient pas supportables en français." His literary skill thus adapted the romances to a public whose taste his own novels had helped to form, and he had the misfortune of seeing his popularity overshadowed by that of an author whom he had himself rendered accessible to his compatriots. For the excitement over *Pamela* was quite as great in Paris as in London. "Without Pamela," wrote the younger Crebillon to Chesterfield, "we should not know what to do or say here." There were, as in England, spurious sequels to the story ; it was even dramatised and parodied. And after the appearance of *Clarissa Harlowe*, the mania increased to such an extent that "they translated English novels all day long."[1]

This admiration is curiously attested by a contemporary French criticism of Clarissa, which appeared first in Amsterdam, and was translated for the *Gentleman's Magazine* of June and August 1749. The writer begins by comparing Richardson's novel with the old French heroic romances, much to the disadvantage of the latter, which he condemns as artificial and extravagant; and though he concedes to Marivaux the honour of endeavouring "to bring back his countrymen to nature," yet he prefers Richardson, on account of his superior morality. "*Marianne* amuses, *Clarissa* not only amuses, but instructs; and the more effectually, as the writer paints nature, and nature alone." He then goes on to show the advantages of Richardson's method of narration by means of letters—a defence which supplied that author with some material for his own vindication in the preface to succeeding editions of *Clarissa*—and gives a short epitome of the plot, and description of the principal characters. His observations are mainly laudatory, but wherever he ventured on an objection, he was answered in a footnote, perhaps by the editor, Cave, who was a personal friend of Richardson. The article is, on the whole, a very interesting and judicious criticism, and anticipates many of the later verdicts on the book.

Sir Charles Grandison does not seem to have

[1] Texte, *Jean-Jacques Rousseau et les Origines du Cosmopolitisme Litteraire*, p. 260.

excited quite as much interest as its predecessors, but on Richardson's death the enthusiasm, to use the words of M. Texte, became a delirium. It was then that Diderot composed at a white heat in twenty-four hours, the celebrated eulogy which, as the editor of *Le Journal Etranger*, where it was first published, remarked, could only have originated " in those moments of enthusiasm when a tender and deeply affected spirit submits to the pressing need of giving outward expression to the sentiments that weigh upon it." But however exaggerated the panegyric may appear to us, it found many admirers, for its magnificent and studied eloquence simply gave voice to the prevailing enthusiasm, and what that enthusiasm was may be judged from the following extracts.

"This author never deluges the pavement with blood; he does not transport you into distant lands; he does not expose you to the cannibalism of savages; he never loses himself in magic realms. The world where we live is the scene of his action; the basis of his drama is reality; his persons possess all possible actuality; his characters are taken from the midst of society; his incidents from the manners of all polite nations; the passions that he paints are such as I have myself felt; the same objects inspire them, and they have the energy which I know them to possess. The misfortunes and afflictions of his heroes are of the same kind as continually threaten me; he illustrates the ordinary progress of things around me. Without this art my mind, yielding with difficulty to imaginary descriptions, the illusion would be but momentary, and the impression weak and transitory.

. . . . . .

"I still remember the first time that I chanced upon the works of Richardson. I was in the country. How deliciously did their perusal affect me. With every passing minute I saw my happiness diminish by a page. Very soon I experienced the same sensation as men feel who have lived together in intimate friendship and are on the point of separation. At the end I felt as if I were left all alone.

. . . . .

"He bequeathed to me a lasting and pleasing melancholy; sometimes my friends perceive it and ask me, What is the matter with you? You are not the same as usual; what has happened to you? They question me about my health, my fortune, my relations, my friends. O my friends, *Pamela*, *Clarissa*, and *Grandison*, are three great dramas! Torn from reading them by important business, I felt an overwhelming distaste for it; I neglected my work and returned to Richardson. Beware of opening these enchanting books when you have any important duties to perform.

. . . . . .

"O Richardson, Richardson, first of men in my eyes, you shall be my reading at all times! Pursued by pressing need; if my friend should fall into poverty; if the limitations of my fortune should prevent me from giving fit attention to the education of my children, I will sell my books; but you shall remain on the same shelf as Moses, Euripides and Sophocles, and I will read you by turns." [1]

After this immoderate laudation it is not surprising to find that Diderot's novels show very clear traces of his hero worship. *La Religieuse*, which he produced in the year preceding the Eulogy, has many points in common with Richardson's works, as well it might have, seeing that during its composition he continually imagined that he heard the lamentations of Clementina, and saw Clarissa's phantom flit before him; and some critics ascribed the superiority of this novel over his earlier ones to the fact that he had in the meanwhile become acquainted with the English writer.

A still more famous disciple was Rousseau, whose *Nouvelle Héloise* was published in 1760. The resemblances between the two novelists were so striking that people at once began to make comparisons, not at all to the liking of Richardson. He disapproved of Rousseau, and "was so much disgusted at some of the scenes, and the whole tendency of the New Eloisa, that he secretly criticised the work (as he read it) in marginal notes; and thought with many others that this writer 'taught the passions to move at the command of vice.'" [2] There is no doubt, that though he must have been flattered by Rousseau's

---

[1] Diderot, *Works*, v. 212-227.
[2] Nichols, *Literary Anecdotes*, p. 598.

obvious imitation of Clarissa, he would have
earnestly repudiated the idea of any similarity of
morals or sentiment; he did not realise in the
least what dangers might lurk beneath his own
exaltation of sensibility. Yet Julie, Rousseau's
heroine, consoles herself on her deathbed with
words that exactly express the state of mind
which Richardson had first made fashionable.
"On ne sait pas," said she, "quelle douceur c'est
de s'attendrir sur ses propres maux, et sur ceux
des autres. La sensibilité porte toujours dans
l'âme un certain contentement de soi-même,
indépendant de la fortune et des evènements." [1]
So that, after all, there is a certain distinction
in suffering, and our deepest grief may be the
occasion of sincere enjoyment.

But this is not the only resemblance between
Clarissa Harlowe and *La Nouvelle Héloise*. There
is also a certain resemblance of plot. Julie is in
love with her tutor St Preux—whence the title of
the book; her father is bent on marrying her to
an old friend of his own, M. de Wolmar. St
Preux, wishing, for Julie's sake, to conceal his
connection with her, and with the help of "Milord
Bomston," an English nobleman who also admires
the heroine, but sacrifices his feelings to her
happiness, goes abroad, and in his absence Julie,
from a conviction of duty, marries her elderly
suitor. The sequel describes her home at Clarens,
where St Preux visits her and is cordially received
by her husband. But after a time, finding his

[1] *La Nouvelle Héloise*, Sixième Partie, M. de Wolmar à St Preux.

suppressed passion stronger than ever, he again retires, and the story ends with the death of Julie, not from disappointed affection as might be supposed, but from the effects of an accident.

The chief resemblance in plot is therefore the struggle between personal inclination and filial duty, for in each case the heroine is urged to give up her lover in favour of the suitor chosen by her parents. But while Clarissa is ready to leave her home rather than submit, Julie will not accept the asylum in England which Lord Bomston offers to her and St Preux ; she prefers to involve herself in a network of deceit, and, while acting the part of a dutiful daughter, carry on a clandestine love affair in her parents' house. It is hardly comprehensible that a heroine of such faulty character should develop into the saintly mistress of the home at Clarens. In the second part of the story her character is clearly modelled on that of Clarissa, but in the earlier chapters there are striking dissimilarities. Julie, ardent, weak and sensual, is utterly opposed to Clarissa, whose haughty modesty will not admit more than "a conditional liking" for the one man to whom she has ever had the slightest inclination. Julie takes fire at once, but Clarissa's affection is the slow growth of months, nor does it ever attain the dimensions of a passion. Clarissa's whole energy is directed at preserving what Julie with joyous recklessness flings away; and it is easy to see that the bad moral effect of which Richardson complained depends on the fact that the reader's

sympathy is so strongly enlisted for this indis-
creet and ill-balanced heroine. And while Clarissa
cannot survive the loss of what she holds most
dear, Julie resigns her honour and her lover with
equal impunity, and lives to be the mother of
another man's children, and to reign in smiling
felicity over that scene of domestic bliss which
Rousseau imagined to be a realisable ideal.

The prominence given in the *Nouvelle Héloïse*
to the domestic interest is another point of contact
between the two writers. Richardson's audacity
in taking his characters from the middle and lower
classes has been already noticed; though it may
be observed that as he himself rose in life his
heroes and heroines made a corresponding social
advance. Rousseau's characters, however, with
the exception of the above-mentioned English
nobleman, are all thoroughly bourgeois,[1] a circumstance that was rendered more natural and
probable by the scene of the story—republican
Switzerland. It is worthy of note that it was
with a native of England, whose people had
always preserved a large amount of liberty and
independence, that the bourgeois novel took its
rise; and by a native of Switzerland, where there
was no strong demarcation of rank, that it was
first adopted.

The intense earnestness and didacticism of both
authors is another subject that cannot be omitted
in any parallel between them. But just as

---

[1] Julie's father is proud of his title as Baron d'Étanges, but his
nobility is limited to his name. See Texte, p. 293.

Rousseau was a greater philosopher than Richardson, so the topics of his ethical digressions are much more varied than those of the latter. Rousseau had much wider interests than Richardson, and aimed at a political as well as a social and moral reform; thus his story is divided between two themes, the fate of the lovers, and the exposition of a new economic theory, which, if applied to the state, would cure all the evils that afflicted France. Richardson's didactic purpose is closely interwoven with his plot, but in Rousseau's novel the two threads run side by side; and though the hectic love story leaves an unpleasant impression, the ideal account of a simple, innocent, and pastoral life is full of charm and quiet beauty. It was no accident that in the first part of the book so much space is devoted to an account of corrupt Parisian life, and in the second, to those idyllic scenes at Clarens. The two descriptions are companion pictures, complementary to one another. And if anyone reads *La Nouvelle Héloise* now, it is mainly for the light that these digressions throw on the history of thought in the eighteenth century, for it is distinctly one of those books that have migrated from the boudoir of the lady to the library of the student.

The nature worship that suggested Rousseau's panacea for all moral and political evils is all his own, and one of the points in which he is most strikingly original. "He associated with his other characters this new actor, nature, which often plays the principal part."[1] It was not for nothing that Rousseau had spent his youth in some of the most beautiful and majestic scenery that Europe can boast; and that "the passions that build up our human soul," in his case, as in Wordsworth's, had been associated with high objects and enduring things. The results in the cases of the two men were widely different, for while the solemn grandeur of the English hills gave added serenity to their poet, Rousseau found the Alps only a further stimulus to his already overcharged emotions. The hills and lakes among which he had suffered so keenly were indissolubly connected with his woes, and served as a reminder of them, so that when he laid the scene of his story round Lake Geneva it was natural that he should represent his hero as being affected by his surroundings in the same way as they had affected himself. His most glowing descriptions of natural beauty are always connected with human passion, as when St Preux, in the first rapture of successful love, imagines that the earth is adorning herself with greater loveliness in celebration of his nuptials; or when with his lost mistress he visits the scenes of their former happiness, and bitterly recalls to her memory "le temps qui n'est plus." The eloquence of such passages is inseparable from the passion that inspires it; here are steep rocks and foaming torrents, glaciers and gloomy pines, and in their midst a little patch of tender green adorned with glittering streams and glowing

[1] Texte, p. 304.

flowers. "While comparing so sweet a resting-place with the surrounding objects," says St Preux, "it seemed as if this lonely spot were meet to be the asylum of two lovers, escaped together from the tumult of nature."[1] And it is on this reflection that the whole passage depends.

With regard to the minor questions of form and style, there is one more point in which Richardson's influence is to be seen in Rousseau's work. *La Nouvelle Héloise* is written in the form of letters, and the characters possess an epistolary facility quite equal to that of Clarissa Harlowe or Harriet Byron, and exercise it at equally unlikely moments. St Preux, for instance, waiting for the approach of Julie at the crisis of their love, takes up his pen to describe his sensations, though it is difficult to believe that so excitable a person would have been capable of holding one at that moment. But such improbabilities are inherent in the method, and must be forgiven on the same grounds as those of Richardson.

Rousseau's great and immediate popularity does not seem to have interfered with that of Richardson, which, on the contrary, gained ground in France up to the time of the Revolution. Enthusiastic visitors flocked over to London to seek out the Flask Walk at Hampstead, where Clarissa found a temporary refuge, or to weep at the modest tomb in St Bride's. Mdme. de Genlis, who visited England in 1785, tells how she wrote

[1] *La Nouvelle Héloise*, Quatrième Partie, De St Preux à Milord Édouard.

to Richardson's son-in-law, Mr Bridgen, "though he was somewhat rude in manner," because she was anxious to see an original portrait of the novelist that was in his possession. "I went over his house with great interest, and saw the original picture of Richardson ; he was fair, short in stature, rather fat, and his physiognomy and eyes were expressive of the greatest mildness. . . . I had the pleasure of sitting in Mr Bridgen's garden on the bench on which Richardson used to sit, the right arm of the seat opened, and held an inkstand ; here he used to compose and write a great part of the morning."[1] Mdme. de Genlis goes on to relate how Mr Bridgen offered her the original MSS. of *Pamela* on condition that she would translate it herself, and on her refusal to do so promised to send her instead a miniature copy of the author's portrait. Among other notable visitors was Mdme. de Staël, who has left it on record that the elopement of Clarissa was the great excitement of her own girlhood.

It is not difficult to account for this enthusiasm. The "classical" movement had exhausted itself; in France as in England there existed a general restlessness among the younger writers, a half unconscious desire to shake off the yoke of ancient literary formulæ. The very absence of art in Richardson's novels was to them an additional attraction ; after such prolonged subjection to form it was refreshing to turn to the thing itself, and to restore to it its proper precedence.

---

[1] Mdme. de Genlis, *Memoirs*, vol. iii.

There was a vast amount of deep and sincere emotion surging beneath the rigid artifices of the "grand style," which was only too ready to escape as soon as an opportunity presented itself; and Richardson by concentrating his attention on what he wished to say, and ignoring questions of form, gave courage to others, who, better trained in the prevailing literary traditions, would have hesitated to break loose from them. And the lyrical nature of his work, the expansiveness and lack of reticence which are sometimes so distasteful to an English reader, were much more congenial to a race that is naturally more inclined to find a verbal outlet for its superfluous feeling.

But there were deeper and more satisfactory reasons for his popularity than these, which after all would apply only to the educated classes. When Richardson brought the novel into the domain of real life he had no other object than to provide an instructive story for the benefit of youth; he did not at all realise that in making a lady's maid the heroine of his first novel he was really giving voice to the sentiment of liberty and of the importance of the individual, which had been growing stronger and stronger ever since the Revolution of 1689. The popularity of *Pamela* was another testimony to the growing importance of the industrial and trading classes. And this reason applied equally to France, whose revolution was yet to be accomplished—indeed, the seeds thus sown in a soil fertilised by the tears of an oppressed people had no little share in producing the terrible harvest that sprang up a generation later.

Richardson's reputation in Germany was no less remarkable. Mention has already been made of his correspondence with Mrs Klopstock, whose husband wrote an ode on the death of Clarissa, and, it is said, actually solicited political employment in England in order to live near the novelist. But the writer who did most to disseminate his fame in Germany was Gellert, professor of rhetoric at Leipzig, who translated *Pamela* and *Grandison.* "I have formerly," he confessed, "wept away some of the most remarkable hours of my life, in a sort of delicious misery, over the seventh volume of Clarissa and the fifth of Grandison." In 1757 he wrote to Richardson urging him to publish a selection of the letters that had passed between him and his friends, and Richardson actually considered this proposal, though, with becoming modesty, he wrote, "It would be presumptuous in me, in the present state of my health, to think of writing anything more for the public. The letters that have been written to me by several correspondents would, many of them, be worthy of the public eye. I do think that if the writers of them knew of your request and approved of it, and applied to me first to grant it (I not to them for their consent), there might appear anonymously, and with certain restrictions, in the language of your country, and in that only, a volume or two." [1] It was probably this suggestion that gave Richardson the idea of revising his correspondence with a view to its ultimate publication in England (not-

[1] Forster MSS. *Miscellaneous Correspondence.*

withstanding his protest) as well as in Germany ; but, as has been seen, the project was interrupted by his death.

Gellert's translations were not his only tribute to the genius of Richardson, and his admiration found further expression in the lines which he inscribed over his friend's portrait. "This is the creative spirit who, by means of instructive stories, commands us to feel the charm of virtue ; who, by means of Grandison, extorts from the sinner himself a first wish to be pious also. The works which he created, no time can destroy ; they are nature, taste, religion. Immortal is Homer, but among Christians the British Richardson is more immortal still." And, emulous of following in the steps of this immortal, the German professor himself commenced novelist, and produced the long rambling romance entitled. '*Das Leben der Schwedischen Gräfin von G.*' The plot of this novel has much in common with those of the heroic romances, and is constructed with equal disregard to morality; but there are at the same time unmistakable traces of Richardson's influence in the predominance of the feminine interest, and in the fact that the heroine relates her own story ; in the ponderous didacticism, which fits in rather badly with the conduct of even the virtuous characters, and in the introduction of English characters.[1]

Other novelists followed his example ; Hermes, inspired by the praiseworthy desire " to be a German Richardson," produced in 1766 his *Geschichte*

[1] Erich Schmidt, *Richardson, Rousseau und Goethe*, p. 31.

der Miss Fanny Wilkes, which purported to be a translation from the English. The scene of the story is laid in England, and both incidents and characters are copied from Richardson, whose novels the hero, Mr Handsome, recommends to a lady as her best consolation in distress. "Finally, read Grandison, for it is natural that your mind should need distraction, and Grandison is the best book of its kind." Again, the heroine (who after all is not Miss Fanny Wilkes, but a certain Jenny) is subjected to the same kind of trials as Pamela and Clarissa, and emerges triumphant. And the resemblance is completed by the obvious moral intention of the book.

Equally complimentary, though more discriminating, was the admiration of Wieland, who first made Richardson's acquaintance by means of a French translation of *Pamela*. *Sir Charles Grandison* made so great an impression on him that he contemplated a volume of *Letters from Charles Grandison to his pupil Emily Jervois*, and actually composed a drama on the subject of Clementina. But Wieland outgrew his early enthusiasm, and afterwards declared that he did not like "your Clarissa, Charles Grandisons, and Harriet Byrons, for the simple reason that they are too perfect." [1]

This remark was addressed to Sophie La Roche, whose romance, the *Fräulein von Sternheim*, is

---

[1] For a very complete account of Richardson's imitators in Germany see Erich Schmidt, *Richardson, Rousseau und Goethe*, pp. 19-79.

another imitation of the English writer. Sophie La Roche has a further interest for the student of the history of English fiction, inasmuch as she was a great admirer of Miss Burney, whom she embarrassed by an ill-timed visit to Windsor Castle. But this was some years after the appearance of her own novel.

Wieland's tragedy had been preceded by another, written by a still more remarkable person, Gotthold Ephraim Lessing. In his endeavour to reform the German theatre he boldly broke away from French traditions, and in 1756 produced the prose tragedy entitled *Miss Sara Sampson*, which was evidently suggested by *Clarissa Harlowe*. The scene is laid in England, and the heroine is beguiled from her home by a rake called Mellefont, and is poisoned by another woman whom he has deceived. Sara's father goes in pursuit, and reaches his daughter just in time to forgive her.

Lastly, Richardson's popularity in Germany was shown in the same way as in England, by a parody, not of *Pamela* in this instance, but of *Sir Charles Grandison*, which was gently satirised by Musäus in his *Grandison der Zweite*. This parody, first published in the years 1760-1763, is in itself a striking testimony to the duration of the mania, for a parody loses its point as soon as the form it satirises has gone out of fashion, and the last edition of *Grandison der Zweite* is dated 1803. And these years, which witnessed the development of German national literature, were particularly favourable to the reception of new ideas, for the strong young intellects, now approaching maturity, absorbed with surprising rapidity whatever presented itself to their assimilation. Both Wieland and Lessing were men of genius, but there was a greater than these who acknowledged the charm exercised by the little English printer. Goethe has left on record in several places[1] his admiration for Richardson's writing, and though *The Sorrows of Werther* was inspired rather by *La Nouvelle Héloise* than by *Clarissa Harlowe*, the close relation between these books must not be forgotten while considering the literary relations of Germany and England in the eighteenth century. The Wertherism which, in its turn, reacted on England, may thus legitimately be regarded as a link between two such different writers as Lord Byron and Samuel Richardson.

It is plain that an influence so permanent and so widely diffused must have had some substantial and sufficient grounds. How did it come about that Richardson, a man whose first work was produced at the age of fifty-one, exercised so great a power over the rising generation? How can we account for this almost delirious excitement over works that sometimes seem to us so ponderous and so dull?

The answer to these questions will have been partly gleaned from the foregoing pages, but it is convenient to recapitulate them here. Richardson was popular because he gave voice to senti-

---

[1] *Wahrheit und Dichtung*, Part II., Books vi. and xiii. ; *Wilhelm Meisters Lehrjahre*, Book v., Chap. vii.

ments that were already latent in society; it was because he anticipated the younger generation by giving expression to these feelings that he was so much idolized by it. Almost all the characteristics of the romantic school—its disregard of conventional literary form, its exaltation of emotion, its idealization of women, its preoccupation with the theme of education, its recognition of the moral value of the individual, are found in Richardson's novels. And, limiting our enquiry to his native land, it may be further remarked that a society, which notwithstanding its surface corruption was sound at heart, would not long remain content in the spiritual torpor that had overtaken it. The revulsion that is marked by the Wesleyan movement in religion, is marked in literature by the appearance of Richardson. Henceforth the moral tone of the nation becomes healthier. A spirit of philanthropy begins to stir at home, while those "boy patriots," who were destined to win such glory for England abroad, spring into power and manhood. Fielding lays his hand on the domestic sores of the country and works himself to death in the reform of justice; while Johnson, in the midst of men like Reynolds, Goldsmith and Burke, preaches his stern creed of sincerity and independence. But all of these were anticipated by Richardson, and not his least claim to originality is that in an age of selfishness and brutality he appealed to higher sentiments, and awoke true and tender emotions in his readers.

" He found them when the age had bound
  Their souls in its benumbing round ;
  He spoke, and loosed their heart in tears."

It is the mission of some writers to brace and fortify, to preach restraint and self-control. Richardson, coming when he did, rendered a no less valuable service by appealing to the "simple, sensuous and passionate" side of human nature.

BIBLIOGRAPHY

I. The Forster Manuscript

This manuscript is contained in the Forster Library at the South Kensington Museum. It consists of more than eight hundred letters written by Richardson and various correspondents, the chief of whom are Lady Bradshaigh; Mrs Chapone, senior; Aaron Hill; Thomas Edwards; Mrs Scudamore; and Eusebius Sylvester. There are also many anonymous compliments on Richardson's novels, and various poems and sonnets by T. Edwards, Miss Mulso, Miss Highmore, John Duncombe, and John Chapone. The majority of the letters in this collection were not printed in Mrs Barbauld's edition of the Correspondence, which, however, contains many letters absent from the Forster Manuscript, the most remarkable being those between Richardson and Lady Bradshaigh before she made herself known to him, and the correspondence with Miss Mulso.

Many of the letters in the Forster Manuscript are autographs, while others are transcripts made by Richardson's daughters. They are nearly all carefully docketed, in his own hand, with their date and subject-matter. They are contained in six folio volumes, as under :—

Folio XI.—

Correspondence with Lady Bradshaigh, beginning May 10, 1748, ending with a letter to Miss Patty Richardson (afterwards Mrs Bridgen), dated April 25, 1762.

Folio XII.—

(1) Correspondence with T. Edwards, Dec. 2, 1748-July 30, 1756.

Folio XII.—continued—
  (2) Correspondence with Mrs Chapone, senior, April 23, 1751-Nov. 26, 1753.

Folio XIII.—
  (1) Correspondence with Mrs Chapone, senior (continued), Nov. 26, 1753-June 20, 1759.
  (2) Correspondence with Aaron Hill, March 6, 1735-Aug. 11, 1749 (also contains letters from Astræa and Minerva Hill and Urania Johnson).

Folio XIV.—
  (1) Correspondence with Mrs Urania Johnson, July 23, 1750-Sept. 9, 1758.
  (2) Correspondence with Mrs Scudamore (Miss Westcomb), Miss Righton and others.
  (3) Correspondence with Miss Westcomb (afterwards Mrs Scudamore), April 14, 1748-Oct. 1, 1754.
  (4) Correspondence with Eusebius Sylvester, Aug. 22, 1754-July 26, 1756.

Folio XV.—
  (1) Correspondence with Eusebius Sylvester (continued), Aug. 10, 1756-Aug. 21, 1759.
  (2) Correspondence *re* Clarissa Harlowe by various writers.
  (3) Correspondence *re* Clarissa Harlowe and Sir Charles Grandison by various writers.

Folio XVI.—
  (1) Correspondence *re* Pamela by various writers.
  (2) Miscellaneous correspondence, chiefly consisting of poetical pieces.

II. Works

Works of Samuel Richardson. With a Sketch of his Life and Writings by the Rev. E. Mangin. London, 1811.

The Novels of Samuel Richardson. To which is prefixed a memoir of the author [by Sir Walter Scott]. The Novelists' Library. Vols. vi-viii.

The Works of Samuel Richardson. With a prefatory
chapter of biographical criticism (reprinted with
additions . . . from " Hours in a Library "), by
Leslie Stephen. London, 1883.

An address to the Public on the Treatment which the
Editor of the History of Sir Charles Grandison has
met with from certain booksellers and printers in
Dublin. Including observations on Mr Faulkner's
Defence of himself. London, 1754.

Æsop's Fables. With Instructive Morals and Reflections Abstracted from all Party Considerations,
Adapted to all Capacities, and Designed to
promote Religion, Morality, and Universal Benevolence. London, 1740. (Probably by Richardson).

Case of Samuel Richardson of London, Printer, with
regard to the Invasion of his Property in the History
of Sir Charles Grandison, before publication, by
certain Booksellers in Dublin. London, 1753.

Christian Magazine. Edited by Richardson and Mau-
clerc. London, 1748. (Mentioned by Nichols, but
not in the British Museum).

Clarissa Harlowe, or the History of a Young Lady.
Published by the Editor of Pamela. London, 1748.

——— Second edition. London, 1749.

——— Fourth edition. London, 1751.

——— Sixth edition. London, 1768.

——— Seventh edition. London, 1774.

Another edition. Dublin, 1780.

Another edition. London, 1784.

New edition. London, 1785.

Another edition. The British Novelists. Vols. i-viii.
1810.

Tauchnitz edition, 4 vols. 1862.

History of Clarissa Harlowe. Abridged by J. H. Emmert in The Novelist, vol. ii., 1792.

Clarissa. A novel. Abridged by E. S. Dallas. 1868.

Clarissa Harlowe. New and abridged edition by Mrs Ward. Part of Railway Library. London, 1868.

Another edition, 1890.

Clarissa, or the History of a Young Lady. Condensed by C. H. Jones. New York, 1874. Part of Leisure Hour Series.

Collection of the Moral and Instructive Sentiments . . . contained in the Histories of Pamela, Clarissa and Sir Charles Grandison, A . . . to which are subjoined two letters from the editor of those works. London, 1755.

Correspondence of Samuel Richardson, author of Pamela, etc. Selected from the original manuscripts, to which are prefixed a biographical account of that author and observations on his writings, by A. L. Barbauld. London, 1804.

The History of Sir Charles Grandison. In a series of Letters published from the originals, by the editor of Pamela and Clarissa. London, 1754.

———— Second edition. To which . . . is added . . . a brief History . . . of the treatment which the editor has met with from certain booksellers and printers in Dublin.

———— Third edition. London, 1755.

———— Sixth edition. London, 1770.

———— Seventh edition. London, 1776.

———— Eighth edition. London, 1796.

Another edition. London, 1781.

Another edition. London, 1786 (Part of the New Novelists' Magazine).

Another edition. By L. Aikin, afterwards Barbauld. The British Novelists. Vols. ix.-xv., 1810.

Another edition. The seven volumes comprised in one. London, 1812.

Cooke's edition. Embellished with engravings. London, 1817.

History of Sir Charles Grandison, abridged by T. H. Emmert. The Novelist. Vol. i., 1792.

History of Sir Charles Grandison. A new and abridged edition by M. Howitt, 1873.

Sir Charles Grandison. [Six short extracts.] With six illustrations from the original copper-plates, Leadenhall Press, 1886.

Letters from Sir Charles Grandison. Selected with a biographical introduction and connecting notes by G. Saintsbury. London, 1895.

Negotiations of Sir Thomas Roe in his embassy to the Ottoman Porte. Edited by Samuel Richardson, 1740.

One Hundred and Seventy-three Letters Written for Particular Friends on the most Important Occasions. By the late Mr Richardson, Author of Clarissa and Sir Charles Grandison. Seventh edition (no date).

Pamela; or Virtue Rewarded. In a Series of familiar letters from a beautiful young damsel to her parents. London, 1740.

———— Second edition. London, 1741.

———— Sixth edition.

———— Tenth edition. London, 1771.

Another edition. To which are prefixed extracts from several curious letters written to the editor on the subject. London, 1785.

Cooke's edition. Embellished with engravings. London, 1800 (?).

A new edition, being the fourteenth. London, 1801.

New edition. Berwick, 1816.

Another edition. (With plates.) London, 1825.

Another edition. Edited by T. Archer. London, New York, Guildford, 1873.

Another edition. Halifax, 1878.

Pamela; or Virtue Rewarded. London, 1891. (Part of Routledge's Florin Library).

The History of Pamela. (An abridgement.) Edinburgh, 1817.

Pamela's Conduct in High Life (A sequel to Richardson's Pamela). London, 1741.

Six original Letters upon Duelling. In Literary Repository, 1765.

Tour . . . through Great Britain, A. With very great additions, improvements and corrections by Samuel Richardson. London, 1742.

———— Another edition, 1748.

———— Another edition, 1753.

———— Another edition, 1762.

Another edition. Tour through the whole Island of Great Britain, A. . . . originally begun by the celebrated Daniel De Foe, continued by the late Mr Richardson, 1769.

———— another edition, 1778.

III. Translations and Adaptations

Clarisse Harlowe. Traduit sur l'édition originale par l'Abbé Prevost, précédé de l'éloge de Richardson par Diderot. Paris, 1845-6.

Clarisse Harlowe. Traduction nouvelle et seule complète, par M. le Tourveur.

Clarisse Harlowe, par Jules Janin, précédée d'un essai sur la vie et les ouvrages de l'auteur de Clarisse Harlowe. Bruxelles, 1846.

Istoria di Miss Clarissa Harlowe. Lettere inglesi di Richardson per la prima volta recerte in Italiano.

Clarisse Harlowe, drama, etc. [founded on Richardson's novel of Clarissa Harlowe], 1788. Dinaux (P.) *pseud.* [P. P. Goubaux.]

Clarissa Harlowe. A tragic drama. . . . Adapted from the French by J. H. Lacy and J. Courtney.

Clarissa ; ein . . . Trauerspiel . . . nach Anleitung der bekannten Geschichte, 1765.

Clarisse Harlowe. Opéra, etc. (founded on Richardson's novel, Clarissa), 1896. Barbier et Chouvens.

Clarissa, ein burgerliches Trauerspiel in drei Aufzugen (and in prose) nach Anleitung der bekannten Geschichte von J. H. Steffens. Zelle, 1765.

Nouvelles Lettres Anglaises, ou Histoire du Chevalier Grandisson. Augmentée de huit lettres . . . avec figures (Traduit par A. F. Prevost d'Exiles).

Nuove Lettere inglesi orvero storia del cavalier Grandisson. (Translation from the English). Venice, 1784-9.

Historia del Caballero Carlo Grandisson . . . puesta en Castellano par E. T. D. T. Madrid, 1798.

Grandison der Zweite, oder Geschichte des Herrn von N——. In Briefen entworfen. Eisenach, 1760-2.

Paméla ; ou la Vertu Recompensée. Traduit de l'anglais par A. F. Prevost d'Exiles. (A translation of vols. i. and ii. only).

L'Histoire de la verteueuse Pamela dans le temps de sa liberté jusqu'à son mariage. Traduit de l'anglais de Mr Grandisson. Frankfort, Leipzig and La Haye, 1771.

Hanes Pamela; neu Dbiweirdeb wedi ei wobrwyo. Cærfyddin, 1818.

Pamela. A comedy founded on Richardson's novel, by James Love, 1741.

Pamela Nubile. Farsa in Musica. (Founded on Richardson's novel). Padua (?), 1810.

Pamela. Nova comedia intitulada: A mais heroica virtude ou a virtusa Pamella (in three acts and in verse). Composta no idiomo Italiano (by Goldoni, under the title of Pamela Fanciullo) e traduzida (and altered) ao gosto portugez. Lisbon, 1766.

IV. CRITICAL AND BIOGRAPHICAL

Barbauld, A. L. Biographical Account prefixed to her edition of Richardson's Correspondence. London, 1804.

——— Vie de Samuel Richardson, avec l'examen critique de ses ouvrages. 1808.

Birrell, Augustine. Obiter Dicta. London, 1896.

Candid Examination of the History of Sir Charles Grandison. London, 1754.

Coleridge. Table Talk. Bohn's Edition, p. 295.

Conjectures on Original Composition. In a Letter to the Author of Sir Charles Grandison. London, 1759.

Diderot. Éloge de Richardson. Works, v., 212-227.

Dobson, Austin. Eighteenth Century Vignettes. Second Series. Richardson at Home.

Donner, J. O. E. Richardson in der deutschen Romantik.

Gentleman's Magazine, June and August, 1749.

Hazlitt, W. C. English Comic Writers. Lecture vi.

Keyber Conny (pseud.). Fielding? An Apology for the Life of Mrs Shamela Andrews, in which the many notorious falsehoods and misrepresentations of a book called Pamela are exposed. London, 1741.

Laroummet. Marivaux. Sa Vie et ses Œuvres. Troisième Partie, chapitre ii.

Le Breton. Le Roman au dix-huitième Siècle, chap. v.

Mangin, E. Preface to Richardson's Works. London, 1811.

Nichols. Literary Anecdotes of the Eighteenth Century, vol. iv., No. 18.

Oliphant, Mrs. Historical Sketches in the Reign of George II., chap. x. London, 1869.

Povey, C. The Virgin in Eden. . . . To which are added Pamela's Letters, proved to be immodest romances. London, 1741.

Remarks on Clarissa addressed to the Author. London, 1749.

Schmidt, Erich. Richardson, Rousseau and Goethe. Ein Betrag zur Geschichte des Romans im 18 Jahrhundert. Jena, 1875.

Scott, Sir W. Lives of the Novelists.

Stephen, Leslie. Hours in a Library, vol. i. London, 1892.

Texte. Jean Jacques Rousseau et les Origines du Cosmopolitisme Littéraire. Paris, 1895.

Traill, H. D. The New Fiction. London, 1897.

Villemain. Cours de Littérature Français. Tableau du dix-huitième Siècle, Deuxième Partie, Deuxième Leçon.

V. Magazine Articles [1]

Clarissa Harlowe—
Westminster Review, 91, 48.
St James', 23, 21.

[1] The first number in these references refers to the volume, the second to the page.

Clarissa Harlowe—continued—
St Paul's, 3, 163.
Tinsley, 3, 311.
Christian Remembrancer, 56, 330.
Living Age, 87, 92.

Life and Correspondence of Richardson—
Edinburgh Review, 5, 23 (by Jeffrey).
Littell's Museum of Foreign Literature, 7. 1, 104;
32, 41.

Morals and Manners in Samuel Richardson's Novels—
National Review, 14, 321; same art. Living Age,
183, 771.

Novels and Characters of Samuel Richardson—
Cornhill, 17, 48; same art. Living Age, 97, 131.
Spectator, 56, 1284.
Saturday Review, 55, 114.

Samuel Richardson—
Blackwood, 105, 253 (by Mrs Oliphant); same art.
Living Age, 101, 67.
Fraser, 61, 20; 71, 83; same art. Living Age, 84,
215.
Fortnightly, 12, 428 (by H. B. Forman).
Contemporary Review, 44, 529 (by H. D. Traill);
same art. Living Age, 159, 345.
Gentleman's Magazine, n. s., 44, 74; same art.
Living Age, 184, 459.

Samuel Richardson At Home—
Scribner's Magazine, 14, 375 (by Austin Dobson).

Sir Charles Grandison—
Chambers' Journal, 30, 193.

Stephen's Edition Richardson's Novels—
Athenæum, '84, i. 399.

INDEX

A

ADDISON, 139,
Adventurer, The, 96.
Æsop's Fables, 40.
Amelia, Fielding's, 74, 115, 162, 269.
Anna Howe, 204.
Arcadia, Sydney's, 130, 142.
Arden of Feversham, 131.
Aretina, 137.
Austen, Jane, 172, 270-271.

B

B., Mr (in *Pamela*), 156, 168.
Barbauld, Mrs, 10, 12, 20, 29, 30, 31 ; 164.
Beowulf, 125.
Berger Extravagant, Le, 135.
Bevis of Hampton, 128.
Boyle, Roger, 138.
Bradshaigh, Lady, 7, 11, 17, 49, 52, 55, 65, 71, 104-111, 112, 266.
Brooke, Henry, 250, 268.
Brunetière, F.; *quoted*, 137.
Burney, Frances, 172, 269, 270, 288.
Butler, Samuel, 138.

C

Canons of Criticism, Edward's, 101.
Carter, Elizabeth, 53, *note*; 67, *note*; 95, 111, 113.
Case of Samuel Richardson, Printer, etc., 54.

Cassandre, 134, 137.
Caxton, 127.
Cecilia, Miss Burney's, 270.
Chapone, Hester Mulso, afterwards Mrs, 47, 52, 55, 76, *note* ; 95-98, 119, 265.
Chapone, John, senior, 71.
Chapone, John, junior, 55, 92, 94.
Chapone, Sarah Kirkham, afterwards Mrs, 92-94.
Charlotte Grandison, 169, 233-239.
Chesterfield, Lord, 44, 47, 53 ; *quoted*, 249.
Chudleigh, Miss, 48-49.
Cibber Colley, 17, 45, 47, 48, 49, 55, 63, 86-88.
Clarissa Harlowe, 15, 44, 45 ; analysis of plot, 173-186 ; criticism, 186-208 ; character of Clarissa, 190-198.
Clélie, 96, 134, 137.
Clementina della Poretta, 228, 261.
Cleopatra, 96, 137.
Collection of Moral Sentiments, etc., Richardson's, 62.
Collier, Miss, 71, 107, 111.
Conjectures on Original Composition, Young's, 121.
Corney House, 18, 19.
Crebillon, *quoted*, 272.
Cry, The, Sarah Fielding's, 111.

D

Daily Journal, Richardson, printer of, 16.

Daily Gazette, Richardson, printer of, 16.
David Simple, 74, 111.
Defoe, Daniel, 141.
Dela Fayette, Mdme., 133.
Delany, Dr, 91.
Delany, Mrs, 67, 72, 91.
De Musset, Alfred, *quoted*, 272.
Desborough, Mrs, 72.
Dewes, Mrs, 91, 92.
Diderot, 274 ; his eulogy of Richardson, 274-276.
Distressed Mother, The, 163.
Duncombe, John, 98-100.
Duncombe, Susannah Highmore, afterwards Mrs, 12, 21, 52, 98-100.

E

EARLE, John, 138.
Edgeworth, Miss, 172.
Edwards, Thomas, 55, 59, 60, 63, 100-103.
Emily Jervois, 145, 239.
Emile, Rousseau's, 269.
Euphues, Lyly's, 130, 131.
Evelina, Miss Burney's, 270.
Every Man in His Humour, Jonson's, 131.

F

Faerie Queene, The, 128.
Familiar Letters, Richardson's, 23-29.
Fasts and Festivals, Nelson's, 256.
Faulkner's *Account of Fulham*, 20.
Feminead, The, 99.
Fielding, Henry, 1, 13, 35, 36, 38, 73, 112, 120, 172, 259, 269.
Fielding, Sarah, 71, 74, 111.
Fool of Quality, The, 250, 268.
Fräulein von Sternheim, Das, 287.
Furetière, 134, 135 ; *quoted*, 248.

G

GARRICK, David, 47, 80.
Gellert : His translations of *Pamela* and *Sir Charles Grandison*, 285. Correspondence with Richardson, 285, 286.
Genlis, Mdme. de, 283.
Gentleman's Magazine, 113, 273.
Geschichte der Miss Fanny Wilkes, 287.
Gesta Romanorum, 127.
Gil Blas, 38, 133, 144, *note*.
Goethe, 289.
Goldsmith, Oliver, 122.
Governess, The, Sarah Fielding's, 111.
Grandison der Zweite, 288.
Gray, Thomas, *quoted*, 264.
Greene, Robert, 132.

H

HAMILTON, Anthony, 140.
Harlowe family, The, 206-208.
Harriet Byron, 53, 87, 145, 228-233, 261.
Hermes, author of *Miss Fanny Wilkes*, 286.
Highmore, the artist, 75, 107.
Highmore, Susannah, *see* Duncombe.
Hill, Aaron, 18, 31, 33, 34, 41, 45, 63, 71, 73-80.
Hill, Astræa and Minerva, 82-86.
Hill, Urania, *see* Johnson.
History of Mrs Beaumont, The 13.
Hogarth, 118.
Holy Living and Dying, Taylor's, 256.
Hudibras, 138.
Huet, The Abbé, His definition of romance, 133, 134.
Humphrey Clinker, 140.
Huon of Bordeaux, 127.

I

Ibrahim, 96.

J

JEFFREY, Lord, His criticism of the *Familiar Letters*, 30.
Johnson, Dr, 47, 50, 71, 113, 118-121, 258.
Johnson, Urania Hill afterwards Mrs, 46, 55, 80, 81.
Joseph Andrews, 38, 74, 129.
Journal Etranger, Le, 274.
Journal of the Plague, Defoe's, 141.
Jowett, Dr, *quoted*, 209, 249.

K

KIRKHAM, Sarah, *see* Mrs Chapone, senior.
Klopstock, the poet, 285.
Klopstock, Mrs, 115-117.

L

LA BRUYÈRE, 138.
La Calprenède, 134.
Lady Davers (in *Pamela*), 168.
La Roche, Sophie, 287.
Leake, Elizabeth, *see* Mrs Richardson.
Leben der Schwedischen Gräfin von G. Das, 286.
Le Grand Cyrus, 137.
Lessing, Richardson and, 288.
Letters from Charles Grandison to his pupil Emily Jervois, 287.
Letters on the Improvement of the Mind, 97.
Le Sage, 133, 144 *note*.
Lovelace, 15, 141 ; Character of, 198-204.

M

MACKENZIE, Sir George, 137.
Mackenzie, Henry, 140, 268.
Magdalen Charity, 110.
Man of Feeling, The, 268.
Man of the World, The, 140.
Manley, Mrs, 138.
Manon Lescaut, 272.
Marivaux, 147, 273.
Memoirs of a Cavalier, Defoe's, 141.
Memoirs of the Comte de Grammont, 140.
Minto, Professor, *quoted*, 141.
Miss Sarah Sampson, 288.
Moll Flanders, 255.
Monmouth, Duke of, 1.
Montagu, Lady Mary Wortley, 44, 53 ; *quoted*, 233.
More, Hannah, *quoted*, 7.
Morte d'Arthur, 127.
Mrs Jewkes, 157, 169.
Mrs Shirley, 8, 142, 239.
Musäus, author of parody of *Sir Charles Grandison*, 288.

N

NASH, Thomas, 132.
New Atalantis, The, 138.
New Way to Pay Old Debts, A, 131.
Night Thoughts, Young's, 44, 121.
Northanger Abbey, 271.
Nouvelle Héloise, La, compared with Clarissa Harlowe, 276, 282.

O

ONSLOW, the Speaker, 41, 47.
Osborne, the printer, 22, 30, 34, 40.
Oronooko, 255.
Overbury, Sir Thomas, 138.

P

Pamela, 21, 22, 23, 30-32, 35, 36; compared with *La vie de Marianne*, 148-152; origin of story, 153; analysis of plot, 156-163; criticism, 163-71; character of Pamela, 163-168.
Pamela in High Life, 35.
Parthenissa, 138.
Paysan Parvenu, Le, 148.
Pilgrim's Progress, The, 128, 138.
Pilkington Letitia, 71, 88-91.
Piozzi, Mrs, *quoted*, 121.
Polexandre, 96.
Pope, Alexander, 17, 18; his criticism of Pamela, 31; Pope and Hill, 78; Pope and Edwards, 101, 102.
Practice of Piety, 256.
Prevost's translations of *Pamela* and *Clarissa*, 270.

R

Rambler, The, 50, 51.
Ranelagh, 31 (and *note*).
Recuyell of the Histories of Troye, 127.
Reich, Mr, 117.
Religieuse, La, 276.
Richardson, Mrs Elizabeth, 16, 60, 61, 67, 75, 76.
Richardson, Mrs Martha, 10, 16.
Richardson, Patty, 64.
Richardson, Polly, 63, 107.
Richardson, Samuel, his parentage, 1; birth, 2; education, 3, 4; apprenticed to John Wilde, 8; journeyman printer, 9; master printer, 10; first marriage, 10; early love affairs, 11; connection with Duke of Wharton, 14; prints *True Briton*, 15; prints *Daily Journal* and *Daily Gazeteer*, 16; death of first wife and second marriage, 16; rents house at North End, 19; writes *Pamela*, 23; *Familiar Letters*, 23; edits *Letters of Sir Thomas Roe*, 39; and *Æsop's Fables*, 40; revises *Defoe's Tour through Great Britain*, 40; prints Journals of the House of Commons, 41; correspondence with Hill about *Clarissa*, 41; publishes *Clarissa*, 44; visit to Tunbridge Wells, 46; correspondence with Lady Bradshaigh, 49; contributes papers to the *Rambler*, 50, 51; engaged in composition of *Sir Charles Grandison*, 51; publishes *Sir Charles Grandison*, 54; correspondence with Eusebius Sylvester, 56-58; removes to Parson's Green, 59; Master of Stationers' Company, 60; rebuilds offices in Salisbury Court, 61; publishes Maxims from Novels,62; his daughters, 63, 65; his wife, 66-68; his will, 68, 69; his death, 70; character, 71-74; personal appearance, 75; assists Aaron Hill and family, 81; correspondence with Astræa and Minerva Hill, 82-85; friendship with Cibber, 86-88; assists Letitia Pilkington, 89; correspondence with the Chapone family, 92-95; *Feminead* addressed to him, 99; friendship with Edwards, 100-103; and Lady Bradshaigh, 104-111; friendship with Sarah Fielding and Elizabeth Carter, 111, 113; correspondence with Mrs Klopstock, 115; friendship with Johnson, 119, 120, 121; and Young, 121; Young's Verses on Richardson, 123; clumsy con-

struction of his plots, 243, 246;
his prolixity, 249; minute description, 250-254; his didactic aim, 254, 255; bad
taste, 256, 257, 260; shrewd
maxims, 257, 258; his humour,
259; sentimentality, 262; his
prose style, 264, 265; his influence in England, 265-271; in
France, 271-284; in Germany,
284-289; reasons for his popularity, 289, 290.
Richardson, William, 69 and
note.
Rivington, the printer, 22, 30.
Robinson Crusoe, 142, 255.
Roe, Sir Thomas, 39.
Roman Bourgeois, Le, 135.
Roman Comique, Le, 135.
Rousseau, Richardson's influence
on him, 276; comparison of
La Nouvelle Héloïse with
Clarissa Harlowe, 276-282.

S

SCARRON, 134, 135.
School for Scandal, The, 260.
Scott, Sir Walter, 172; quoted,
220, 229.
Scudéry, Mdme. de, 134.
Serious Reflections of Robinson
Crusoe, 142, 143.
Shamela Andrews, The History
of Mrs, 36-38, 73.
Slocock, Dr, 31.
Sir Charles Grandison, 51, 52,
53; pirated by Irish book-
sellers, 54; analysis of plot,
210-219; character of Sir
Charles, 220-226.
Sir William Harrington, The
History of, 76.
Smollett, Tobias, 172.
Sorel, 134.
Spectator, The, 50, 51, 139, 162.
Stäel, Mdme. de, 283.
Stephen, Leslie, quoted, 163, 220.

Swift, Jonathan, 88, 143.
Sylvester, Eusebius, 57, 58, 71.
Sydney, Sir Philip, 130.

T

TALBOT, Miss, 53, note; 67,
note; 69.-
Tatler, The, 139.
Tender Husband, The, 163.
Texte, quoted, 196, 273, 280.
Thackeray, 46; quoted, 172.
Tillotson, quoted, 220.
Theophrastus, 138.
Tom Jones, 51, 140, 250.
Tour through Great Britain,
Defoe's, 41.
Trevelyan's Life of Macaulay,
172.
Tristram Shandy, 267.
True Briton, The, 14, 15.

U

Unfortunate Traveller, The,
132.

V

Vie de Marianne, La, 147, 148;
compared with Pamela, 148-
152.
Villemain, quoted, 198.

W

WALPOLE, Horace, 31, note;
44.
Warton, Thomas, 102, 228.
Warburton, William, 101, 103.
Webster, Dr, 71.
Webster, the poet, 198.
Wharton, Duke of, 14, 199.
Wieland, Richardson's influence
on, 287.

Wilde, Allington, 10.
Wilde, John, 8, 10.
Wilde, Martha, *see* Mrs Martha
   Richardson.
Williams, Mr, 169.
Woman killed with Kindness,
   A, 131.

Y

YOUNG, Dr, 44, 121-123.

Z

Zayde, 133.